The Best American Food Writing 2018

GUEST EDITORS OF
THE BEST AMERICAN FOOD WRITING

2018   RUTH REICHL

The Best American Food Writing 2018™

Edited and with an Introduction
by RUTH REICHL

Silvia Killingsworth, Series Editor

A Mariner Original

HOUGHTON MIFFLIN HARCOURT

BOSTON • NEW YORK   2018

hmhco.com

ISBN 978-1-328-66224-8 (print)   ISBN 978-1-328-66308-5 (ebook)
ISSN 2578-7667 (print)   ISSN 2578-7675 (ebook)

Printed in the United States of America
DOC 10 9 8 7 6 5 4 3 2 1

Contents

Foreword

I soon saw, as I considered every aspect of the pleasures of the table, that something better than a cook book should be written about them; and there is a great deal to say about those functions which are so ever-present and so necessary, which have such a direct influence on our health, happiness, and even on our occupations.

—Jean Anthelme Brillat-Savarin

THE MOST COMMON question I was asked while working on this volume was, "How does it not already exist?" Houghton Mifflin Harcourt has been publishing anthologies of fiction, travel writing, essays, and poetry dating back over a hundred years, and it seems impossible that the first *Best American Food Writing* collection won't have appeared until thirteen years after the launch of a website named *Eater,* nine years after Michael Pollan's best-selling *In Defense of Food,* and four years after the *New York Times* changed the name of its "Dining" section to "Food."

It is apparent that food as a topic is perennial, but food writing itself has not always been taken seriously (except when it has). My coeditor, Ruth Reichl, gets at this in her introduction. For a long time in America, mass-market food writing lived in the domestic realm of the kitchen, closely aligned with women's interests. In Orville Prescott's 1942 *New York Times* review of Mary Frances Fisher's *How to Cook a Wolf,* he writes, "For a mere male book reviewer who has never become even a naturalized citizen of that foreign country, the kitchen, a good deal of the ground covered in 'How to Cook a Wolf' is terra incognita." This is markedly not the case in France, where cooking is historically a male-dominated sport. Gastronomy is its attendant fine art, codified by Marie-Antoine Carême in the nineteenth century, further refined by Auguste Escoffier, and then reimagined by Paul Bocuse and other celebrated giants in the twentieth. Ironically, it took a woman named Julia Child to translate all that Cordon Bleu knowledge into the modern American imagination.

But what would anyone write about food that wasn't a recipe? For starters, memoirs, like A. J. Liebling's scenes of extravagance in Paris, such as *Between Meals,* and Jim Harrison's self-described "food bullying" in 2002's *The Raw and the Cooked* (encouraged by none other than the great appetite of Orson Welles). There has also been great food journalism, from John McPhee's multipart *New Yorker* reportage devoted to the orange to the lyrical travelogues of *Saveur.* Just as Reichl resisted labeling herself a "food writer," so too did *New Yorker* writer Calvin Trillin insist that a 1985 story about Memphis barbecue was about Memphis and not the barbecue. Fair enough, but the title of the story is "Thoughts of an Eater with Smoke in His Eyes." In the modern age, criticism reigns supreme in food writing, though its merits as a form are the source of lively debate (you will soon see on which side we the editors fall). The country's top practitioners can make or break restaurants and are themselves the subject of magazine profiles. In the democratic age of the Internet, even independent food bloggers and Yelpers can make themselves heard on a large scale.

Indeed, at no point during the making of this book did I or anyone ask, "Why food?" In her 1943 *The Gastronomical Me,* Mary Frances Fisher anticipated the question:

> The easiest answer is to say that, like most humans, I am hungry. But there is more than that. It seems to me that our three basic needs, for food and security and love, are so mixed and mingled and entwined that we cannot straightly think of one without the others. So it happens that when I write of hunger, I am really writing about love and the hunger for it, and warmth and the love of it and the hunger for it.

It seems more useful to ask why Fisher's prolific and peerless work (W. H. Auden called her America's greatest writer) was ignored for so long. When a man has a sensualist awakening spurred on by a childhood memory of his aunt's small cakes dipped in tea, he has invented a literary device; but when a woman makes sense of modern life and her relationships through food (*Heartburn, Tender at the Bone*), she is relegated to the shelves of domestic dramedy (whither Liebling?).

Most American consumers didn't get "serious" about reading about food until swashbuckling, piratical chefs like Marco Pierre White Jr. and Anthony Bourdain chronicled their days of slinging knives and profanity around high-end kitchens in displays of male dominance and ego. (If only they knew how long women have been swearing in kitchens.) Like Bill Buford's Mario Batali, these men were handled like rock stars, with carnal appetites and tempers that ran as hot as their burners. In them we see the first seeds of the rise of the celebrity chef and the cult of personality in the kitchen, and the modern view of innovative chefs as artists.

Food is paradoxically trivial. We need it to survive, but it can also be an absurd thing to spend a lot of money on, because in the end you don't even get to keep it. But it's not ephemeral, either. Food is an inescapable physical necessity, and over thousands of years we have continued to iterate novel ways of consuming it. One of the many things that separates humans from most of the animal kingdom is our deep and abiding love of inducing the Maillard reaction—when amino acids and sugars react at high temperatures to brown food and create complex and appealing aromas. Thanks to writers like Harold McGee and J. Kenji López-Alt, the chemistry and history of food science are just as essential to our recipe development as cultural histories.

Humans have also made food fun. It can be frivolous and ridiculous yet filling all the same. The little details of what celebrities like to eat are some of the most humanizing trivia out there, like Steve Jobs's all-fruit diet, M.I.A.'s truffle french fries, and Courtney Love's toast soldiers. Jeff Gordinier has called writing about food working on the "pleasure beat," since most of what we pay for at a restaurant is someone else entertaining our senses. Some have found ways to wring the pleasure (or at least the gustatory part of it) out of food by rendering it efficient, like the powdered meal replacement known as Soylent or the failed startup Juicero, whose only product was a $400 Wi-Fi-connected juice squeezer. Even so, these food hacks were covered in both traditional and food media with great relish. One of the more memorable pieces of food media of the past few years was the viral food diary of Amanda Chantal Bacon, the wellness entrepreneur and founder of Moon Juice. Her daily routine as published on Elle.com involves mushroom protein powders, seawater electrolytes, and something called "brain dust." Suffice it to say that we love to consume stories about consumption in all its forms.

Food can also be an ethical conundrum for eaters in an age where certain resources have become scarce and animal health and safety are being sacrificed in the name of mass quantity (not to mention the health and safety of the planet). Much ink has been spilled in this arena by Michael Pollan, from *Omnivore's Dilemma* to *Food Rules,* in which he advises us to "eat food, not too much, mostly plants." Humans evolved to like hot, cooked food and animal proteins, which are arguably both things that made humans what they are today. But that doesn't mean they have to or even should continue to do so, because the path of evolution is neither a value judgment nor a proscription.

To complicate matters, we've turned food and all its components into economic consumption items, and food products are developing at an exponential rate. Food as a commodity is an endlessly renewable source of controversy and drama as well as moral debate. It also becomes a socioeconomic concern: who has access to what and why? In food there is plenty of science—chemistry, largely—as well as junk science. The media loves a study that will sign off on red wine, chocolate, and the power of kale to change lives. Food can foster health and its opposite: we now know that processed meats are classified as carcinogens, but we also have the technology to engineer meat. In light of all these facts, what would Mark Bittman tell us to make for dinner?

For me, food has always been a given, and largely the organizing principle of my life. My family moved around from East Coast to West, for a time living abroad, in Paris. Some of my earliest food memories are of living in Paris at a time when the only reminder of home was McDonald's. You could get Cheerios only through your friend's parents who worked at the American Embassy, and no matter how much fancy French cheese and red and yellow food dye my father used, he could never replicate the powder-based boxed mac and cheese of our suburban youth. (I know what you're thinking: who goes to France and wants to look back on her American staples? A five-year-old, that's who.) But oh, the éclairs! And the

baguettes. It is my strong personal stance that Americans' relationship with bread is troubled at best. Infinitely more novel than sliced
bread is the pure chemistry and curiosity of human patience that
is a good loaf.

After college I moved to New York City to work in magazines.
After a year and a half I was working at *The New Yorker*, as the A-issue
editor. I would spend late nights at the office, but whenever I had
the chance, I'd travel downtown for dinner and send my parents
a postcard from the restaurant. The only time in my life I have
ever felt like I knew something David Remnick didn't was when
he looked on in bafflement as my colleague Amelia Lester and I
discussed which new restaurants we had been to recently and what
we'd ordered. He shook his head—the sex, drugs, and rock 'n roll
of his youth had been supplanted by . . . ricotta gnudi and hay-
smoke-infused whiskey cocktails? I couldn't blame him; it sounded
unbelievably lame.

But for us it was honest. Amelia was a far-flung Australian who
found her way in New York through bars and restaurants, and I
a transplanted Californian raised on *Cook's Illustrated* and stop-
watch-timed backyard grilling, who learned that going out to dinner could be as much a cultural event as a trip to the Met. As Jeff
Gordinier told *The Ringer* in 2017, "The defining pleasure of the
sixties was music. To some extent, the defining pleasure of the seventies was film. The defining pursuit of our time now is food." Chefs
were our rock stars, bespoke cocktails our drugs, and gut-busting
meals our orgies. Remnick recognized that passion and put pens
in our hands—we both reviewed restaurants for the magazine's
"Tables for Two" section until we left.

It used to be that food writing was confined to food publications,
but with the splitting open of the media—the various print con-
tractions, online expansions, and crossover in coverage—you're
as likely to see a story about flavored soda in the *Wall Street Journal*
as you are in *Bon Appétit*. I have always been grateful to the space
that *The New Yorker* made in its pages for food writing, even in the
smallest doses.

Food is the ultimate modern topic, now that we know enough
about it to discuss it and analyze it and manipulate it to death. How
do you get kids to eat X? How do you make sure you get enough
Y? Why is organic Z so expensive? Each and every human anxiety
can be co-opted by food. Are you getting enough? Are you eating

too much? Is it being raised ethically? Can it make you live longer, grow more beautiful hair, and have lower taxes? We are doomed to wonder about food as long as we shall live, and this is part of what makes us human.

Food is an expression of human culture. It is not just a trend, or a light, fluffy topic best suited to service journalism and domestic interests. For me it is the one true topic, evidenced by the most oft-quoted aphorism of Jean Anthelme Brillat-Savarin: "Tell me what you eat and I'll tell you what you are." If humans are made of stardust, so too are they made out of sandwiches and carrots and gallons of coffee. At first blush, the subtitle of Brillat-Savarin's famous *Physiology of Taste,* "Meditations on Transcendental Gastronomy," reads as obscure and almost stubbornly academic. But upon closer inspection it is utterly precise: thoughts on food and beyond. Quite simply, food transcends, and the real reason this book took so long to exist is that it's still hard to say so with a straight face.

It has been a great honor to work on this inaugural collection of *The Best American Food Writing,* and I hope it is the first of many to come. I can only wonder at what we might have missed or left out (a list of notable essays appears at the end of the book), which only energizes me to cast an even wider net on the next go-round. May this volume sustain you until then. I owe a debt of gratitude to my editor, Naomi Gibbs, and to the brilliant Ruth Reichl for her enduring wisdom. Onward and upward with food!

SILVIA KILLINGSWORTH

Introduction

FOOD WRITING IS STEPPING OUT.

It's about time.

For far too long it's been the timid little sister of the writing world, afraid to raise its voice. Food writers were missionaries of the delicious, celebrating rural simplicity—usually in other countries —or luxuriating in the extravagance of urban fare. Sensual and sensuous, their tools were travel and nostalgia. One sent you back to better times, the other off to explore new places. They leaned on descriptions of flavor and aroma, and their ultimate desire was to make you very, very hungry.

But that was in another time, an era when America's interest in food was so minimal that serious writers refused to choose it as their subject. It was, they thought, beneath them. I plead guilty: fifty years ago, when I began to write, I bristled at being labeled a "food writer." Back then food writing was tepid stuff, created primarily by women for women. As far back as the thirties Mary Frances Fisher used only her initials, hoping readers would think she was a man and take her seriously. Forty years later, I understood: "I'm a writer," I kept insisting, "not a food writer."

I had my heroes, of course—Fisher, A. J. Liebling, Joseph Mitchell, Joseph Wechsberg—but they all belonged to the past. By the time I entered the field, food writing was held in such contempt that when Jacques Pépin, studying for a PhD in philosophy and literature at Columbia, proposed writing a doctoral thesis on the history of French food in the context of French literature, he was turned down flat. He'd planned to start with Ronsard's "Apology to a Field Salad," go on to the wedding feast in *Madame Bovary*, and of course deal with the famous madeleine. But it was not to be. "Cuisine," his adviser pontificated, "is not a serious art form. It's far too trivial for academic study."

This situation endured for a very long time. As recently as twenty years ago, when my first memoir was published, bookstores had no idea what to do with it. The biography people refused to embrace a book about adventures at the table. "We don't keep it on the main floor," one salesman told me when I asked where I might find the book. "It's about food." He made a contemptuous gesture and pointed upstairs. "Go look in cookbooks." But the cookbook people were equally disdainful. "What we sell," they told me, "are recipes." The notion that food writing might offer more than advice about ingredients struck them as absurd.

A few years later, when I arrived at *Gourmet* magazine, little had changed. My publishers were horrified when I suggested that an epicurean magazine should offer its readers more than recipes, restaurants, and resorts; the old formula, they said, was working very well. Any hope that readers might think otherwise were soon dashed; when we began stretching the boundaries to include literary articles by prominent writers, many longtime readers howled in protest.

I couldn't help thinking about that as I read the articles that series editor Silvia Killingsworth chose for consideration for this book. Immersed in a fabulous feast of words, I thought how thrilled I would have been to have had such bounty when I still had a magazine. Back then only a handful of writers were willing to tackle food subjects, and it took great persuasion to get the best to change their minds. Even later, after *Gourmet* readers had broadened their outlook, many writers still refused to believe that subscribers to an epicurean publication were interested in articles venturing beyond entertainment.

The situation so distressed me that when I addressed the American Society of News Editors twelve years ago, I used my time to beg them to start covering food. I began by saying, "I'd like to try and convince you that many of the important issues we're dealing with today are, ultimately, about food. And that they belong not only in food sections, where, in my opinion, they do not often enough appear, but also very much on the editorial pages of our newspapers."

I was desperately trying to prove that what we eat has an impact on our lives extending far beyond the table.

That speech would be ridiculous today: over the past few years Americans have changed their minds about food. We've shaken off our indifference, transformed our outlook, and recognized that food offers a unique perspective on almost every subject. Nothing could make me happier. These days so many writers are fascinated by food that it's difficult to pick up a newspaper or magazine without finding an article focused on some aspect of edible culture.

What happened?

I hate to admit this, but much of the credit goes to food television, which turned chefs into celebrities and made cooking cool. An entire generation grew up watching smart, articulate people talk about food in interesting ways; the result is that young Americans are the most sophisticated eaters this country has ever raised. Millennials have tugged food into the realm of popular culture and given restaurants a new kind of respect. Previous generations went to restaurants to celebrate special occasions, but eating out has now become an everyday occurrence. Food used to be something to eat; now it is something to talk about, as important as music, art, and movies.

The Internet certainly played its part. As we spend increasing hours buried in our computers, the very fact that food can't be virtually consumed gives it a special resonance. You can, of course, post pictures of what you're eating—people do that by the millions —but that's no substitute for the scent of onions caramelizing in butter, the sound of stock burbling on the stove, or the shocking coldness of an ice cream cone. And no photograph will ever be as thrilling as a slice of chocolate cake. Even the most avid technocrat must occasionally escape from virtual space, and what better place to do it than the kitchen, with all its dangerous knives and delicious aromas?

This grand passion for food eventually led to questions; it was pretty much inevitable. Where, we began asking, is our food coming from? What is going into it? Who's in charge? The answers have been unsettling: modern technology has changed the way almost everything we eat is raised, caught, created, consumed, and transported. These days it's impossible to ignore the fact that this has reshaped not only our bodies but also our communities and the way we relate to each other. Food is, in a very real sense, redesigning the world.

In the face of all this, is it any wonder that writers in almost every field have embraced food? That has created yet another dramatic shift. Ten years ago a book called *The Best American Food Writing* would have been filled with articles gleaned from epicurean publications. Not anymore. These articles come from an enormously wide swath of publications: literary magazines, newspapers, science journals, business publications, sports magazines, and the Internet. It's become abundantly clear that no matter which corner of the world you're focused on, food has something important to tell you.

When I became a food editor, my mantra was that every great writer has at least one good food story in them, and I made it my job to ferret that out. But it turns out I was wrong; every writer has at least a dozen great food stories, and they are now producing them at an unprecedented pace.

It's exciting — and daunting. Choosing the articles for this book was one of the hardest tasks I've ever faced. It would have been easy to fill these pages with moving personal essays about growing up and discovering the wonderful world of flavor. I was certainly tempted. I love rich, delicious prose, and I could sit for hours reading Tejal Rao tell about growing up with cookbooks. Few people describe food as poetically as Ligaya Mishan. And reading Wyatt Williams is always a pleasure.

I'm also easily seduced by writers who travel to places I've never been and return with fabulous tales. I loved tagging along with Anya von Bremzen as she uncovered the glories of Baku. Alex Halberstadt's lyrical visit to a Japanese temple opened up a whole new world to me. And when John T. Edge takes the great American smokemaster to Spain, I'm thrilled to be there with them.

But other voices clamored to be heard. Angry voices. Raucous voices. Impolite voices. This was the year when race, class, and gender became fodder for food writers, and many spoke up with clearheaded rage. I dare you to read Amanda Cohen's screed on women chefs without laughing, crying, and ultimately searching your conscience. Lauren Michele Jackson, Marissa Higgins, and Lauren Collins each had a similar effect on me, and I both wept and winced as I read their words. This is the new sound of food writing — muscular, passionate, powerful, and intent on fomenting change.

For many years we turned a blind eye to the important part politics play in deciding what we eat. Our ignorance is over: food writers are embracing the subject with renewed rigor. As Jane Black chronicles the revenge of the lunch lady, she takes us deep into the complicated world of the school lunchroom with all its messy local politics. Clint Rainey explores the convoluted place that cheese now occupies on the national table, offering up a very clear picture of the profound impact government policy has on our daily diet. And when Ligaya Mishan examines the effect immigration policy has had on Asian-American food, she also explores what it is like to be caught between the obligations of inheritance and the desire for self-expression. This is a story about the third generation, about what happens when the food of other places becomes the food of America.

But there's another, equally compelling side to that particular coin. When Julia O'Malley tells us about a talented young hunter, she is really asking a profound question: what happens when the ancestral foodways of native cultures bump up against modern mores? It's an ethical issue, and the answers are uncomfortable.

For most of human history raising food has been man's major occupation, and agriculture has a unique way of connecting the past to the present. Food writers are beginning to understand what farmers have always known: plants are, in a very real sense, living history. Agriculture has always had an honored place at the food-writing table, but it's different today. When Shane Mitchell looks at rice, he sees not just a grain but a crime. Ted Genoways takes us down to the farm, hoping to show us how profoundly modern production has changed the lives of farmers. And although Harold McGee begins with a simple question, his answer goes beyond yes and no to look at the unique way that cooking and science might interact.

I've chosen writings from across the spectrum, hoping to offer a snapshot of the way America eats at this very moment in time. And so I've included restaurant reviews. Restaurant critics are no longer content to be simple consumer reporters telling us where to spend our money, and the best are bending the form. They've become cultural critics, because they understand that where we choose to eat tells the world not only who we think we are but also who we want to be.

Restaurants themselves have been constantly evolving, and our view of them is evolving as well. In the past, chef profiles tended to be pleasant little personality pieces focused on what some famous person was cooking and an attempt to understand the reasons why. We would have learned about their childhoods, their families, their homes. But restaurants have become big business, and the profiles I've included here go beyond personality to examine the new face of chefs who are intent on turning themselves into valuable brands.

Food in America is an almost $6 trillion industry, so it should come as no surprise that some of the best food writing takes us deep into the world of business. But here too food writers are bringing something special to the table, offering us another way of peering behind the curtain.

"Produce," says Dana Goodyear as she explores the strawberry business, "is war!" Her reporting goes beyond market share and dollars to demonstrate something crucial about the intersection of agriculture and business. Beth Kowitt explores the brave new world of alternative meat, beginning with this rather startling statement: "Animals are lousy tools for converting matter into muscle tissue." Building on that, she initiates us into the mysteries of a world that did not even exist a few years ago. And that, of course, is the point; both writers are scrutinizing a brave new world in an attempt to find out what these foods can tell us about the people we've become.

Although food writing is turning up in the most surprising places, I did not expect to find it in a magazine dedicated to competitive sports. "The NBA's Secret Sandwich Addiction" is a testament to the central place food has come to occupy in modern culture. More than that, it is incontrovertible proof of food writing's uncanny ability to delve into the secrets of hitherto hidden worlds.

While many food writers are busy tearing down walls to create transparency, others take the long view. For these writers food is simply a jumping-off point, a way of talking about larger issues. In many ways these are the most satisfying pieces, because they offer us the entire world in an oyster, an orange, or a country store. These writers start small and think big, reminding us along the way that this thing that we do, this activity that keeps us alive, can be a way of making sense of the world. These writers insist that we pay attention to our food, pointing out that it is something to cherish and protect. In the end their words are a reminder that in an increasingly complicated world, focusing on food can be a way of finding grace.

This is the first time this series has included a volume on food writing, and I am honored to be the inaugural editor. My one regret is for the many wonderful words that got left on the cutting-room floor, the many talented writers I could not include.

Still, all those lost articles give me hope. They are proof, if we need it, that food writing is not only alive and well but growing bolder every day. These days most bookstores have entire sections on food history, food memoir, food novels, and I like to think that if Mary Frances Fisher were still with us, she would no longer feel the need to hide behind her initials. I hope that no university will ever again sneer at the notion of a food-focused thesis. As for me, these days I not only admit to being a food writer, I do it with great pride.

RUTH REICHL

The Best American
Food Writing 2018

Revenge of the Lunch Lady

FROM *The Huffington Post/Highline*

IN THE FALL of 2009, the British celebrity chef Jamie Oliver arrived in Huntington, West Virginia, which had recently been named the unhealthiest city in America. Huntingtonians were suffering in record numbers from diabetes and heart disease. They were being destroyed by the mountains of burgers and fries and nuggets that filled their restaurants, schools, refrigerators, and arteries. They were fulfilling the prophecy that this generation of children would be the first to live shorter lives than their parents. Oliver had come to save them—and to film a season of his new reality show, *Food Revolution*.

The first thing he saw when he walked into the kitchen of Central City Elementary School was the breakfast pizza. It looked like you remember school pizza: a rectangle of bleached dough spackled with red sauce and melted cheese. What made it breakfast, presumably, was that each slice also had crumbles of sausage scattered across it. That, and it was 7:40 a.m.

Oliver was disgusted by the school's freezers (an "Aladdin's cave of processed crap"), by the "luminous" strawberry milk that kids poured on their cereal, and by the instant potato pearls that tasted like "starchy fluff with off nuts in it." To his astonishment, all of these foods were considered part of a healthy diet by the standards of the U.S. government.

"This is where it's at, guys," he said as he strode through the cafeteria. "This is the future of America sitting here, having pizza for breakfast."

The locals were even less enthusiastic about Oliver than he was about the breakfast pizza. Being tarred as the least healthy place in America by the Centers for Disease Control and Prevention had unsettled Huntington, a former railroad town at the intersection of the Rust Belt and Appalachia. The city, like so many others, had been ravaged by America's manufacturing collapse, and it seemed as if the only time anyone paid attention to it was when something bad happened. In media coverage of the CDC report, out-of-town journalists gleefully reported that half of Huntingtonians over the age of sixty-five had no teeth.

Now some fancy chef—a foreign one, no less—was scrutinizing how unhealthy they were on national television. To Huntingtonians, it seemed like the latest insult in a lifetime of ridicule and humiliation. When Oliver went on a local radio show, the DJ, Rod Willis, lit into him. "We don't want to sit around and eat lettuce all day," Willis said. "I just don't think you should come in here and tell us what to do. I mean, who made you the king?"

Oliver had expected this reaction. He had seen it before, when he filmed a similar show in an industrial area of England. ("Same shit, different country," he told me.) But Oliver genuinely wanted to help, and Huntington's rejection seemed shortsighted to him.

Oliver had made his name in the late 1990s on a television show called *The Naked Chef*—not because he cooked in the nude, but because of his stripped-down approach, which emphasized fun rather than precise measurements or techniques. By the time he turned twenty-five he had cooked for the prime minister and established a mini media empire that included a contract that reportedly paid him over $1 million a year to serve as the face of British retail giant Sainsbury's. He could have continued on this path, making insane money flacking pots, pans, and other products, as celebrity chefs do. Instead he decided to use his power to champion a series of culinary crusades, including revamping school meals to showcase fresh food rather than, say, Britain's beloved Turkey Twizzlers. That kids were the focus was essential; study after study had shown that lifelong eating habits are formed at a young age. And when kids eat well, they also perform better academically. In the U.K., Oliver had won the argument. The 2005 reality TV series, *Jamie's School Dinners,* resulted in a government investment of over $1 billion to overhaul Britain's disgraceful school meals.

Despite the locals' resistance, it looked as if Oliver was replicating that success in Huntington. He built a gleaming cooking center in a long-empty building downtown. He introduced a range of made-from-scratch school dishes—beefy nachos, tuna pasta bake with seven vegetables, rainbow salad with creamy dressing. And he did righteous battle with the unimaginative bureaucrats who seemed to want kids to keep eating the same sludge. In scene after scene, Rhonda McCoy, Cabell County's uptight and slightly menacing schools food-service director, reminded the chef that his revolution had to conform to the government's endless standards and regulations. "I just wanted to cook some food," a baffled Oliver protested. "This is like a math test." When the show aired, McCoy's in-box filled with hate mail from around the country. At home, there was grumbling that she should resign.

But there was a problem with this made-for-TV narrative—several, actually. Shortly after Oliver left, a study by the West Virginia University Health Research Center reported that 77 percent of students were "very unhappy" with his food. Students who relied on school meals for nearly half of their daily calories routinely dumped their trays in the trash. Some did it because they hated the taste, others because it became the cool thing to do. And while Oliver's meals used fresh, high-quality ingredients, many turned out to be too high in fat to meet the U.S. Department of Agriculture's standards. Within a year, McCoy said, the number of students eating school lunch fell 10 percent, forcing her to cut her budget and lay off several cooks.

In almost every respect, it would have been easier for McCoy to drop this grand experiment in school-lunch reform that had been foisted on her. Her employees were overworked, and the fresh food was more expensive, even after McCoy abandoned the free-range chicken and organic vegetables that Oliver had insisted on (and that school officials say ABC Productions had paid for). There's only so much you can do when you have $1.50 to spend on ingredients for each meal. But over the next few years McCoy accomplished exactly what Oliver had set out to do himself: she saved school lunch in Huntington and proved that cafeteria food isn't destined to be a national joke.

To those unfamiliar with the absurdist theater of school lunch, it is puzzling, even maddening, that feeding kids nutritious food should be so hard. You buy good food. You cook it. You serve it to hungry kids.

Yet the National School Lunch Program, an $11.7 billion behemoth that feeds more than 31 million children each day, is a mess, and has been for years. Conflicts of interest were built into the program. It was pushed through Congress after World War II with the support of military leaders who wanted to ensure that there would be enough healthy young men to fight the next war and of farmers who were looking for a place to unload their surplus corn, milk, and meat. The result was that schools became the dumping ground for the cheap calories our modern agricultural system was designed to overproduce.

This tension has played out over and over again, with children usually ending up the losers. A case in point: In 1981, America was awash in surplus dairy. The government's Inland Storage and Distribution Center—a network of tunnels beneath Kansas City, Missouri—was filled with 200 million pounds of cheese and butter, stacked "like frozen pillars and stretching over acres of gray stone floor," according to the Associated Press. In an effort to ease the glut, the USDA purchased millions of pounds of dairy for schools. But according to Janet Poppendieck, a professor at Hunter College who specializes in poverty and hunger, this encouraged dairy farmers to keep on milking. So in 1986 the government had to create a new program, the Whole Herd Buyout, which paid farmers to slaughter the dairy cows. The government then bought the beef, which was turned into hamburger, taco meat, and so on for school lunch.

That flood of meat and dairy hiked the fat content of school meals just as the country was descending into an antifat frenzy. In 1990 the federal government issued new dietary guidelines, declaring that a healthy diet should contain no more than 30 percent fat, with a 10 percent cap on saturated fat. But cafeterias simply had too much of the wrong food to comply. In a USDA study of 544 schools conducted several years later, only 1 percent met the requirement for overall fat and just a single school had managed to keep saturated fat to a healthy level. The deeply conflicted nature of the program was showing itself once again.

Since the 1990s the USDA has made many improvements—it now requires that canned vegetables have less salt and insists that ground beef be 95 percent lean. But school lunch is still a disgrace, and the timidity of Congress is largely to blame. In 2011 the USDA proposed limiting the amount of potatoes and other starchy vegetables permitted in school lunches so that cafeterias could make room for healthier options. But the Senate, led by members from two top potato producers, Maine and Colorado, killed the idea in a unanimous vote. Then there's the pizza lobby. When the 2010 revision of nutrition standards increased the minimum amount of tomato paste required for pizza to count as a vegetable from two tablespoons—the typical amount found on a slice—to half a cup, the National Frozen Pizza Institute and other groups howled, and Congress opted for the status quo. The idea that pizza might not be considered a vegetable was apparently un-American.

What makes school lunch so contentious, though, isn't just the question of *what* kids eat but of *which* kids are doing the eating. As Poppendieck recounts in her book, *Free for All: Fixing School Food in America,* the original program provided schools with food and, later, cash to subsidize the cost of meals. But by the early 1960s schools weren't receiving enough to feed all their students, and many pulled out of the program. As a result, middle-class students, whose parents could cover the difference between the government subsidy and the actual cost of a meal, ended up benefiting the most from school lunch, while the truly needy went hungry. This moral failing became clear in 1968, when a landmark report called "Their Daily Bread" revealed that only one third of the 6 million children living in poverty were receiving free or subsidized lunch. Schools' ability to pay for food was so limited that one in Mississippi rotated 100 lunches among more than 400 students, while another in Alabama had just 15 meals for 1,000 needy kids. School lunch had its first official scandal.

In response, Congress, which had preferred to let schools decide who got to eat and who did not, established a three-tiered system. Students from families with incomes up to 25 percent above the federal poverty line—about $3,300 for a family of four, or around $24,000 in today's dollars—were entitled to free meals. Those from families with incomes between 25 and 95 percent above the poverty line paid a reduced price, while everyone else paid the full price. (Just to make things extra-confusing, schools also received a small subsidy for those meals as well.) This system had the virtue of guaranteeing that the poorest children would be fed. But it also transformed school lunch from a program designed to feed *all* students into one for the poor.

Once school lunch was perceived as welfare, it became a target.

President Ronald Reagan, elected in 1980 on a promise to slash domestic spending, attacked the program. It was one thing to help the genuinely needy, Reagan's budget director, David Stockman, declared, but it was "wasteful" to support middle- and upper-class families who could afford to buy lunch. What he didn't mention was that the cutoff for a free meal was nowhere near a middle-class income and excluded many kids who needed the help.

Still, Congress agreed to cut the small subsidy for full-price lunches by more than a third. The effect was quick and severe. Lunch prices rose, and in the space of just three years, more than a quarter of the kids in the full-price tier stopped buying school lunch. With fewer students participating and smaller reimbursements for each meal served, schools lost their (already limited) economies of scale. The ensuing budget crisis forced schools to seek out even cheaper food—the highly processed stuff, such as chicken nuggets and corn dogs, that they are now condemned for serving. And on it goes.

Not that any of these cautionary tales have diminished the Republicans' desire to gut the program. In 2014, now House Speaker Paul Ryan said that public assistance, including school lunch, offered a "full stomach and an empty soul" because it made kids reliant on government handouts. With the party now in control of Congress and the White House—and with Michelle Obama, the program's greatest defender, gone—school lunch is as vulnerable as it's ever been.

One Republican strategy to hobble school lunch involves changing an innocuous-sounding proposal called the Community Eligibility Provision. The formula for CEP is complex, but it essentially allows schools in high-poverty areas to provide free meals to all students. This alleviates the administrative burden of keeping track of who qualifies for which tier and allows money that would normally be spent on administration to go instead toward paying cooks or buying better food.

Judging by its popularity among food-service directors, CEP has been one of the most successful innovations in school-lunch policy in decades. Studies show the program reduces the long-standing stigma for kids getting free lunch and enables those who don't qualify for subsidized meals but who actually need them to eat if they're hungry. This prevents situations like the one that took place last fall, when a school cafeteria worker in Pennsylvania resigned after having to take away the lunch of a first-grader whose parents failed to pay their bill. Not surprisingly, CEP has been embraced in impoverished areas like North Dakota, Kentucky, Tennessee, and West Virginia, where food-service directors have been forced to hire collection agencies to chase down parents who haven't paid for their kids' meals.

Conservatives insist that it's not the taxpayers' job to cover for negligent parents. Todd Rokita, an Indiana Republican who chairs the House subcommittee that oversees school food, called CEP "perverse," alleging that it incentivizes schools to give free meals to students who either already pay or are capable of paying for school lunch. This despite the fact that schools, like most places in America, have become increasingly segregated by socioeconomics over the past two decades. So the throngs of coddled middle-class kids Rokita thinks are eating for free don't actually exist.

Rhonda McCoy is emphatic that kids shouldn't be punished for their families' financial situations. "It's not their fault that the parents didn't pay the bill," she said. Before CEP, she remembers getting calls, which she said "broke my heart," about students who chose to go hungry rather than have an embarrassing conversation about money. But if Rokita wins this battle, more than 7,000 schools, feeding nearly 3.4 million kids, will once again have to start charging for some meals. In West Virginia the new formula would exclude 327 schools, including all 26 in Cabell County. "This would all be over," McCoy told me. "It would kill us."

There are people who are comfortable with silence, and then there is Rhonda McCoy. Even the most innocuous question can bring conversation to a halt. When I asked her once what she likes to cook for dinner, she looked startled, then tucked her hands beneath her thighs and swung nervously back and forth in her swivel chair. She never answered. And it wasn't as if I were a stranger; we'd known each other for six years.

I have learned not to take this personally. Jedd Flowers, Cabell County Schools' voluble, upbeat director of communications, has worked with McCoy for eleven years. But when I wondered aloud to him whether McCoy had any grandchildren, he shrugged and said he really didn't know. Maybe one or two. "She's CIA," James Colegrove, another longtime colleague, told me. "I call her Secret Squirrel."

This does not make McCoy a lousy coworker. Nearly everyone I spoke to—from a school dishwasher to the county superintendent—mentioned that she has a way of making people feel part of something. She's fastidious and never misses a deadline, they added. She doesn't pick favorites, and the cooks who make far less than she does notice that she works as hard as, if not harder than, they do. Frances Hickman, the cafeteria manager at Cabell Midland High School, has served under four different food-service directors in her thirty-three-year career. But she told me (after McCoy left the room, since she couldn't bear hearing a compliment) that she'd never met a person so skilled at her job and can't imagine working for anybody else now. "When she goes, I go," Hickman said.

A crucial part of McCoy's appeal is that she is a West Virginian—an insider, one of them. She grew up in Lincoln County, a rural area at the edge of the southern coalfields, the poorest region in a very poor state. Her family, like many others, had a garden where they grew much of what ended up on the kitchen table. And the tastes of those homegrown meals left a mark. She told me that it took years before she could bring herself to eat a canned green bean from the supermarket. She wanted the students in her district to have a real relationship with food.

Long before Oliver had ever heard of Huntington, McCoy had begun to improve the meals in Cabell County. Notwithstanding what *Food Revolution* viewers saw on TV, McCoy's cafeterias were downright enlightened by the dismal standards of America's school-lunch program. In 2008 the West Virginia Board of Education had imposed tough new rules that required meals to include fresh fruits and vegetables, lean meats, whole grains, low-fat milk, and water. McCoy, a registered dietician with twenty-five years of experience, pushed her district even further. One of the first things she did was remove the saltshakers from cafeteria tables—a move that prompted students to steal salt packets from fast-food restaurants and create a black market for them at lunch. At a time when 94 percent of U.S. schools were failing to meet federal guidelines, Cabell County hit, and often exceeded, every one.

This was a surprise to Oliver's advance production team, which assumed that the schools in America's most unhealthy city would serve junk. "That," Jedd Flowers said, "is when the show became about 'fresh.'"

McCoy was a proponent of fresh food. But she recognized that kids had to *like* what they were eating — and that she had to be able to pay for it. She started by assembling a group of cooks to rework Oliver's recipes so they reflected local tastes. A friendly competition developed over who could come up with the best adaptation. The snap peas with mint, a quintessentially English combination, lost the mint; the garlicky greens became a lot less garlicky; the cinnamon in the chili was eighty-sixed. That McCoy let the cooks decide what tasted good made them feel important and helped win them over to the new, more labor-intensive way of doing things.

At every level, practicality took precedence over idealism. Where Oliver had been skeptical of government handouts on principle, McCoy happily accepted 2,000 cases of raw chicken from the USDA, because it left her more money to spend on fresh fruits and vegetables. Where Oliver had insisted the cooks peel and slice 50 pounds of carrots, she ordered presliced frozen coins that were ready to cook. McCoy also holed up in her office writing federal and state grants for money to buy equipment. It is an arduous, unsexy process, exactly the sort of thing she's great at. In the first year after Oliver left, she was able to secure an extra $50,000 for her district.

McCoy has been smart about spending the money, using a lot of it to pay for new equipment that's expected to save the district thousands in the long term. Take the tilt skillet, a hulking, $15,000 vat about the size of a six-burner stove that can cook up to 60 gallons of food. Before the cooks had one, making enormous quantities of chili, taco meat, or spaghetti sauce was backbreaking work. For each batch, cooks had to use several big stockpots. The process took hours, the pots were heavy to lift, and it was awkward to transfer the finished sauce into containers. A slosh or two inevitably ended up on the floor. But kids really like chili and tacos and spaghetti, which meant that cooks spent too much time making red sauce. Now, with the tilt skillet, the whole thing takes a few hours, doesn't make a mess, and yields enough sauce for more than a month.

It's weirdly beautiful watching one of McCoy's kitchens at work. At many U.S. schools, the food arrives ready to be reheated. Mixing a jar of commercial sauce into boil-in-the-bag pasta is considered "cooking." But at Cabell Midland High School, the eighteen cooks — all women, all dressed in medical scrubs, all engaged in constant small talk with one another — start arriving at 6 a.m.; it's the only way to make sure that lunch is ready for the first wave of students, who eat at 10:49. Over the course of one morning I watched two cooks quarter red potatoes and toss them in olive oil with a shake of garlic powder and paprika, then move on to rubbing chicken breasts with a seventeen-spice seasoning. I saw cooks top rounds of pizza dough with homemade tomato sauce and cheese and mix olive oil and vinegar for salad dressing. (Commercial dressings, packed with sodium and calories, undermine the health benefits of most salads.) One cook's full-time job consisted of making home-made desserts and fresh bread—fluffy, delicious Parker House rolls whose yeasty scent wafted down the school's hallways.

The only items not regularly made from scratch are the ones for breakfast. Some, like the heat-and-eat whole-wheat sausage bis-cuits, looked fine. Others, including the sausage-stuffed pancake on a stick, could have made a school lunch most-wanted list. When McCoy saw me inspect one, she blushed and opened her mouth to explain, but ultimately said nothing. To make breakfast from scratch, a cook told me apologetically, "we'd have to get here in the middle of the night."

I didn't taste the pancake on a stick. But the chicken and roasted potatoes at lunch were pretty good. I might have used a little more salt, but then I don't have the USDA looking over my shoulder when I cook. Were it not for the red plastic tray, I would not have even known this was school lunch, so tight are my associations with metallic-tasting green beans, bland pizza, and desiccated crinkle fries. I was impressed.

The kids? Not so much. The first few times I visited Cabell Mid-land, in 2013 and 2014, most students didn't have much to say about the improved quality of the food. They didn't hate it; it just didn't register as anything special. Tori Evans, a junior who ate school lunch every day, declared the chicken and potatoes "okay," but rated the salad as "boring." Asked what the cooks might do to make it better, she answered, "Put ham in it."

But the students have apparently gotten used to it. The younger ones don't know any different, and with the older kids it helps that fast-food restaurants have adopted the lingo of "fresh." McDonald's now boasts of using "freshly cracked" eggs and is even trying out nonfrozen beef for its hamburgers.

McCoy has also gotten kids to accept better food by buying sea-sonal produce from enterprising student farmers. She didn't do this to mimic what was happening in Berkeley or Brooklyn—nor does it make her job any easier. The first crop of local peppers she purchased from a student arrived covered with dirt, not clean and shiny like the ones from a mega-distributor. But she understood that kids are more likely to try something if a friend had a hand in growing it. It was just another way for her to build a healthier food culture in a place that had been colonized by the drive-through. McCoy has since helped several students win grants to buy seeds and equipment. One of McCoy's first student farmers, Zachary Call, was so successful that after graduation he continued to farm full-time—no small feat on the industrial western edge of West Virginia. All told, McCoy now buys more than $85,000 a year in local produce.

It's an article of faith that processed food is cheaper than the good stuff. But each one of the made-from-scratch meals that McCoy dishes out costs only $1.50 in ingredients—about 2 cents less than when Jamie Oliver arrived. Counterintuitively, it is the huge number of students served (about 10,000 a day) that makes the numbers work. The more kids who eat, the easier it is to achieve economies of scale. And McCoy couldn't have done that without the Community Eligibility Provision.

CEP lets schools feed everyone for free. But the trick is that schools are reimbursed only for the number of meals actually served. So if the kids don't eat all of the meals that are prepared, the county has to bank the losses. McCoy needed her conservative, cash-strapped board to accept that risk.

Her pitch to the board was a meticulous demonstration of how CEP could work. Each year, beginning in 2012, she added a few schools and watched what happened. At Huntington High School, where McCoy worried that teenagers would shun hot lunches—even free ones—she conducted a pilot before officially signing up. The school went from serving 700 or so meals a day to nearly 1,300. Because of successes like this, she earned the board's trust and was the first food-service director ever to be invited to join the superintendent's cabinet and the weekly meetings where big decisions were made. "She knows her figures," said William Smith, Cabell County Schools' superintendent. "By the time it came to make the decision [to implement CEP at all schools], we knew it was working." When I returned to Huntington last fall, the number of students eating school lunch had jumped 15 percent.

Oliver, for his part, has moved on from school lunch. He had little success delivering change in the second and final season of *Food Revolution,* in Los Angeles, and in 2015 he admitted to a British magazine that his campaign to improve school meals had failed because he hadn't applied himself single-mindedly to the issue and because eating well was a "very posh and middle-class" concern. Oliver has since focused his attention (and his television time) on railing against the ubiquity of sugar and raising awareness of so-called Blue Zones, areas of the globe where healthy diets help a surprising number of residents live to one hundred or more.

Still, he told me that he is proud of all that he accomplished in Huntington. In an email interview, he called McCoy's efforts "amazing" and suggested that this is exactly how he hoped things would go. "My part involved putting a spotlight on the town," he said. "Ultimately, when it comes to making a real change, only local people can help local people."

The success that McCoy has achieved in Cabell County is rare, and was due to a propitious confluence of factors. Not every district has such a supportive superintendent, for instance, or such an overwhelming determination to prove a reality TV star wrong. But what McCoy did isn't magic. Much of what made the Huntington experiment work is transferable to other places—so long as they have someone like McCoy.

Schools need an ambitious leader at the helm, one who understands both nutrition and how to manage complex operations. In the mid-2000s I visited two schools in the Boston suburbs that were minutes away from each other but belonged to different districts. In the one run by a motivated dietician, the food was colorful, fresh, and reasonably tasty. In the other, administered by a disinterested box-ticker, the food was appalling: stuff like chicken nuggets packed with fillers, gray hamburger patties, bagel dogs.

"You have to have someone who goes against the flow at every turn," says Toni Liquori, executive director of School Food Focus, a nonprofit that pushes for better school meals. "How can this be more whole? How can I get fresher? You have to be driven to do that or you will coast along and hit all the targets that are in the standards, because they are pretty low."

The problem is that it's hard to find people like McCoy. There's been a historical lack of respect for her job that is reflected both in the pay and in the hiring standards. Forty-one states have no requirements at all for food-service personnel, according to the National Association of State Boards of Education's most recent assessment. And in states that do, like Mississippi, they often are as minimal as a high school diploma or its equivalent. West Virginia has the most stringent standard by far, though that isn't saying much: it mandates competency tests for all staff and specifically requires food-service directors to have a college degree and a minimum of six hours of nutrition training. In 2015 the USDA issued its first professional standards for school nutrition directors, and it required continuing education too. But these standards apply only to new candidates, so real change could take a generation.

The best school food-service directors are the ones who are able to tap into, or build, a culture around healthy eating. In Burlington, Vermont—where even the airport has a local-foods café —Doug Davis spends about a quarter of his $1.1 million budget on goods from local farmers. In Detroit, Betti Wiggins, a leader in urban farming, opened up her own 2-acre farm to help feed the system's 46,000 students. And in the university town of Oxford, Mississippi, Eleanor Green created a comprehensive gardening and education program that offers, among other things, a weeklong "Carrot Camp" for elementary-school students. What connects these seemingly disparate efforts (and McCoy's in West Virginia) is that each one makes school lunch more enticing without resorting to the cheap trick of always serving pizza. This helps to boost the number of children eating lunch, which in turn gives districts more money to spend on further improvements to their programs. It's a virtuous cycle.

Obvious as it sounds, one effective way to spend that extra money is on kitchens you can actually cook in. As the School Lunch Program turns seventy, many school kitchens are almost as old, and the ones in new schools are often no more than a warming oven in a glorified closet. The shift to processed food has helped to hasten this neglect. But it is important to note that it was the decision to wipe out federal funding for kitchen equipment under Ronald Reagan that started the problem. For twenty-seven years Congress provided zero dollars to upgrade or improve kitchen equipment. It took until 2009—and a near collapse of the economy—for Congress to appropriate $100 million to it as part of a sweeping federal stimulus. (Due to pent-up demand, the USDA received requests for more than $600 million.)

The ability to cook doesn't just produce better food. It allows schools to adapt to America's regularly shifting nutrition standards; we live, after all, in a country where the "right" diet can swing from low-fat to low-carb seemingly overnight. Cooking also gives a school the ability to tweak what it serves and accommodate changing tastes. By contrast, if a school depends on a food conglomerate to change its menu, it might wait years for new products to make their way through research and development and food-safety testing.

Schools that have received USDA funds for equipment prove that it doesn't take much money to make a big difference. Garnet J. Robertson, an intermediate school in Daly City, California, for example, didn't have a full-service kitchen, and its aging oven broke so often that staff frequently had to use the microwave in the teachers' lounge to warm up food. In 2015 the administration spent about $12,000 on a three-door refrigerator and a new warming oven, which allowed the school to sign a better contract for meals and to store fresh fruits and vegetables. At Perry County Central High School in Hazard, Kentucky, staff struggled to serve students fresh vegetables because the cafeteria line equipment couldn't hold both hot and cold items; the only space for a salad bar was a far-off corner of the cafeteria. With $25,000 from the USDA, the school purchased new lines, each with an integrated salad bar and stations with variable temperature settings, which made it easier to get fresh produce on the students' trays. Even Congress recognizes the importance of these contributions. Since 2010 it has allocated another $115 million to kitchen equipment.

Still, no one in McCoy's position can ever assume that the government will make serving kids healthy meals at school any easier. Menus and budgets and staff need to be shuffled around constantly to keep up with the whims of a superior or the politics of the moment. The day after Donald Trump was elected, I sat with McCoy in a dimly lit conference room in the school board's offices. We were both in a daze, short on sleep after watching the returns late into the night and trying to grasp what his unexpected presidency might mean for her program. CEP could be eviscerated. So could state budgets, which subsidize the salaries of her cooks. And at the local level, William Smith, Cabell County's thoughtful, supportive superintendent, had announced he would retire in June. Who knew? Maybe the new boss would decide that sports or music was more essential than homemade food.

What McCoy had done in Huntington was exactly the kind of thing Republicans claim to celebrate. She wasn't a Washington bureaucrat telling people to do it her way or no way at all; she was a well-intentioned local who had figured out what made sense for her community and acted on it. Now, as it began to grow dark outside, she confronted the fact that her last six years of work might be undone. "Any part of it could change overnight," McCoy told me. She was incredulous in a way I'd never seen her. "A child can come to school all day and not eat," she continued. "Little ones. First-graders." She lowered her voice to a whisper. "How do you tell a child they can't eat?" A few moments later she shook my hand and said goodbye. Then she returned to her office and got back to work.

New York. Chicago. Detroit. Portland? Making the Case for a New American Pizza City

FROM *Portland Monthly*

THIS IS PORTLAND pizza. Sarah Minnick barrels down I-5 last summer, fast and furious, homebound from a conference on Cascadian grains in Mount Vernon. She can't wait to get back to Lovely's Fifty-Fifty, her North Mississippi Avenue restaurant, a sort of locavore pizza think tank. In the back seat: a cache of multicolored snapdragons. Flour to flowers, what grows around here drives Lovely's strange and wonderful flavor expeditions. Who puts snapdragons on pizza? (Who puts snapdragons on anything?) But Minnick is lost in a reverie. "Snaps, man, they're really hard to explain," she says when I happen to cold-call in the moment. "A little sweet, a little rosy, *very* floral." Her plan: confetti them over a bacon-cheese pizza—a princess birthday party, with pork.

No, *this* is Portland pizza: Imagine Sunday-night lasagna. Your sister in curlers. Robert De Niro's unhinged Johnny Boy dancing to "Mickey's Monkey." It's not your life; it's Martin Scorsese's. But it *is* the Defino pie at Scottie's Pizza Parlor: a moment that crackles, alive with tactile pockets of baked cheese. In the pizzeria of macho Gotham fantasy, you imagine an oven guy built like a Lucchese foot soldier. Scottie Rivera, the twenty-eight-year-old owner here, is a sprite in pizza socks and an apron emblazoned with the words

PIZZA MANIA. Yep, you're in Portland, down the rabbit hole. The kid studies pizza theory like a paleontologist puzzling over what ancient animals might have looked like. During a ten-year quest, he distilled 1970s New York, *Mean Streets* New York, into pie form. No one gets a crust like this. But you won't find Sinatra or DiMaggio on the shop's "Wall of Fame." Rivera enshrines his own idols, Julia Child and Ruth Bader Ginsburg among them. He also loves New Mexican green chiles.

Wait, *this* is a Portland pizza: Pizza Hut meets *No Reservations.* Blunt included. That's just the rough outline at Pizza Jerk. During the shop's short history in Northeast, Tommy Habetz and friends have tossed Portland's indie ethos into a punk-rock pizza joint for families: studied, stoner-satisfying pies, with Fugazi and grade schoolers raging in the background. Pizza Jerk pies often seem to bring all the threads of the city's interconnected food culture together in eighteen-inch beasts.

Take the "Thai pizza." The lore I've heard traces the pie's DNA to a random joint in the jungle outside Chiang Mai, the city that often inspires Andy Ricker and his famed Pok Pok minichain. Ricker discovered lemongrass-singing northern Thai sausage—vibrant, coarse, and funky. Olympia Provisions now produces it, an epic Portland collaboration to begin with. Next chapter: JB Tranholm, once Ricker's right hand at Pok Pok, is now Pizza Jerk's "chef de cuisine." (Yes, this is a red-checked-tablecloth joint with retro video games *and* a head chef.) He gives this very Thai thing a new identity, crumbled with fried shallots, hot chiles, and basil over a buttery crust ripped from Habetz's Connecticut youth.

You can't make this stuff up. It's Portland pizza.

As it turns out, Portland pizza is many things, beholden to no doctrine, only to open minds and a willingness to get serious about quality. That it's even worth talking about is a recent development —Portland used to be a pretty sad pizza town. A few great pies busted out over the years. But mostly, veggie pizzas heavy enough to mug Luca Brasi ruled the day.

The city's collective dough is rising at last, with a voice and unmistakable taste of place. Portland might even be America's most original pizza destination. (No, I'm not saying it's better than New

York, so sit back down and put your head on your desk.) I've been on a pizza bender recently, thinking about all this, checking in on the places defining a very local slice.

At Lovely's, Minnick has emerged as the Alice Waters of pizza, with a near-spiritual connection to Oregon's most adventurous farmers. She builds toppings from whatever they drop off—stinging nettles, quinoa greens, maybe bok choy raab, backed by unusual regional cheeses. Lovely's makes its superb sourdough crust with locally milled grains that change with the season. The results may not be pizza as you know it. But I'm embarrassed for most other pies when I dig into one of these chewy, sour, flavor-rich wheels, and I may not be alone. Minnick recently shared a stage at a food conference in Milan with Franco Pepe, the pizzaiolo behind Pepe in Grani outside Naples, considered perhaps the world's greatest pizza shop for its profound evocation of land and place. After finding kinship with Minnick's philosophy during a Portland visit, Pepe invited her to collaborate on a double-onion pie. They communicated with their hands and beloved ingredients. She's now learning Italian to talk to him.

Meanwhile, Habetz, once a protégé of New York Italo-imperialist Mario Batali, later cofounder of Bunk Sandwiches, has found his destiny as something of a pizza genius. Few places have an old-school/new-school/out-of-my-mind game like Pizza Jerk. Where else can you order a half-and-half that combines major-league pepperoni and a Chinatown-riffing dan dan pie? Jaded *Bon Appétit* called the Jerk "America's Pizzeria of the Year" for 2016.

Also reaching peak Portland pizza: Ken Forkish, who pioneered his own Italy-meets-French-boulangerie style on the east side eleven years ago. Ed Levine, founder of the popular New York–based blog *Serious Eats,* calls him "one of the world's great pie men," and when you eat a spicy soppressata pie at Ken's Artisan Pizza, it's hard to disagree. No bones about where his heart lies—these twelve-inchers demand engagement with their rustic crust. Forkish's recent scholarly book, *The Elements of Pizza,* is a must for home cooks hoping to pass for pros. For him, a New York immersion was not just book research but a challenge, and last year he opened downtown's Trifecta Annex to prove it. "I'd put our slices against any in New York," he told me recently. After a slow start, I must say they're darn good, thin and crispy in all the right places.

Some of Portland's pizza makers channel East Coast heroes

through an Oregon bread baker's heart, which is why our dusky, muscular rims often taste like exaggerated ciabatta. Apizza Scholls, founded in 2005 with roots in an earlier sourdough bakery, still protects its dough art like a samurai warrior: no more than three ingredients, no phone orders, no screaming kids, nothing to detract from the sheer enjoyment of a beautiful neo-Neapolitan crust. The place can be a pain, but you can't help respect it: the super-creamy ricotta pools, the tongue-sized bacon. The menu rarely changes, so it's easy to forget that seven nights a week, arguably one of America's top twenty pizzas is emerging from an electric oven on SE Hawthorne.

Superstars aside, legit pizza has spread to all corners of the city. Neighborhood spots like Concordia's Red Sauce (family game boards, springy-crisp dough, house meats), NE Killingsworth's Handsome Pizza (exploring whole grains), and the East Glisan Pizza Lounge (home of the meatball pie) are budding enthusiasts to watch as they dig into their own niches. Southeast's Renata found a groove in San Franciscoesque pies marked by good char and big flavors. At Scottie's, Rivera is *the* up-and-comer, with straight-up thin crust, bright sauce, homemade everything, and a classic slice menu: pepperoni to margherita to bianca.

And who knows what will come of the new Heart Pizza, from zeitgeist-savvy entrepreneur Micah Camden (Blue Star Donuts, Little Big Burger) and his gifted, how you say, *emotional,* chef, Morgan Brownlow? Except this: it's gonna be interesting. Two of the city's most complicated personalities are joining forces on a venture inspired by Brownlow's cooking at one of Portland's most exciting and fraught restaurants ever, Clarklewis. Multiple locations are already in play, testing a new model: fast food meets cheffy wood-fired pizza, ready to go in mere minutes. Early versions are still in shake-out mode, but I enjoyed—on many, many levels—an effort called the Peasant pizza, an ode and a wink to Clarklewis's legendary salad of chicory, walnuts, and pancetta. Over in the 'Couv, Forkish's longtime oven man Alan Maniscalco makes his mark at Rally Pizza, keeping things more playful than his former boss (a meeting of Canadian and belly bacon: the Piggy Back). It's one of several artisan projects north of the Columbia. The most fascinating sits in a blue trailer in a Hazel Dell parking lot bordered by abandoned buildings that look like remnants from Hurricane Katrina. Inside, as a little fire rages, a Japanese guy trained in Sorrento makes true

Neapolitan pizza, besting any challengers in Portland. In this unlikely corner of the metro area, forty-three-year-old Daisuke Matsu-
moto uses only fine-grained *doppio zero* Caputo flour, paying close
attention to the fundamentals of flash-fired Naples dough. At last
count he was laying as many as six slices of La Quercia prosciutto
on an $11 pie. Customers tailgate in the lot. If the romance of food
is a state of mind, this cart with the operatic name Pizzeria La Sor-
rentina captures it.

All this is merging into a quantifiable style, even if harder to explain
than the taste of snapdragons. Typically a regional pizza genre —
Detroit's gooey, cheese-crispy squares or New Haven's coal-charred
ovals and rectangles, say — is defined by a set of shapes, thickness
specifications, and baking methods, highly codified and endlessly
replicated at local shops. They inspire biblical feuds over origin stories and "authenticity." Stumptown's pizza is the opposite. No two
joints are alike. Portland has no prescriptive, handed-down food
culture, so our pizza makers freely sample American styles and the
Naples mothership, adding personal choices and oddball preoccu-
pations, adhering to our unofficial food motto: no idea forbidden.
    In the end, commitment and originality are the litmus tests at
these self-created schools. Only slackers aren't making their own
mozzarella. If you're not tapping world-class Oregon produce, go
home. Foragers and growers are adding to the mix. Sure, you can
find a fine sausage pizza here. But at Lovely's, just for example, you
can dig into fresh sheep cheese and nostril-flaring "green-in-snow"
mustard greens, bred by a farmer specifically to thrive in Oregon's
rainy chill. It can send a shiver down your spine.

The founding father behind our declaration of pizza independence is surely Mark Doxtader. In 2001 the guy had never laid a
brick when he decided to build a massive wood-burning oven in
the back of his pickup truck and haul it to the Portland Farmers
Market. On Day One, at about 4 a.m., his father drove behind him
to the downtown site, packing extra mortar in case disaster struck.
Hours later Doxtader lit a fire with fresh-chopped wood; when the
coals burned brightly, he laid down a vision of flatbread and apples
from his farm 30 miles south. He called it Tastebud. The combo
tasted like smoke and earth. It tasted like playing your own damn
music. It tasted like the future of Portland pizza.

Tastebud would birth a Multnomah Village restaura. staffers top pies with dill pickles and peaches. But far beyon oven, Doxtader's influence can be felt across town, from Lovely's to Pizza Jerk. Consider Tommy Habetz, on track to be Batali's disciple when he moved here in 2002. For a hard-core East Coaster, Portland pizza was unworthy, "hippie-dippie," as he once put it. (He wasn't wrong.) One day at the farmers' market he happened on Tastebud's apple-laden sausage slice.

It was one moment in a journey to Habetz's self-discovery. He learned to trust himself, *his* tastes. Doxtader, he says, helped set him free. Most pizza shops look to respect tradition or jump on bandwagons. The overriding impulses of a Pizza Jerk pie are basically "What is Tommy craving?" Korean barbecue, apple pie, lamb sausage and mint, roasted beets and goat cheese, even a vat of creamy al dente penne alla vodka have gotten the Jerk treatment.

The Jerk's latest passion is Detroit style, *sort of:* deep-dished and über-cheese-crisped in a cast-iron pan. It's as American as a pie gets, like eating a loaf of bread over grilled cheese and adding a refrigerator binge—so wrong and yet so right. Daily options are available, but ask and they'll make any pizza the cast-iron way. No house rules. Sure, edges can be too burned; experiments might fizzle. Other places may have the consistency thing down. Pizza Jerk takes us into the mind of a chef. Maybe—like all these mothers of inventions, these avatars of self-expression and keepers of the flames—it may even give us a glimpse into our soul.

"I so want a mezza pizza," Habetz moaned recently. I hope he follows through. That would be Portland pizza.

stina Tosi Has a Cookie

м *Eater*

A FEW MONTHS ago Christina Tosi met a cookie she expected to be meh. "It was called salted caramel crunch, and I thought it was going to be a total snoozefest," she said. After all, these days a cookie carpet-bombed with salt is old hat. But this confection, discovered in an airport, blew Tosi's mind. "Imagine a butter cookie with raw sugar on top, with hints of kosher salt—it was toffee bits and these pretzel rounds folded in so every time you thought you were getting a toffee bit, you got this amazing, salty, multi thing."

It wasn't simply that it was delicious, it's that it was familiar. "It makes me laugh because I'm like, *I did that*," she said. "Like, no one put pretzels in cookies. Like, holy shit, nine years ago this was not a real thing in the world." When Tosi first started peddling baked goods, it was the halcyon days before Instagram. Before unicorn freakshakes, rolled ice cream, and Oreos with Oreo filling—back when people could still get it up for flourless chocolate cake on a square plate. Her creation, this airport cookie's godfather, was laden with potato chips, coffee grounds, butterscotch, chocolate chips—and pretzels. Tosi called it the Compost Cookie (later registering the trademark, because she's smart) and it was weird. Subversive, even. It, along with a black hole of butter and two kinds of sugar called the Crack Pie, ushered in the era of the Stunt Dessert —FOMO-inducing, insulin-spiking sweets consumed as much for the performative pleasure as for the sugar rush, from slutty brownies to anything off the Cookie Dough Cafe menu and the incalculable number of crummy Cronut clones.

Marrying salty with sweet predates Christina Tosi, no doubt—

hat tip to Dorie Greenspan's salted chocolate chip cookies of 2006, and hell, who hasn't had a Snickers bar?—but the high-low mix of Snyder's of Hanover and Barry Callebaut, with a soupçon of stoner fantasia, is pure Milk Bar, which Tosi founded in 2008 as a small part of David Chang's Momofuku insurgency. It's the bakery that attracted a forty-five-minute wait at the opening of its D.C. location, baked Taylor Swift's enormous birthday cake, and prompted Chrissy Teigen to Instagram its delights to her 14.1 million followers.

When I met Tosi, now the CEO of Milk Bar, for tea in Williamsburg back in December, she had just come off the red-eye she takes back and forth from Los Angeles to New York every weekend when filming on her other job: since 2015 she has served as a judge for *MasterChef* and *MasterChef Junior,* the competitive cooking franchise on Fox that's popular enough to merit its own cruise. In between guiding and (gently) crushing children's dreams and running the ever-expanding Milk Bar empire—twelve locations in North America and counting—her side hustles have included posing for Corcoran Group Real Estate (in a campaign shot by Annie Leibovitz), starring in a Subaru ad, and consulting on Kellogg's NYC, a café that sold bowls of cereal for $7.50 to tourists in Times Square—an idea that sounds like a grim, halfhearted joke about the state of the universe but was so successful that the café is moving to a bigger location downtown in a few months.

Slight, pale, with an old-timey face that evokes Vermeer's *Girl with a Pearl Earring* (especially when her hair's covered by a bandanna), Tosi, who is thirty-five, is often dressed like a big kid from the cover of a Judy Blume novel, with a preference for stripes, overalls, jeans, and, almost always, Converse All Stars. Unless she has a meeting—where she'll wear a little more jewelry and maybe short-heeled booties—or when she's getting married. For her summer-camp-themed, restaurant-industry power wedding to Will Guidara, one half of Make It Nice, the restaurant group behind the (possibly) number-one restaurant in the world, Eleven Madison Park, and the NoMad, she wore J.Crew. It rained, they had the tallest Milk Bar cake on record, and she looked radiant under her plastic poncho.

Tosi's childlike qualities, unfussy air, and lack of pretension are disarming, making her particularly winsome as a judge on *Master-Chef*—she's tough but fair, a solid foil for the blustery, irascible charms of one of her costars, Gordon Ramsay. It's also probably why

Tosi is so often characterized in interviews as playful or ebullient, like a cheerleader, or Samantha from *Bewitched,* or maybe Taylor Swift, who's besties with Tosi's bestie and occasional collaborator, the supermodel Karlie Kloss. But the blonde she most resembles to me is Tracy Flick from *Election,* punctilious and unflinching. The notion of a universally sunny, conspicuously inoffensive purveyor of cookies, cakes, and soft-serve ice cream has a broad, easy appeal, but it's inexhaustible reserves of grit that alchemize folksy sweets into a food empire. "I'm never ever, ever, ever the smartest person in the room," she said. "But it's not about smarts. It's about will."

Every Milk Bar location carries a couple dozen items, from Bagel Bombs to soft-serve to the also thoroughly trademarked Crack Pie. What every Milk Bar doesn't have is that fresh-baked-cookie aroma, the enticing fragrance staged to sell million-dollar condos. Milk Bar's Williamsburg commissary, the 11,000-square-foot commercial kitchen in Brooklyn that supplies all of its New York and Toronto shops and its online store, smells incredible, though. Like throw-back supermarket vanilla flavoring, the see-through kind, not what Ina Garten calls the "good" stuff—a raw, primordial, cake-batter fragrance. It's kind of like how McDonald's fries *smell* bright yellow and Jamba Juices emit some tropical-fruit scent that doesn't exist in nature. It's more an aroma of general deliciousness than anything specific—a scratch-n-sniff sticker of a baked good.

Tucked behind the Williamsburg store, the commissary is Milk Bar's NYC base of operations. It's a space big enough to host a good-sized rave. On the wall near the front is an area dedicated to Milk Bar's Hardbody of the Month, a collage of hastily photocopied and enthusiastically decorated pictures of the team's hardest-working members. The rest of the commissary is perhaps better understood as a 3D model of the way Tosi's brain works. It's shrewdly mapped out with stations, and the accompanying walk-in fridges are positioned closely together. Products with multiple components—like cakes, which contain various fillings and different-flavored layers and need to be assembled before they are packaged—move through the kitchen systematically and chronologically, so that the finished product lands in the fridge closest to its shipping area. In the same way that chefs pride themselves on a scrupulously organized and maintained mise en place for optimal efficiency in the kitchen, Tosi and the team tinker with the layout constantly.

Tosi, as a whole, is big on tinkering. On the day I met her at the kitchen, she'd arrived with pistachio cookies that she insisted everyone under her employ sample. Near the R&D area, a nook tucked behind the dry-goods storage racks, is a stack of brown boxes. "I went a little crazy on Goldbely," she said, opening the box closest to her. "I bought all the pound cakes they had to offer. I'm always curious how other people do it."

Tosi and Courtney McBroom, a former Milk Bar employee who helped write and test recipes for Milk Bar's two cookbooks, eyed a yellow bundt cake, breaking off small pieces with their hands. "The texture is nice and moist," said McBroom, another blonde with an open face, who hails from Texas.

"No, it's almost angel food cakey," Tosi said, smushing it between her fingers and popping the mass in her mouth.

"Okay, it's not that moist," McBroom demurred, crumbling a morsel. "But it's still good in a weird way. It's better than the ones we've been doing, but it almost . . ."

McBroom and Tosi looked at each other while chewing. "I wonder what that's from," Tosi said.

"It's like cream cheese," McBroom said, checking the ingredients to confirm. "It kind of dissolves on your tongue."

"That's the emulsifier, the cream cheese," Tosi agreed.

This, ad infinitum, is how Tosi and her team deduce that corn cookies need golden flaxseed meal to be chewy, or that a pinch of citric acid makes Birthday Cake frosting really sparkle, or that there's a special textural alchemy when you mix grapeseed oil and buttermilk for your cakes. Though it's been said roughly one million times in a thousand different ways that nostalgia is Tosi's "secret ingredient," the ethos, really, is what her team refers to as Tosi's "pure approachability." But as accessible or sentimental as her food tastes, it requires a fiercely analytical and precise mind to make a Milk Bar Birthday Cake reminiscent of an old-school birthday cake from a box. This is why Milk Bar recipes are exhaustive, harrowingly convoluted ways of getting to a particular flavor destination from our collective youths. Liberating textures or flavors that would otherwise stay trapped inside the minds of Nabisco food scientists is not easy.

Milk Bar currently employs 220 people, 50 of them in the New York commissary, with more around the holidays. When you're hired as a pastry cook, you start at the bottom, and that means spending a few months at the standing Hobart—a human-sized mixer where you negotiate with a 500-pound blob of cookie dough, as unwieldy and unaccommodating as a futon mattress, and try to coax it into hotel pans. If you don't master the cookie dough, you never level up. "It's a very individualistic sport," Tosi said. "Working the 140-quart is only for the people that mean it. It's stamina, it's love, it's care, and there's no one to complain to."

After cookie dough, you're moved on to ice cream. "Soft-serve is more about blending, technique, and the balance of flavor," Tosi said. "If you think about making a cup of tea, you have hot water and a tea bag, but it depends on how hot your water is, how long you steep, the tea-leaf mixture, how fine the mesh of the bag is, how humid the day is, and the temperature of the kitchen. When we make Cereal Milk soft-serve, we take cornflakes and toast them and grind them down. If someone grinds the toasted cornflakes a little more or less, the surface area is different. And inevitably we're using organic, farm-fresh milk, and where we buy our whole milk the cows are eating in different pastures, so the nuances of the flavors of the milk are different—so it holds notes of cereal milk differently. All of those things make a difference, all of which make me go, 'Why in the world did I decide making food for a living was a good idea?'"

Alison Roman, a food writer and cookbook author who worked at Milk Bar in the early days—her most enduring contribution is an apple pie cake that is filled with liquid cheesecake—recalled Tosi's exacting standards. "There was this chocolate soft-serve," she told me. "It was brownie, and I made it a thousand fucking times and Tosi would be like, 'No, it needs more this.'" *This* was the key to some elusive flavor profile known only to Tosi. "Part of the challenge for Milk Bar was that you were making things that had never been made before, so there was no reference," Roman said.

If you're able to make it through the gauntlet, after a year, you'll finally be allowed to touch a cake. These secrets are among Milk Bar's most valuable launch codes. Despite the nondisclosure agreement that you have to sign when you're hired (and the multiple trademarks), Tosi hasn't gone after former Milk Bar employees who have erected copycat bakeries. She's simply quietly lost respect for them while she's gone on to develop new techniques. "I believe in sharing recipes," she said. "We have cookbooks. But we know why we're adding ingredients. We know why we're adding this much salt and this much baking powder. We're the ones who are going to do it the best, because they're ours."

Tosi's easygoing pluck is, however, piqued by corporate copycats. When Ben & Jerry's announced a new run of flavors called Cereal Splashback, a clear rip-off of Cereal Milk soft-serve, it was a buzzkill. "I'm bummed," she said about her state of mind when everyone texted her the news. "Why couldn't [Ben & Jerry's] just come to us? Like, I'm not trying to say I'm Jimmy Fallon or Stephen Colbert, but I think they would have gotten so many more cool points and authenticity points in doing something together." It's inevitable that other sweet shops and brands ape your best concepts; just ask Dominique Ansel. The only consolation is that imitators are merely catching up, and when they do, they won't do it quite as well.

If there's a specific era that dominates Milk Bar's brand identity, with its chalkboard menus, bright-pink logo, and rainbow sprinkles, it's the '80s. Part *Punky Brewster* and part Lisa Frank, a lot of the attitude comes from its founder, who grew up in Virginia. When I asked Tosi what table she sat at in the high school cafeteria, she told me, "I was always a 'march to the beat of my own drum' person." She recalled a cross-country practice where she wore "spandex shorts with the map of the world in blue and gray velour." Her friends were cool, but she insists she wasn't. "I was in Dorkestra," she said. "I was in all AP classes. I was a no-nonsense person."

Tosi's house was the spot where all the kids would go after school to ransack the pantry. Snacks were plentiful, as were sheet pans full of fresh baked goods, and her mom was usually at the office. "My mom raised us to be super-independent people," Tosi said of her and her sister. Her parents, who'd been separated since her early childhood, finally divorced when she was fifteen. Her mother, whom she lived with, remarried, and her stepfather traveled a lot for work. "The day of your sixteenth birthday you get keys to the family minivan, you get your credit card and your chore list." Baking was part of that—part chore, part birthright. "We baked cookies as kids and we'd bring them to someone we didn't know who was sick in the hospital," she explained. "That's the tradition of our family. You can never go home to visit my mom or my grandma for some R&R. That's not a thing."

Tosi's freshman year of college was spent at the University of Virginia. While her peers rushed sororities and turned up at frat parties, Tosi got a job. "Those southern schools, you go to college to meet your girlfriends and your husband," she said. "That's not my thing." First she worked at Bed Bath & Beyond, but when she transferred to James Madison University, where she majored in applied mathematics and Italian—"There was a lot of ego and kind of stuff about elitism that just didn't sit right with me," she remembers of UVA—Tosi began working at a microbrewery in Harrisonburg called Calhoun's. She started out as a hostess, put in hours on the waitstaff, and eventually muscled her way into the kitchen as a prep cook. It was an inauspicious start, but she was hooked. "It was my social outlet," Tosi said. "I like the renegades in the kitchen. I like the restaurant life. I was like, school is fine, but I'm not trying to go do a keg stand."

Tosi's love of the kitchen prompted her to begin researching culinary school. She enrolled at the French Culinary Institute (now International Culinary Center) and moved to New York, where she'd go to school during the day and work at night. Living in a tiny walk-up in Nolita, she started out as a reservationist at Aquagrill, worked her way up to maitre d', and then friends of friends introduced her to the pastry chef at the hyper-soigné Bouley, where she worked for two and a half years. From there she staged at Wylie Dufresne's now-defunct molecular gastronomy mecca, wd~50. Tosi, being Tosi, didn't just walk into a job at wd~50; she kept showing up for no money for a full year before one opened up.

In 2005 she made herself indispensable by volunteering for the herculean task of writing wd~50's Hazard Analysis Critical Control Point plan, a tangle of health department bureaucracy that details everything a restaurant kitchen does in terms of food safety, from how it handles raw produce to the minimum temperature of roast beef. A job typically reserved for food scientists, it's such a monumental pain in the ass that by 2011, Mario Batali's restaurant group declared it wouldn't even bother with sous vide cooking, just to avoid revising its HACCP. Tosi, of course, basked in the challenge. "I like to always be in over my head," she said. "I'm at my happiest, and most challenged, and typically most successful when like the water is somewhere between here"—her hand hovered at her forehead—"and here." She stretched a slender arm way above her head. "I like the constant pursuit of better, bigger, stronger, faster."

Around that time David Chang had just tossed $1,500 worth of vacuum-sealed food thanks to the watchful eye of the New York City

Department of Health and Mental Hygiene, which relished raining fines down on kitchens for preparing sous vide foods without an established protocol. Chang called up Dufresne, a friend and a chef he'd long admired, to ask him about Tosi. "I asked for help," Chang told me over the phone. "Back then, before the Internet, you just heard about the people who were good. She was always on my radar, and when I got in trouble with the health department because I was organizing my foods in Cryovac, she helped me get out of purgatory."

Before she knew it, Tosi was doing everything at Momofuku—in fact, her unofficial job title was "et cetera." She ran payroll, helped out on the line, managed restaurants, and ordered supplies like an office assistant. "She's so goddamned smart," Chang said. "So regiment-oriented. It's what I don't have. People forget or else they don't know that she's a mathematics major." Nothing was too arduous or too menial, and after full days she'd hone recipes into early morning and bring baked goods into work the next day. Desserts were her in. At the time Momofuku had no pastry program, offering spicy ginger chews or Hershey's Kisses with the bill. An early creation, a Tristar strawberry shortcake recipe, was such a resounding success—tart, sweet, and a little salty—that Momofuku began integrating more sweets across the restaurants, like soft-serve ice cream and deep-fried apple pie, just like the kind you used to get at McDonald's before 1992, when they started baking them.

When the laundromat next to Chang's Ssäm Bar cleared out in 2008, Tosi opened Milk Bar in the space that November. Then she didn't sleep for two years. Open until 2 a.m., partly to complement Ssäm Bar's late-night menu, Milk Bar was the rare bakery positioned as a pit stop for East Village bar crawls. Tosi dubbed it "Dairy Queen with pork buns." It was an immediate hit, with hypebeasts queued out the door as people clamored to devour Blueberry & Cream Cookies and Candy Bar Pie, washed down with corn-flake-suffused milk. Despite the potential to blanket the city immediately, over the next few years Milk Bar grew deliberately, opening just three more locations by 2011.

"It's scalable," Sujean Lee, who came on as Milk Bar's COO at the end of 2016 from Greek yogurt monolith Chobani, told me over lunch. "But how long it's taking is a conscious decision on Tosi's part. It's a conscious evolution." Since Lee's arrival nine months ago, she's overseen store openings in the Financial District, West Village, and their now westernmost outpost, Las Vegas. This accelerated expansion is likely to continue, with their eagerly anticipated Los Angeles flagship slated to open early next year on Melrose.

Business appears to be brisk, but Milk Bar is tight-lipped about actual sales figures. Lee framed the metrics in the most Milk Bar–possible way by telling me that last year they sold 600,000 B'day Truffles and about 300,000 Compost Cookies, and that they go through nearly 200,000 pounds of flour and over 100,000 pounds of butter annually. It's fantastic and whimsical to picture heaping, toppling mountains of scrumptiousness akin to however many Ding Dongs you need to get to the moon and back, but what that means for Milk Bar's finances remains deeply mysterious.

In terms of branding, since 2014 Momofuku Milk Bar has quietly become simply Milk Bar. "I've never been as involved as people think," Chang told me. "No matter what the fuck I say, people just assume it's a Momofuku product. We even dropped the Momofuku, so I don't even know what the fuck's up with that."

"Milk Bar is mine," Tosi said. "Dave would never disagree with that. And Momo will always be him." Momofuku Holdings, the umbrella company for all of Chang's businesses, remains a key investor in Milk Bar, though the bakeries operate independently from the other restaurants in Momofuku Group. No one would tell me precisely how the ownership of Milk Bar is split up, nor how much equity Tosi actually has; Milk Bar declined to comment on who owns the majority stake in the business.

In the last few years Momofuku Holdings appears to have shifted gears for stratospheric growth: in addition to Milk Bar's recent expansion, Momofuku has launched a delivery-only restaurant in New York and moved into fast food. They've also sold a minority stake for an undisclosed sum to Matt Higgins and Stephen M. Ross's RSE Ventures, a firm that is invested in stuff like a drone-racing league and VR events. More recently Chang hired Harvard MBA and hospitality vet Alex Munoz-Suarez, formerly of the Batali-Bastianich empire, to act as Momofuku's president. But Milk Bar insists there's minimal meddling, with Chang, Munoz-Suarez, and RSE considered valued advisers above all. "There's a lot of email-forwarding," Milk Bar's Lee said. "Like, 'Hey, not for me but for you?'"

The clarity of the delineation between Momofuku and Milk Bar operations might be a factor in the success of the enduring

Chang-Tosi collaboration, which stands out in a streak of Chang partnerships that have ended abruptly and unceremoniously. Most recently, *Lucky Peach,* the quarterly he founded with Peter Meehan, folded earlier this year despite critical and commercial success. Last year Booker and Dax, the highly acclaimed bar that Dave Arnold operated in the original Milk Bar space, shuttered with little warning; its future remains up in the air. And this past spring a tenured hospitality exec replaced longtime Chang business partner Andrew Salmon as president of Momofuku. (Last year Salmon became an adviser to Milk Bar; he was not made available for interview.)

Tosi's stamina could be a matter of will. Mettle. A testament to her high pain threshold or her corn-fed predilection for the "right thing to do." But this wildly discounts not only her agency in the matter but her patent shrewdness. "Everyone's here because they want to be here, right?" she told me, rolling her eyes when I asked whether it's hard to work with Chang. "Like, no one's putting a gun to anyone's head."

"The easiest way to get along with Dave," she said, "is to prove that you care and that you mean it even more than him."

In many ways Tosi is of the last generation for whom selling out is even a thing. You can tell she cares by how often she talks about it in interviews. But scaling a business is by nature selling out, even when it's cast as a way to share Tosi's delicious treats with as many people as possible. It's particularly dicey because the margins on sub-$3 cookies are murder and each competitive advantage won at the hands of economies of scale feels to her like a compromise.

The decision to spring for the cookie-scooping machine four years ago was just one example. "I held out as long as possible," she said. "I could scoop cookies faster than anyone else and that was my business model. But I know better than that. That's not a responsible thing for me to do. But it also means the cornflake-marshmallow cookie is the same cookie but texturally its nuances are different. It's the same recipe, but it's a different cookie." With each acquisition—a mechanized hamburger-patty stamp that's been modified for cake truffles, a $60,000 flow-wrap machine to package cookies in cellophane—Tosi's struggled with the death of the romance. "They used to make English muffins to order," Meehan, the former Chang collaborator who was always around in the early days, said. "There was a crazy preciousness to the food they did."

In Milk Bar's first year, cookies were baked fresh and handed to you on a plate or in a box or paper bag. "We were super-worried that the packaging would feel less personal," she said of their current cellophane sheaths. "It's one of the things that made me the most sad about the original Milk Bar." It's a piece of Milk Bar lore that curmudgeonly food critic Alan Richman bought two dozen cookies to serve to his friends and, finding them broken, emailed her with some constructive criticism. "You can't bake a bunch of cookies and sell them fresh right out of the bakery case and expect them to stay in one piece," she said.

Milk Bar started selling packaged cookies as "day-old" goods for 50 cents cheaper, until they realized that people wanted them not only because of the discount but because you could save them for later or send them to friends. "I think it was one of the most challenging moments, deciding to put the cookies in bags," she said. "They're still obviously every bit as fresh, but for me, that was the moment I had to decide."

Scaling's also tough when your founder's afflicted with a conscience. "There's no such thing as an overnight baker at Milk Bar," she told me over tea. "Everyone gets to leave. That's important to me." Health insurance is also important to her. As are dental and vision and paid time off for hourly employees. Milk Bar offers four weeks paid maternity and paternity leave, and while she doesn't give stock options or have a bonus pool, she hopes to someday soon. "I don't have that part of my act together yet, but that is so representative of what I believe in."

Another indication of how Milk Bar is evolving is Milk Bar Life, the umbrella brand under which it peddles gluten- and dairy-free options, as well as pressed juice. If you're a longtime Milk Bar patron, the juice feels like an odd move—in fact, the knee-jerk instinct is slight disappointment. Same goes for their yogurt parfaits, or Brekkie Cups, which sound bafflingly Australian. Tosi's past collaboration with Karlie Kloss, called Karlie's Kookies, inspired the line of cookies now under the Milk Bar Life umbrella, which are no longer affiliated with the supermodel. (MB HQ swears it's still all love, though.)

These changes can be seen as brand dilution, though Milk Bar insists they're part of a rejiggering, addition and not subtraction. "Juice is the newest addition to Milk Bar because it's the newest addition to my life," Tosi said. "Why am I going elsewhere to get juice when I can make juice here?" (It's worth noting that if the margins on cookies suck, the wiggle room on cold-pressed juice is somehow worse, even at $5.25 a bottle.)

To be truly approachable, Tosi has made peace with the idea that Milk Bar must be everywhere, from a collaboration with JetBlue where premium customers can opt for Milk Bar juice, a cookie, or a bagel round (they're not called Bagel Bombs because . . . well, airplanes) to cookie mixes at Target to that full-body-eyeroll-inducing Kellogg's-branded café in Times Square. The dream is for Milk Bar is to have an online ordering system that eventually rivals Domino's in terms of coolness and interactivity—and to one day have wedding cakes delivered by drone.

Still, there will always be an emo core to Milk Bar, one true to Tosi's heart as a home baker. As all-consuming as her life has become, Tosi maintains a cake list—like some sugar-slinging Santa Claus, everyone important to her gets a cake when she thinks they deserve one, by any means necessary. "She's relentless," Chang said. "Every birthday, every special occasion. I don't know how she does it. I recently got married. We eloped, and somehow—I don't know how —that fucking cake got to where I was."

This gives Tosi enormous pleasure. "Who gets surprised anymore?" she said. "No one goes out of their way to surprise anyone. That's why I started baking in the first place."

I've Worked in Food for Twenty Years. Now You Finally Care About Female Chefs?

FROM *Esquire*

IT IS AN exciting time to be a woman in the food industry! Many food writers know that we female chefs are shy and retiring creatures, ready to bolt like startled deer at the first sign of loud noises, bright lights, or press coverage. In consideration of our delicate feelings, they have decided we should be written about only twice a year. Our first moment comes with the new Michelin guide, at which point the requisite articles appear asking where all the women/black/Hispanic chefs are and why they have been underrepresented in the nominations again. Then, when the James Beard Awards are announced, those same pieces get dusted off and republished.

But now John Besh's sexual harassment allegations have provided women with another chance to get in on some of that boys-only press coverage. For the past two weeks my Twitter feed and email in-box have been filled to overflowing with food journalists begging me to Come Forward with My Story, demanding that I Make a Statement, encouraging me to Speak Out. Apparently the rules have changed. Women may not have value as chefs, but as victims we're finally interesting!

Only a real grouch would point out how depressing it is that what's gotten food writers actually excited about covering female chefs is their sexual assaults, not their approach to food.

Warning: I am about to display anger. When women display this emotion, it is known to cause discomfort, headaches, and nausea.

Let me make it clear to those who've asked for my comment:

Yes, I have experienced things in the food industry that would be considered sexual harassment and assault.

No, I will not be your headline.

Make no mistake about it, I think it's long overdue that women feel safe enough to come forward and speak about the assault and harassment they experience in restaurants, and I'm glad reporters are holding the perpetrators responsible. This is 100 percent a good thing. But if the press had been as eager to celebrate the talents of female chefs as they are to discuss their victimization, we wouldn't be in this position in the first place.

Women are second-class citizens in the restaurant world. We have less access to investors and are perceived as less profitable investments because in large part we have smaller profiles than male chefs. We get nominated for fewer awards, our restaurants get reviewed less often, and we get less press coverage than men.

Women need safe places to work. But until the playing field is financially level, there will never be safe places, because we will never be able to control our own futures. The odds are against us getting the award that drives business into our dining rooms. We are statistically less likely to get the review that makes all the difference. Maybe if women in this industry felt like they had the same opportunities, they would be able to leave abusive kitchens faster. Maybe then they wouldn't feel like they had to endure the unendurable. Maybe male chefs would view them as equals, not as targets.

I've been in this business for twenty years, and I don't think I'm owed anything except equality of opportunity. But don't ignore me, marginalize me, cut me out of your coverage, and then ask me to be your victim. Don't pack your headlines with the hot young men, the male-dominated restaurant groups, the macho celebrity chefs, and then expect me to be impressed by your sudden outrage.

You're probably saying, "You talk a big game, young lady, but where's your proof?" Well, I read in an article (Just kidding! My husband read it to me) that men like numbers, so I put some together for you.

Over the past twelve months, the *New York Times* has written major reviews for forty-four restaurants. Six of those kitchens are run by women.

In the past twenty-seven years, 361 James Beard Awards have been given out. Eighty-one of them have gone to women.

Since 2000, *Food & Wine* has selected 192 of the Best New Chefs in America and given them extra coverage. Twenty-eight of them have been women.

Of the seventy-two Michelin-starred restaurants in New York, six are run by women. Of the fourteen restaurants in the U.S. with three Michelin stars, none have female chefs.

I'm sure you're thinking, *Fewer women get awards and press coverage because there are fewer women in the restaurant business.*

My simple feminine intuition crumbles before your rigorous logic, but below you'll find a list of sixty-five women who are executive chefs, executive sous chefs, or restaurant owners in New York City alone. I just made this list off the top of my head, but I bet if a man put it together it would be twice as long and twice as good.

Maybe every single one of us is a terrible cook? It's possible, but isn't it a convenient coincidence that the worst cooks happen to be female? Or African-American? Or Hispanic? Because let's not forget that if you're a chef of color, your numbers are even worse than those of women.

Since I can barely do my own job, I shouldn't make suggestions to other people on how they should do theirs. But here's a fun game we can play, press friends: For one year, put your headlines where your outrage is and give half your coverage to women. For every review of a restaurant led by a male chef, run a review of a restaurant led by a female chef. If you call some male chefs for comment on an article, call the same number of female chefs. A male chef gives you his recipe for the ultimate potato salad? Then run a piece where a female chef tells you how to cook the perfect pasta.

On the one hand, *how dare I tell you how to do your jobs! Journalistic integrity!* On the other hand, you're not exactly writing about nuclear proliferation. What's stopping you from trying this? Do you think your readers value women so little they'll stop reading? I wonder where they got that idea.

But really, I just came here to say thank you to the press. Thank you for finally letting me know what us ladies have to do to get your attention. As you've made clear, it doesn't matter how well we cook. It only matters if a man wants to grab our pussies.

Female Chefs in New York, Off the Top of My Head

1. April Bloomfield — Spotted Pig, The Breslin, The John Dory, Salvation Taco, Tosca
2. Alex Raij — El Quinto Pino, Txikito, La Vara, Tekoá
3. Missy Robbins — Lilia
4. Gabrielle Hamilton, Ashley Merriman — Prune
5. Einat Admony — Balaboosta, Taïm, Bar Bolonat
6. Lynn Bound — 54 Below
7. Sara Jenkins — Porsena, Porchetta, Nina June
8. Julie Taras Wallach — Tipsy Parson
9. Barbara Sibley — La Palapa
10. Suzanne Cupps — Untitled
11. Melissa Rodriguez — Del Posto
12. Jody Williams — Buvette, Via Carota
13. Rita Sodi — I Sodi, Via Carota
14. Angie Mar — The Beatrice Inn
15. Jean Adamson — Vinegar Hill House
16. Emma Bengtsson — Aquavit
17. Caroline Fidanza — Saltie
18. Lidia Bastianich — Felidia, Becco, Del Posto, Esca
19. Rebecca Charles — Pearl Oyster Bar
20. Alex Guarnaschelli — Butter
21. Leah Cohen — Pig & Khao
22. Hong Thaimee — Ngam, Thaimee Box, Thaimee at McCarren
23. Sawa Okochi — Shalom Japan
24. Sarah Sanneh, Carolyn Bane — Pies 'n' Thighs
25. Anna Klinger — Al Di La
26. Lauren DeSteno — Marea
27. Susan Povich — Red Hook Lobster Pound
28. Sohui Kim — The Good Fork, Insa
29. Mary Redding — Mary's Fish Camp
30. Ann Redding — Uncle Boons
31. Duangjai Thammasat — Ayada
32. Gazala Halabi — Gazala's Place

33. Sripraphai Tipmanee—Sripraphai, Qi Thai Grill
34. Rawia Bishara—Tanoreen
35. Patti Jackson—Delaware and Hudson
36. Wafa Chami—Wafa's Express
37. Julieta Ballesteros—La Loteria
38. Ratchanee Sumpatboon—Larb Ubol
39. Pam Panyasiri—Pam Real Thai
40. Hillary Sterling—Vic's
41. Ivy Stark—Dos Caminos
42. Mary Cleaver—The Green Table, The Cleaver Company
43. Denisse Chavez—Taqueria El Atoradero at Parklife
44. Katherine Fuchs—The Thirsty Koala
45. Amy Scherber—Amy's Bread
46. Melissa O'Donnell—Lil' Gem
47. Isa Chandra Moskowitz—Modern Love
48. Paola Bottero—Paola's
49. Kristin Sollenne—Bocca Di Bacco
50. Anita Jaisinghani—Pondicheri
51. Janine Booth—Root & Bone
52. Christina Tosi—Momofuku Milk Bar
53. Simone Tong—Little Tong Noodle Shop
54. Zhu Rong—Hao Noodle and Tea by Madam Zhu's Kitchen
55. Clare de Boer, Jess Shadbolt—King
56. Claire Welle—Otway
57. Umber Ahmad—Mah-Ze-Dahr
58. Victoria Blamey—Chumley's
59. Jocelyn Guest, Erika Nakamura—White Gold Butchers
60. Daniela Soto-Innes—Cosme, Atla
61. Sarah Nelson—Beauty & Essex, The Stanton Social
62. Lucero Martinez—Pampano

Secrets in the Sauce

FROM *The New Yorker*

IN FEBRUARY OF 2015, Kathleen Purvis, the food editor of the *Charlotte Observer,* drove to Birmingham, Alabama, to attend Food Media South, an annual symposium. The keynote session, "Hey, You, Pitch Me Something," was meant to be a friendly wind-down to a weekend of talks. Participants were invited to get up in front of the editor of the Web magazine *The Bitter Southerner* and, well, pitch him something.

There were several hundred people in the room. Purvis knew that in the name of politeness she should probably stay quiet, but she couldn't resist the opportunity to "toss a good word grenade," she recalled later, into a clubby crowd that she felt tended to overlook, along with chiffon cakes and canning, some of the most complicated questions about southern cuisine. She raised her hand, and the editor nodded her way.

"Men are the new carpetbaggers of southern food writing," she said.

He replied, "Sold."

The resulting essay argues that "the southern food-writing world has been unduly influenced, usurped, yes, even invaded, by a barbecue-entranced, bourbon-preoccupied and pork belly–obsessed horde of mostly testosterone-fueled scribes," who dwell on hackneyed tales of southern eccentricity without developing "the clear-eyed vision" to see them in a contemporary light. The piece generated controversy, though not as much as Purvis's investigation into the racial dimensions of the practice of putting sugar in cornbread. "Honest to God, I really hate that hokey-jokey Hey-us-southerners-aren't-we-cute stuff," she told me. "I've always said that my beat is food and the meaning of life."

Gamely, the organizers invited her to the conference the next year as a speaker. "I was getting ready to get up and talk," Purvis said. "I was sitting there very quietly in a corner, and a woman came up to me and said, 'So, is it okay to go back to the Piggie Park?'"

The woman was referring to Maurice's Piggie Park, a small chain of barbecue restaurants established in West Columbia, South Carolina, in 1953. The original restaurant occupies a barnlike building on a busy intersection and is presided over by a regionally famous electric marquee that features the boast WORLD'S BEST BAR-B-Q, along with a grinning piglet named Little Joe. The Piggie Park is important in the history of barbecue, which is more or less the history of America. One reason is that its founder, Maurice Bessinger, popularized the yellow, mustard-based sauce that typifies the barbecue of South Carolina's Midlands area. Another is that Bessinger was a white supremacist who in 1968 went to the Supreme Court in an unsuccessful fight against desegregation, and in 1974 ran a losing gubernatorial campaign, wearing a white suit and riding a white horse.

In 2000, when the Confederate flag was removed from the South Carolina statehouse dome, Bessinger raised Confederate flags over all his restaurants. (By then there were nine.) A king-sheet-sized version went up over the West Columbia location, where he had long distributed tracts alleging, for example, that "African slaves blessed the Lord for allowing them to be enslaved and sent to America." He was a figure whose hate spawned contempt, leading a writer from the *Charleston City Paper* to fantasize about how "Satan and his minions would slather his body in mustard-based BBQ sauce before they dined."

In 2007 Bessinger, who suffered from Alzheimer's at the end of his life, handed the business over to his two sons, Paul and Lloyd, and a daughter, Debbie. In the months before his death, in 2014, they took down the flags and got rid of the slavery pamphlets. "Dad liked politics," Lloyd, who serves as the public face of the operation, told a reporter. "That's not something we're interested in doing. We want to serve great barbecue."

By the time the news reached Kathleen Purvis, she hadn't eaten Bessinger's barbecue in nearly three decades. She grew up in Wilson, North Carolina, where her father was an R.C. Cola salesman and barbecue sauce is made with vinegar. Early in her career she'd become a fan of the Bessinger family's line of packaged foods— "handy for a quick dinner when I was working nights"—but, she wrote, in an article in the *Observer* in December, "when I learned about Bessinger's history, I stopped buying his products. I followed a simple policy on the Piggie Park: I didn't go there. Ever." During the flag scandal, thousands of South Carolinians made the same call, going cold turkey. "I first made Maurice's acquaintance when I was a child," the barbecue expert William McKinney wrote on the website of the Southern Foodways Alliance. "His barbecue was sold in the freezer aisle of the grocery store. It would bubble up in our family's oven, its orange sauce as vivid as a river of lava. My mother would pack his barbecue in my lunch bag routinely, and I ate those sandwiches all the way through high school, wrapped up in aluminum foil and still a touch warm once lunch time came around." It was as though Jif peanut butter or Katz's Deli had become irredeemably tainted.

The Piggie Park had bad vibes, but it retained a pull on the community. For barbecue obsessives, it held a special fascination as one of the few restaurants in the country to still cook entirely over hickory wood, using no electricity or gas. One prominent Columbia resident, a black man, told me that he was addicted to Bessinger's sauce but that he would never admit it in public. The regime shift, then, represented a touchy moment. Some people wanted to go only if things had changed (but if they were going to go, they wanted to get there before things had changed too much). For others, no amount of change was ever going to mitigate the legacy of a man who had caused so much hurt. Even asking if it was okay to return was a form of blindness to that pain. "They could change the last name, redo the building, then dig the old man up . . . it still wouldn't matter to those who continue to carry the 'chip on the shoulder' mentality," a man named James Last, of Wilmington, North Carolina, wrote in response to Purvis's article, prompting Durward White, of Katy, Texas, to reply, "Are you saying no matter how vile and disrespectful his actions were we should move on? People still can't move on from Tom Brady and deflate gate and that was 3 years ago."

*

Barbecue might be America's most political food. The first significant reference to it that the barbecue scholar Robert F. Moss has
been able to find is in *The Barbacue Feast: or, the three pigs of Peckham,
broiled under an apple-tree,* an account of a 1706 banquet in Jamaica.
The revelers were English colonists, but the pigs were "nicely
cook'd after the West Indian manner": whole, over coals, on long
wooden spits on which they turned as a cook basted them in a spicy
sauce (green Virginia pepper and Madeira wine), using a foxtail
tied to a stick. Native Americans on the East Coast of North America used similar cooking techniques. But the main thing about barbecues is that they were social affairs, a day's entertainment for the
community. Between 1769 and 1774, George Washington attended
at least six of them, he wrote in his diary, including "a Barbicue of
my own giving at Accotinck."

A whole hog can feed as many as a hundred people. Barbecues,
often held on the Fourth of July, became overtly political in the nineteenth century. As Moss writes in *Barbecue: The History of an American
Institution,* they were "the quintessential form of democratic public
celebration, bringing together citizens from all stations to express
and reaffirm their shared civic values." They adhered to a ritual-
ized format: parade, prayer, reading of the Declaration of Independence, oration, and dinner in a shady grove near a drinking spring,
after which dignitaries gave a series of "regular" toasts (thirteen of
them, on patriotic subjects), followed by "voluntary" toasts from
the masses (thirty or forty, on issues ranging from local elections to
the free navigation of the Mississippi, or whatever else happened
to be the day's concerns). Often the festivities turned rowdy. If an
antebellum politician had wanted to rile folks up about building a
wall, he would have done it at a barbecue.

Before the Civil War, enslaved men often cooked these civic
meals. They prepared their own feasts too, either sanctioned by
their owners or organized on the quiet. Much of the planning for
the rebellions organized by Gabriel Prosser and Nat Turner took
place at barbecues. After emancipation, black men continued to
be some of the country's leading pit masters, catering enormous
spreads that featured everything from barbecued hogs, shoats,
chickens, and lambs to stuffed potatoes, stewed corn, cheese relish,
puddings, coffee, and cigars. In 1909 the *Times* noted the death of a
man born around 1865 on a plantation in Edgefield County, South
Carolina. "Pickens Wells, one of the most famous barbecue cooks

in the South, dropped dead today while preparing a barbecue," the item read. "Pickens prepared the famous barbecue at which President Taft was the guest of honor last Winter. White men here are raising a fund to erect a monument to the negro as a tribute to his fidelity and character."

Barbecue restaurants, like lunch counters, played an outsized role in the desegregation battles of the 1960s. In Birmingham in 1964, Ollie McClung, of Ollie's Barbecue, challenged the legality of the Civil Rights Act, arguing that the restaurant's practice of deny- ing sit-down service to black customers was none of the federal gov- ernment's business, since Ollie's, a mom-and-pop operation, wasn't involved in interstate commerce. Pointing out that 46 percent of Ollie's' meat came from out of state, the Supreme Court upheld the act's constitutionality in a 9–0 ruling. It included a concurring opinion from Justice Hugo Black, an Alabamian who reportedly voted over the objection of his wife, a regular diner at Ollie's.

In 1964 Maurice Bessinger was the president of the National Association for the Preservation of White People. On August 12 of that year, Anne Newman and a friend drove to the West Colum- bia Piggie Park. They stopped outside the lot for curbside service. A waitress emerged and, seeing that they were black, returned to the building without speaking to them. Then a man with a pad approached the car but refused to take their order, even though white customers were being served. In *Newman v. Piggie Park Enter- prises, Inc.,* the district court asserted that "the fact that Piggie Park at all six of its eating places denies full and equal service to Negroes because of their race is uncontested and completely established by evidence," but it concluded that the restaurants, because they were principally drive-ins, weren't subject to the public-accommodation provision of the Civil Rights Act. When a higher court reversed the ruling, Bessinger appealed to the Supreme Court, claiming that being forced to serve black people violated his religious principles. He lost, in a unanimous decision. (Justice Ruth Bader Ginsburg recently cited the case in her Hobby Lobby dissent.) In *Defending My Heritage,* Bessinger's 2001 autobiography, he claims that he and his family always treated black people well, citing his father's prac- tice, at a restaurant he owned, of giving a black employee discarded food and old grease. (Then he says that they fired her for steal- ing half a ham.) He writes, "I have concluded that the civil rights movement is a Satanic attempt to make it easier for a global elite, a group of extremely wealthy men with no Constitutional or national or cultural loyalties, working at an international level to eventually seize power in this country."

Bessinger launched his run for governor from his cattle range, which he called Tara, after the O'Hara plantation in *Gone With the Wind*. One of his opponents remembered the primary race as "something between a comic opera and depressing satire." Out of seven candidates, including a competing barbecue baron, Bessinger came in fifth, garnering 2.5 percent of the vote. Business suffered, whether from his notoriety or from his distraction. He decided to focus on rebuilding his restaurant empire, betting that people—white people, at least—would eventually forget about his period of activism. Many of them did. The corollary to white innocence is white passivity, the feeling that what one's ancestors did was so messed up that it couldn't possibly make a difference where one eats a barbecue sandwich.

According to his birth certificate, Maurice Bessinger was born on July 14, 1930, on a farm near Cope, South Carolina. It occupied land that had been willed to his mother, Genora, by her grandfather, a veteran of the Civil War. Maurice thought that his real birthdate was probably closer to July 4, as his father, Joseph, went to the county courthouse, where births were recorded, only a couple of times a month. Maurice was the eighth of eleven children. In his autobiography he says that he helped pick cotton from the age of four, using a "small, ten-pound little cloth sugar bag," and graduating, at six, to "a full, 100-pound bag like the grown-ups used." The family ate clabber, cornbread, grits, and vegetables that they grew in their garden. Meat was scarce, eggs occasional. Maurice's grandmother told him that, anticipating the arrival of Sherman's troops, she and her neighbors had buried smoked pork shoulders, hams, bacon, and sausage, covering them with desiccated leaves to disguise fresh digging.

When Maurice was nine, his father gave up farming, selling the family's cow to buy a roadside café from a widow in Holly Hill, about halfway between Columbia and Charleston. Maurice started to work that year at the Holly Hill Café, swatting flies and busing tables. By the time he was twelve, he was living in a small room in the back of the café, getting up at 5 a.m. to run the breakfast shift, spending a few hours at school, and then returning to the restaurant to work. Tired and skinny, he failed fifth and sixth grades. Two Saturday nights in a row the local policeman shot a black man dead. Maurice wrote in 2001 of one incident, "The perpetrator ran, and Mr. Workman dropped him with one shot at about 150 paces!"

By 1946 Joseph had sold the Holly Hill Café and opened Joe's Grill, where he perfected the secret recipe—its mustard kick supposedly inspired by his German roots—for which the family was coming to be known. In 1949, in Maurice's senior year of high school, Joseph died of a heart attack. Despite Maurice's insistence that his father had told him that the business would be his, the restaurant went to one of his brothers, who was seven years older and had come back from the war with three Bronze Stars and a Purple Heart. Furious, Maurice joined the army and shipped out to Korea.

In the aftermath of the fight over Joe's Grill, many of the eleven siblings struck out across the state to set up their own enterprises. The Bessinger name now dominates South Carolina barbecue, presiding over a complex diaspora of interrelated but not always amicable interests. "I grew up being told that yellow sauce was my heritage," the journalist Jack Hitt, who was raised in Charleston, wrote in the *Times Magazine* in 2001. "But it's clear that without the siblings' anxieties and their nomadic habits, Joe Sr.'s recipe would have died out after Joe's Grill closed. South Carolina would have remained just another outpost in the national camp of red barbecue sauce."

By 2000 Maurice was easily the most successful of his generation of Bessingers. In addition to the nine restaurants around Lexington County, he had the frozen dinners, a mail-order business, and a bottling plant that distributed his Southern Gold sauce (with a Confederate flag on the label) to three thousand grocery stores along the East Coast, making him the largest barbecue wholesaler in the country. *People* called the Piggie Park "the best all-in-one barbecue restaurant in America." Pat Buchanan, running for president on the Reform Party ticket, held fundraisers at the main restaurant, whose pits burned nonstop. When an economic boycott of South Carolina, led by the state's NAACP chapter, resulted in the removal of the Confederate flag from the statehouse dome, Maurice acted quickly. "I surrounded the city of Columbia with Confederate flags," he later said. "I didn't even tell my wife. I had it all planned."

Acting on a tip, John Monk, of the *State* newspaper, went to the Piggie Park and discovered Bessinger's stock of revisionist literature. The NAACP decided to challenge him next. "We didn't have any idea that we would change his mind," Lonnie Randolph, Jr., the chapter's longtime president, told me. "The goal was to make South Carolina, if there's such a thing, whole again—to let folks know that this isn't the way life should be."

Under pressure from the association, Sam's Club, Walmart, Winn-Dixie, Food Lion, Harris Teeter, BI-LO, Kroger, and Publix stopped carrying Southern Gold. Piggly Wiggly, the lone holdout, said that it would continue to stock the sauce, owing to customer demand. Bessinger was defiant. He likened his treatment to that of Jewish merchants during Kristallnacht and told a newspaper, "Winn-Dixie is going to have to take that name off and call it Winn-Yankee." Eventually Piggly Wiggly dropped his products too. Only months earlier John McCain's presidential campaign had been ruined by a series of robocalls that asked voters, "Would you be more or less likely to vote for John McCain . . . if you knew he had fathered an illegitimate black child?" Still, the views that a person could get away with espousing, at least in public, had changed since the 1960s. Joe McCulloch, a Columbia attorney, recalled, "After that, Maurice became radioactive, as did his barbecue."

Bessinger claimed that his business shrank by 98 percent, amounting to a $20 million loss. Eventually he closed several restaurants and shut down the bottling plant. Nonetheless, he held his ground, portraying himself as a champion of free speech and state sovereignty and vowing, like proud southerners after Sherman's march, to "root hog or die."

In the wake of the controversy, the Bessingers were able to cultivate an alternative clientele. If some diners continued to patronize the restaurants in spite of Maurice's views ("Elton John's gay, but I still listen to his music," one customer told the *Baltimore Sun* in 2002), others showed up explicitly to support his cause ("The man's got the guts to stand up for his beliefs," another said). Glen McConnell, then a state senator, began stocking Bessinger's sauce at CSA Galleries, a Confederate-memorabilia store that he ran with his brother. (I Googled McConnell and was shocked to learn that he is now the president of the College of Charleston.)

Even today a rump of supporters regard Bessinger as the heroic victim of a liberal conspiracy. In 2014 a reader wrote to a local pa-

per that "after Bessinger publicly supported keeping the Confederate Battle Flag on the S.C. Statehouse, his business was sabotaged
by anti-southern activists who would go into grocery stores and sur-
reptitiously open a bottle of Maurice's barbecue sauce and lay it on
the top shelf, ruining a section of merchandise and creating a mess
for the store to clean up."

In January I called Lloyd Bessinger, Maurice's elder son. Our conversation began smoothly, but after a few minutes he asked me if
there would be any political angle to the article I wanted to write,
and when I said yes, things got uncomfortable. He sounded an-
guished as he said that while he was no racist, he did not want
to dishonor his father, whom he had known as a good and loving
man. When we hung up, I was left uncertain whether the changes
that Lloyd and his siblings had made at the Piggie Park were business decisions or evidence of a genuine transformation. Even if he
had taken down the flags, Lloyd had never really explained why he
made the move: out of principle or pragmatism or even, as a local
news channel had reported, because of the rising cost of dry cleaning. ("I think we should all be united by one country and one flag,
the American flag," he said later.) I wrote to him, asking if I could
come to see him in Columbia. "It was nice talking to you today," he
replied, declining. "Hopefully time will heal the past."

One of the reasons I'd become interested in the Bessinger story
is that it struck me as a small, imperfect test case for how to act
in our political moment. Of the many moral issues that have beset Americans since November, one of the most nagging is that of
the once beloved relative who appears at the Thanksgiving table
spouting contemptible ideas. When something or someone you
love troubles your conscience—when your everyday relationships
are political acts—do you try to be a moderating force, or are you
obligated to make a break entirely?

I decided to visit some less fraught outposts of the Bessinger
barbecue empire, hoping to get a sense of what makes yellow-sauce
barbecue—a seemingly minor comfort—something that, like Amazon or Uber, even some people who consider themselves hugely
opposed to the ethics of its purveyors find difficult to renounce. I
grew up in Wilmington, North Carolina, eating barbecue at Flip's
Barbecue House. It occupied a cinder-block building with an orange sheet-metal roof, and its hulking stuffed bear, reportedly shot

by Flip himself, was once named one of the "seven wonders of the Cape Fear region." Because barbecue is an intensely regional food, it's also an intensely emotional one, the sort of thing you wake up in the middle of the night fiending for when, say, you're pregnant and living 3,000 miles from home. I got that. Still, I'd always got over it, even when Flip's closed, in 2013. (If eastern North Carolina–style barbecue is your thing and you can't have it, dump a pork shoulder and all the vinegar you've got into a Dutch oven and let it cook, low, on the stovetop for as long as you can stand to.)

My first stop was Bessinger's Barbecue, which two of Maurice's brothers opened in 1960. I ordered a large barbecue plate. I also got a banana pudding. The restaurant's website features testimonials from customers, including Mr. and Mrs. Stephen Beazley, of Evans, Georgia ("We flew in our private plane to shop for rugs. You were near and looked interesting. BEST BBQ EVER!"), and the television personality Andrew Zimmern ("The best spicy sauce I've ever tasted!"). I found a seat, tore a paper towel from a roll that sat on the table, and started eating. The barbecue was satisfying, full of browned bits and ends, but ever so slightly dry. I kept daubing on more sauce—its bright color suggested a starring role in a stain-removal infomercial—which may have been exactly the point.

After the meal I asked at the counter if any Bessingers were around. Michael Bessinger, a third-generation barbecue man, appeared, with an apron tied around his waist, and led me to an upstairs office. Near the cash register, amid pictures commemorating visits from Elizabeth Dole and Mitt Romney, I'd seen a framed newspaper article in which a relative had spoken frankly of the Bessinger schism ("Everybody wanted to be a chief and not Indians"). Michael told me that his branch of the family wasn't close to Maurice's—they never got together for the holidays, for example —but he seemed to regard his uncle with a sort of detached amusement. "Maurice always liked the spotlight, positive or negative," he said. He said that he too was trying to move forward without disrespecting the past. He was thinking about introducing alcohol and had recently added brisket to the menu—a concession to modern customers' expectations of barbecue, however regionally dubious.

Across town at Melvin's Barbecue, I ordered another barbecue plate, this time with a side of butter beans. It arrived on a stylish brushed-metal tray instead of a plastic plate. A list of the Ten Commandments printed on the side of my cup momentarily counteracted the progressive atmosphere, but then I walked over to the condiments bar and, scanning vats of pickled peppers, noticed a bullet-shaped bottle with a green nozzle. Sriracha! I wondered if Melvin David Bessinger, who in 2004 inherited the business from his father, Melvin, might be the family's great unabashed modernizer, the King Abdullah of yellow-sauce barbecue.

Melvin, who died in 2012, was the fifth child of the eleven Bessinger siblings — the older brother who, after their father's sudden death, Maurice wrote, "was conspiring against me to move me out of the business and take it for himself." (Melvin was equally confident of his status as rightful heir, claiming that when he was ten years old, his father had entrusted him with the secret recipe, promising, "Son, this sauce is gonna make you a million dollars someday.") In 2000, when the NAACP initiated the boycott, Melvin swept in, picking up much of Maurice's forfeited business. Melvin's sauce was called Golden Secret instead of Southern Gold. To dispel the suspicion that the business might be a front for Maurice's — same sauce, Confederate-flag-less bottles — Melvin David issued a press release: "Melvin and his brother do not share political or social views. Despite their being brothers, they do not speak to each other. Melvin's views on the Confederate flag, slavery and race relations are not those of his brother." Maurice angrily told reporters, "I taught Melvin everything he knows about barbecue sauce — but I didn't teach him everything I know."

Melvin David was out of town the day I visited the restaurant, but I reached him on the phone later. "When you come from a large family, not everybody's going to agree," he told me. "Some people can't even get along with a brother and sister — how about if you have eleven and you all went into the same business?" Whatever the extent of the brothers' animosity, he said, Melvin and Maurice had reconciled before Melvin died. "I'm ashamed to use my last name," Melvin David had said in a 2001 interview, a statement he now regretted. "I was being accused of a lot of things, a lot of negative things were coming my way, and it just kind of got to me," he told me. "No doubt this was a great name that we were given when we were born."

Lexington County, which encompasses all but one of the dozen Piggie Park restaurants now in operation, remains a bedrock of hard-right politics. It is the home of Donnie Myers, the prosecutor

known during his decades-long tenure as Dr. Death, for his zeal-
ousness in pursuing capital punishment, and Joe Wilson, the con-
gressman who heckled President Obama during a speech to a joint
session of Congress, shouting, "You lie!" In the 2016 presidential
election, 65.6 percent of the county's residents voted for Donald
Trump.

Lake E. High, Jr., the president of the South Carolina Barbecue Association, agreed to meet me at the original Piggie Park, in
Columbia, one day in January. That morning, while renting a car
in Charleston, I struck up a conversation with a late-middle-aged
white man behind the counter. When I told him I was writing about
Maurice's Piggie Park, he reminisced, "You'd get a few cocktails in
you, drive up, get that big-ass fried tempura onion ring, and yum,
yum, yum." He continued, "All that stuff you see on CNN, the liberal side—that division, that prejudice, that's not who we are."

I took the keys and headed up to Columbia. When I reached
the Piggie Park, I pulled the car in under the same formerly futuristic drive-in canopy where, fifty-three years earlier, Anne Newman had been refused service. I walked into the restaurant, where
High—a big man in a sweater vest, with a mottled complexion and
an omniscient smirk—was sitting at a round table. He explained
that he'd got into barbecue as a challenge. "Somebody said, 'We
got the best damn barbecue in the nation, and the worst judges,'
and I said, 'Well, I tell you what, I think we could fix that,' and we
started the South Carolina Barbecue Association in 2004." When
Anthony Bourdain visited South Carolina for an episode of *No Reservations,* he asked High to show him around. (As for his name,
which he shares with his father, when his great-grandmothers were
squabbling over what to call the coming child, High's grandfather
banged a fist on the table, pointed to a map that was hanging on
the wall, and said, "What's behind me?" "Lake Erie," one of the
great-grandmothers answered. "Well, that's his name.")

In High's estimation, the Piggie Park was "hundred-mile barbecue"—worth driving a hundred miles for. "It's the iconic South
Carolina sauce is what it boils down to," he said, surveying the
restaurant, with its lazy Susans, ceiling fans, and brown linoleum
floor. Country music was playing on the radio; a muted television showed Fox News. The crowd was white, mostly older. In the
guest book I found comments that read, "Where's the flag??!" and
"Thanks for Taking It Down! God Bless!!" Near the entrance a por-

trait of Maurice presided over a shrine of sauces. I ordered some barbecue. The chop was delicate, and the sauce was nearly fluorescent. "It tastes like mustard that's got some mouthfeel to it," High continued. "I'd say it's somewhere in the middle of the light-to-sharp spectrum."

High spoke favorably of the Piggie Park's new management—"Paul and Lloyd, and he's got a daughter whose name I forget, cute girl. They're real dedicated." He had also thought highly of Maurice, who, he said, was always friendly and insisted on top-of-the-line ingredients. "He and Strom Thurmond were talking about all-natural thirty years ago," he said, which seemed a bit like remembering Oswald Mosley for his advocacy of brown bread. I asked whether he thought Maurice's political legacy posed a problem. "It wasn't nearly as bitter as modern day makes it seem," he said. He went on to talk about the trouble with racially interbred societies, the genetic basis of criminality, and his belief that the South should secede. After a disquisition that touched on everything from slavery ("It's been around since Day One, and they talk about it in the Bible") to Trump ("I happened to see him speaking to a crowd before he declared, and I came into the kitchen and I said, 'Lovebug, that man's gonna be president'"), he returned to the Piggie Park. "This is the most taken-for-granted barbecue house in America," he said.

Lonnie Randolph, the NAACP state president who had led the boycott of Piggie Park, told me that Maurice Bessinger was part of an ideological and economic lineage that stretched back to before the Civil War. "He represented a hate that was so deeply rooted," Randolph said. "I knew it was dangerous." He didn't think that it was possible to let the past be the past. "'It doesn't affect me'—white people can say that, because it didn't affect them. But when I think of the damage that has been done, it cannot be undone," he said. Things might be different, he conceded, if the new generation of Bessingers were taking some sort of active steps toward reparation. "But I'm not familiar with them supporting any issues that support the lives of the people he abused for so many years."

Representative Joe Neal, a longtime member of the state legislature and the chairman of the South Carolina Legislative Black Caucus during the flag battles of the early aughts, placed a similar emphasis on the younger Bessingers' actions, or lack thereof, when

I got him on the phone in January. (Neal died the next month.) "I don't think they have to apologize," he said. "I think what people are waiting for is to find out who they are."

After talking to Randolph and Neal, I couldn't stop thinking about Nat Fuller's Feast. Nat Fuller, born in 1812, was a slave who became a celebrated restaurateur, opening the Bachelor's Retreat, a Charleston catering hall famed for its pastries, game, and turtle soup. In April of 1865, two months after Charleston surrendered to Union forces, Fuller orchestrated a grand meal—historians have remembered it as a "reconciliation banquet"—to which he invited dozens of the city's prominent citizens. A society doyenne wrote in her diary of the "miscegenat dinner, at which blacks and whites sat on an equality and gave toasts and sang songs for Lincoln and Freedom."

The evening's menu has been lost to time, but in 2015 a group of chefs and scholars tried to recreate the meal, using dishes that Fuller had served at other events. On a drizzly April night, forty Charlestonians gathered for the feast. "This is the beginning for all of us," B. J. Dennis, a black chef, said, making a toast. Fifteen days earlier Walter Scott, an unarmed black man with a broken brake light, had been shot in the back by a white North Charleston police officer. Two months later the white supremacist Dylann Roof walked into the Mother Emanuel African Methodist Episcopal Church in Charleston and killed nine people, including Clementa C. Pinckney, Mother Emanuel's pastor. Pinckney was at the dinner that night, trying to acknowledge and refute history over watermelon brandy, chowchow, shrimp pie, *chapon chasseur,* and truffled squab served with silver ewers of walnut ketchup.

Before I left West Columbia, I decided to try Lloyd Bessinger one last time. In the wood-paneled office at the main Piggie Park, a secretary invited me to have a seat. Lloyd walked out: trim, mostly bald, wearing navy chinos and a red Piggie Park polo.

Lloyd was as unassuming as his father had been outlandish. His ambition, it seemed, was to be left alone. When I asked about the 2000 boycott, he said, "I try not to think about it that much anymore."

"Do you support white supremacy?" I asked.

"No! Of course not," Lloyd said. "White supremacy is totally wrong—and my father was not like that. He was a southerner and a South Carolinian. He enjoyed reading about the history and the heritage of America." Lloyd had recently been to a friend's funeral at a black church, and "two hundred people were there, and"—he chuckled—"ninety percent of them were black, and that was fine."

I told Lloyd what Lonnie Randolph and Joe Neal had said, that people needed a tangible sign that the Bessinger family understood the pain they had caused, and that until they gave one it would persist.

"Mmmkay," he said. "Well, I don't know how I can do that. I'm not objecting to doing that. I just need to know what that is."

That Lloyd could afford not to have much of an opinion—that he simply didn't have to think about race while making choices big and small—was a privilege he had never considered. He seemed caught between the worlds of his parents and his children, the values with which he had grown up and those he now perceived to be ascendant. I recalled what Kathleen Purvis had said to me about Lloyd: "I felt very sympathetic to him. My family's from Georgia —I have family members who had beliefs, used language that was awful. My grandmother, the last thing she remembered about me when she was disappearing into dementia was 'Oh, yeah, that's the girl that loves black people so much.' That was a very painful thing, and to ask me to denounce my grandmother for that—you can't. So being southern always involves that complicated dance."

"I can't change anything," Lloyd said before I left. "All I can do is speak for myself today. I don't look at race. I look at people. We're all equal, okay?"

In 2009 the Daras family, of Fort Washington, Maryland, moved to Orangeburg, South Carolina. Tommy Daras had just retired from running gas stations. "I'd come down here fishing, and I liked it," he said recently. "I always thought the people were nice, and Florida was too hot."

For a while he and his wife, Deborah, enjoyed the weather and their newfound freedom. Then, in 2015, they spotted a cute brick bungalow on John C. Calhoun Drive, an out-of-business Piggie Park. "We were at home, bored, and decided to clean it up, fix it up, and make some money on it," Daras said. They added teal-and-white awnings and named the place Edisto River Creamery & Kitchen. Daras recalled, "An ice cream shop near a park, how hard could that be?" They hosted such events as Bible studies and a Pokémon Go tournament. Their outdoor sign welcomed hunters and advertised a bacon-palmetto burger. Daras said, "I did notice that there were no black customers"—the population of Orangeburg is 80 percent African-American—"and I was trying to figure that out. Man, why am I not getting their business?"

The Darases bought the property from Maurice Bessinger's children, knowing that a Confederate flag flew on a small bit of land in a corner of the lot. From what Daras understood, the parcel, through some quirk of local real estate history, belonged to the Sons of Confederate Veterans, having been donated to them by Maurice Bessinger in 2005. Daras wasn't a fan of the flag, but it didn't really bother him. It became impossible to ignore, however, when, shortly after the massacre at Mother Emanuel, members of the Sons of Confederate Veterans showed up, took down the flag, and replaced it with a new one that was three times as big. "Before, I'd just sucked it up, but then it was, like, 'Man, I've got to try to do something here,'" Daras said, explaining that he could no longer abide "this huge flag sticking up in the air telling everyone to screw themselves."

Daras reexamined his deed. With the help of a lawyer, Justin Bamberg, he is filing a lawsuit arguing that the corner parcel belongs to him. (The Sons of Confederate Veterans maintain their ownership.) Bamberg, who is thirty, grew up near Orangeburg and now serves as a Democratic member of the South Carolina House of Representatives. I called him to discuss the details of the lawsuit, but as our conversation went on, he started talking about what the Piggie Park had meant to him as a young African-American man. "It was one of those places I remember as a kid, always riding by there, feeling like in some people's eyes I was less a person. I did not go into Maurice's until I was in college," he said, recalling one afternoon when he had felt compelled to just walk into the restaurant, leaving without ordering anything. "It was a personal thing —for so long this place always had control over some part of how I felt. For me, it was like, 'It's gonna end today.'" It will be up to a court to conclude the story of Maurice Bessinger's flags, the last of which is, for the moment, still flying, his final provocation.

On the Ibérico Trail

FROM *Garden & Gun*

THREE HOURS SOUTHWEST of Madrid, in the rocky and arid region of Extremadura, where oak boughs sag with acorns, crumbling Moorish castles loom, and solar arrays tilt skyward, Allan Benton, the fabled Tennessee ham and bacon curer, glimpses a possible future for southern food. Leaning into the lunch counter at a truck stop, between bites of a sandwich layered with Spain's prized *jamón ibérico*, he wonders why this sort of everyday excellence is elusive back home. "Can you imagine getting a ham sandwich like this at a truck stop in Tennessee?" he asks, working that rhetorical in his head, grappling for an answer, burnishing the possibility like a gemstone.

A clutch of drivers elbow for seats at the lunch counter to drink pony beers and fork into potato and egg tortillas. A slot machine blinks and flashes. Benton, who looks (and sounds) like a Jimmy Carter stunt double, stands before a rack of black-footed hams sheathed in plastic netting, suspended in a wire cage that looks as if it were built to hold firearms instead of salt-cured hind legs of acorn-fattened hogs. "We're not there yet," he says, speaking of a South in which cheap burgers and fries are not default road foods and salt-cured artisanal hams are not relegated to special occasions. "And I may not live to see this, but maybe, someday, the kind of hams I cure will make it into truck stops."

Benton's name is synonymous with excellence in all things pork. Before him chefs genuflect. David Chang of the New York City–based Momofuku empire was an early advocate of his salt-and-brown-sugar-rubbed hams. Cassidee Dabney, the chef at Tennessee's lavish Blackberry Farm, proclaims the smoky goodness of his bacon like a storefront preacher.

Yet Benton still works in a cinder-block bunker, hard by the highway in Madisonville, Tennessee, near Knoxville. Forty-plus years after curing his first ham, he answers emails with handwritten letters, closes business deals with handshakes, and smiles an impossibly wide grin that broadcasts warmth and welcome. When he meets someone new, at home or here in Spain, he often leads with a statement and repeats it like a mantra: "I'm a purebred hillbilly, raised so deep in a holler I had to look up to see light." Coming from another mouth, this might sound like false modesty. But as those words drawl from Benton, they mark his honesty, humility, and pride in the place he calls home.

Spain is the right place to ponder the past and future of the southern love for the pig. Spanish explorers introduced pigs to the Americas (as well as diseases that decimated the native population). When de Soto landed, he loosed Ibérico pigs from Extremadura to roam the southern countryside. They prospered. And so did the settlers, who employed Native American techniques to smoke them and adapted European traditions to salt and air-cure them. From those pigs came country ham, red-eye gravy, and lard-rich cathead biscuits. From that landing came Benton's livelihood. Today Spain produces the most dry-cured ham of any country in the world. By the measure of many palates, it also produces the best.

Allan flew here with Sharon, his wife of forty-two years, to grasp the roots of his craft. As he approaches his seventieth birthday, he aims to improve on the revered ham that emerges from his foothills cure house. Now, two days into a weeklong run that has taken us in and out of Madrid and down into the boulder-strewn *dehesa* of Extremadura, he has begun to see life back home against the backdrop of Spain.

At the truck stop, another vision comes into focus. Gazing at one of the stainless-steel racks the Spanish use to cradle hams for carving, he sketches a scene. "I can see one of these in any southern home," he says, peering across the bar, where a woman in a white smock carves stubby slices from a teardrop-bottomed violin of pork. Many who reach his age look back in appreciation of what they have accomplished. Or in mourning for what they have lost. Instead, Benton conjures a future.

"You could crank the ham down in there on Thanksgiving Day, and it would stay on the kitchen counter all through the holidays," he imagines. "And you slice that ham as you need it, for suppers and parties. By the time the meat starts to disappear and you're left with nothing but the hock and foot, it will be time to cook black-eyed peas for New Year's Day."

For centuries ridge-backed Ibérico pigs have rooted the Extrema-dura grasslands, scarfing acorns beneath splayed oak canopies, taking on fall and winter weight before slaughter. Artisans here have long cured the rear legs from those pigs. Hung for two years or more, they yield ham celebrated for the nutty sweetness and silky mouthfeel of its meat and for the healthfulness of its fat, which spiderwebs the flesh, tracing marble threads through a dense field of red. Hams made from those Ibéricos bear lard that doesn't clog arteries. Instead the human body processes it similarly to olive oil. That's why lovers of *jamón* refer to these pigs as four-legged olive trees.

Fifteen years back, when heritage-breed pigs became more widely available in America, Benton began curing hams and bellies from Durocs and Tamworths and Mangalitsas. More recently, as he learned of the superiority of Ibérico pigs and noted that whole Ibérico hams can fetch from $500 to $2,000 in the United States, he resolved to visit their homeland, where storefront vendors style their operations as *museos del jamón* and all strata of society share a reverence for all things cured.

This is the first trip out of the country for Allan and Sharon. But this is not a victory-lap payoff for four decades of grindstone work. He regards the trip as a rolling workshop, a research expedition conducted in feedlots, at dining tables, and in cure houses racked floor to ceiling with salted hams.

Traveling Spain, Benton is wide-eyed and restlessly curious. His palate proves unimpeachable. Drinking rioja, he picks up the lic-orice blush that everyone else misses. Tasting hams, he identifies which were cured from lesser cereal-fed pigs and which came from better acorn-fed pigs. Each taste he savors, and every colleague he befriends, inspires him to ask questions of his own work.

Our party spent the first day bouncing from canteen to canteen in Madrid, drinking vermouth on the rocks, eating anchovies perched on potato chips, and sampling rosy-hued *jamón* shaved into match-book planks and spiraled onto platters.

That night Jaime Oriol, a barrel-chested attorney with a flip of white hair, joined us. A native of Madrid, Oriol worked in New York City for twenty years before returning to live in Spain, where his interests span movie financing, hog farming, and international livestock trade. In 2014 he and his son, Kurt, partnered with the pioneering Georgia farmer Will Harris of White Oak Pastures. Under the banner Iberian Pastures, they flew twenty-three mother and five boar Ibéricos from Spain to South Georgia, where Harris now raises his own four-legged olive trees.

As dinner came to a close and the waiter set down glasses of what tasted like Spanish moonshine, I sketched our plans to travel down to the town of Jabugo, where commercial *jamón* producers cluster. Oriol waved his hand in the air like a soccer referee signaling a red-card ejection. "There's no need to travel there," he shouted, screwing his face into a mask of playful contempt. "I'll show Mr. Benton how we do it. Put the master in my hands."

That is how, after driving 300 kilometers south out of Madrid at close to 200 kilometers an hour, we landed at a truck stop that serves transcendent ham sandwiches. And that is how, later that same afternoon, we arrived on a bougainvillea-draped and pome-granate-tree-flanked terrace alongside a farmworker chapel at Cobacha, the Oriol family farm compound in far southwestern Extremadura, where, our host promised, pigs root happily amid oaks flush with acorns.

A genial wild man, Oriol sets in motion a three-day binge of hospitality and discovery, in which he assumes the role of munificent dictator, focused on feeding us Spain's best while delivering graduate-course lectures in Spanish history, geography, culture, and politics.

Days begin at the Cobacha dining room table, beneath an oil painting of the wave-crashed Spanish Armada. Breakfasts of fried yard eggs and *migas,* a toss of bread crumbs and cracklings, end with oranges plucked from trees in the courtyard. Lunches, eaten in the shadow of a Moorish castle one day, on the veranda of a grand hacienda the next, open with Torta del Casar, a local sheep's-milk cheese that turns gooey after a quick run in the oven. They close with pound cake, topped with more oranges. Somewhere around course three, Ibérico pork always shows.

At their simplest, those Ibéricos yield lunches of roasted pork shoulder, sliced into medium-rare medallions, thatched with lard-fried potatoes, presented in a wash of fat-swirled jus. In the hilltop town of Albuquerque, at the restaurant El Fogón de Santa María, set in a stone-walled fifteenth-century cellar, local pork gains complexity. Over a long and boozy meal, a mousse of chorizo crumbles and cream, reminiscent of feral pimento cheese, precedes lozenges of baby Ibérico, roasted until the flesh turns creamy and the skin crisps to a shingle.

Evenings end on the fieldstone terrace at Cobacha, as the sun fireballs across the coral horizon, backlighting the oaks in psychedelic silhouette. "I didn't just come to Spain," Benton says, clasping his hands prayerfully, looking to the skies, clinking Oriol's wineglass. "I fell into Spain."

From their first meeting, Oriol has referred to Benton as a master. Now that he has the master in his friendly grasp, he aims to school him in *jamón ibérico*. And in the life *ibérico*.

Manuel Maldonado of Albuquerque tops Oriol's list of Spanish cure masters. Ferran Adrià, the most famous chef in Spain and arguably the most influential world chef of the twenty-first century, prefers his hams, which Maldonado rubs with salt from coastal Cádiz and hangs with the hooves facing the ceiling. He is, in short, the Spanish Allan Benton.

Our crew meets Maldonado at his white masonry cure house, skirted by wizened olive trees. With the Spanish master leading the way, Benton reviews processes, tracing the path from pink haunches of freshly butchered pork to two-year-old exemplars, rubbed with olive oil until they gleam beneath the lights. After an hour of inspection, Maldonado directs us to the basement tasting room, where a spread of delicacies awaits. For Benton he cracks open bottle after bottle of tempranillo, slices fat hunks of meat from rosy loins, cuts coins of *pimentón*-blushed chorizo, and shaves stub after stub of sweet ham.

While our group praises Maldonado's handiwork, Benton stands alone in the corner, figuring percentages in his head. The USDA requires him to salt a 25-pound ham for fifty days before hanging it to age, but a Spanish firm can hang the same-sized ham after only twelve days. Benton decides that is why the pork he tastes this morning is sweeter and less salty than what he cures back home. That taste is not new to him. It reminds him of the acorn-fattened hams his grandparents salted and hung in Virginia two generations back, before stricter governmental regulations took effect.

When Benton rests a slice of *jamón* on his tongue and looks up at the ceiling, Maldonado steps to his side. "There is a permanence in your mouth," he says. "It's not salty. It lingers. There is persistence." Benton nods and smiles shyly, thinking of the hams that emerged from that dirt-floored Virginia smokehouse.

In Maldonado, Benton recognizes a fellow member of the artisan fraternity, divided by the Atlantic, united by a belief in the careful manipulation of salt and time. Sensing the bond, seizing the moment, Oriol leans toward Benton, smiling. "In the future you two will do business together," he whispers. "The two masters together! I know it."

The next morning—before we tour an industrial cure facility and, later, a farm where we watch, mesmerized, as sway-bellied Ibéricos sashay across rocky pastureland, rooting for acorns—one of the Cobacha workers meets Oriol at his car. He holds an oak tree bloom in his hand. It's late fall now. Trees are not supposed to bloom until March, he says. When the first frost comes in a month, that oak will probably die. Global warming is a real and persistent threat in Extremadura.

Benton arrived in Spain as he began to consider changes in how he sources pigs. In Extremadura he has seen much that is ancient, and much that he would like to replicate. But he also now understands that while the Spanish have a long head start on pig raising and ham curing, they too confront a range of challenges. Acorns, which drop from oak trees here each fall and blanket the savanna, vary year to year. Sweet one season, bursting with the nut meat on which Ibéricos feast, they can be fibrous and nutrient-poor the next. As new markets for Ibérico hams have opened, demand from the United States and China has stressed supply chains. Some years there aren't enough acorns to feed the Ibéricos. To make matters worse, a blight sometimes hits the trees, rendering the leaves brown, the branches withered, the acorns scarce.

"We have been slaves to the acorn," Oriol says, standing by a fence at Cobacha, watching baby Ibéricos scamper by like windup toys. Evidence of that reliance is everywhere at Cobacha. A bronze sculpture of a pig rooting beneath the oaks dominates a credenza opposite the fireplace. Acorns decorate the living room rugs and the serviceware that graces his dining room table. While reverence for the acorn remains, the resolve to find alternatives intensifies.

Across Spain, Oriol and many of his friends have begun experimenting with feeds that might serve as substitutes for or supplements to acorns, which Ibéricos typically eat in the last three months before slaughter. Benton's grandparents, who cured the hams that set his forever standard, fed their pigs on windfall acorns. Back in Tennessee, as Benton made plans to raise his own pigs, he had begun looking for a feed that might render the same fat and flavor.

Not long before he set out on this trip, a University of Tennessee researcher confirmed his hunch that a diet of sunflower seeds might yield similar fat quality in pigs. Benton had begun to imagine how this could play out. He contacted a farmer who might raise the pigs. And he eyed a parcel of land just down the road from his cure house where they might roam freely.

Before Benton set his plan in motion, the professor advised him to wait and see what he would learn in Spain. Traveling Extremadura, he has learned that while the Spanish draw on a deeper trove of experience, they too must bridge gaps between old and new, between tradition and innovation. Watching a pack of Ibéricos root the grasslands, marveling at his good fortune to be here, now, Benton turns toward Oriol. "You are asking the same questions I am," he says. "And I had to come all the way to Spain to meet you."

Many of us dream big dreams while traveling. We resolve to study French or learn the mandolin. We conspire to buy a second home by the water or in the mountains.

Travel offers perspective. When the voting rights activist Fannie Lou Hamer journeyed to West Africa, she came home with new ideas about the power of landownership. The Birmingham, Alabama, chef Frank Stitt returned home from France, where he worked for the writer Richard Olney, with a new appreciation for Alabama farm goods. Travel through Spain has convinced Benton that his dreams of a ham-focused future are realizable. Talking with fellow masters like Maldonado, he has recognized that while Spanish ham is celebrated, what he does is rightly comparable. Tasting his way through Extremadura, he has learned to value anew the excellence of his own craft. Informed by what he has gleaned, Benton may gently rethink his techniques. But he won't reinvent them.

Before we return to Madrid and, eventually, home, Benton loops back to Albuquerque. From Maldonado, the master, he buys ham for everyone. For his colleagues back in Madisonville. For his traveling companions. We tuck packets of the good stuff in our luggage and begin worrying whether we'll clear U.S. customs with our prizes.

Two days and one transoceanic flight later, a customs agent in Atlanta asks Benton if he has returned with any meat products. His fellow travelers have already waltzed through the checkpoint, believing that our white lies and sins of omission were justified by the acorn-fed payoffs, when the Tennessee cure master, who values the contents of his luggage more than any of us covet ours, tells the truth. Soon he's unzipping his bag, rummaging through dirty socks to remove packet after packet of claret-colored *jamón* slices that spangle like mica beneath the fluorescents. Faced with the knowledge that his *jamón* may soon be bound for the trash, he makes one last effort to fix the memory of that Ibérico on his palate. "May I step aside here and just eat my ham?" he asks. That's impossible, says the woman in the blue uniform. "If you ate that food here, you would be making this space into a restaurant."

Back home, when Benton applies what he has learned in Spain, he won't have Maldonado's *jamón* to taste and compare. But he will have company. Will Harris and Oriol have already set a winter date to slaughter their first Georgia Ibéricos. Benton hopes to salt-cure one of those prizes in Madisonville. When he does, the Tennessee cure master will rely on recollections of Extremadura, the promise of sunflower crops to come, and memories of his grandparents' Virginia smokehouse, tucked so deep in a holler he had to look up to see sunlight.

Bringing in the Beans

FROM *Harper's Magazine*

THE BRIGHT-GREEN HULK of our John Deere combine harvester crept across the field of soybeans. It was late in the day, early October, the sun low. A cloud of hulls and chaff spewed from the back of the combine, then swirled up around us and blazed in the glow. Sealed in the dustless quiet of the cab, Rick Hammond steadied the wheel with one hand and punched coordinates into a touchscreen computer with the other. The reel of the harvester head spun steadily below us like the paddle wheel of a river steamer, standing up stalks so that the toothed blades could cut a dozen rows at a go. The feed auger corkscrewed the cut plants into the mouth of the combine, where a throbbing set of threshers splintered the dry pods, collecting the oily seeds inside and sending them spiraling up to the grain tank behind Rick's chair. Harvested beans ticked against the back window like a light summer hail. The only other sounds were the Ponglike beeps from the computer.

"Okay," Rick said at last, marking the final coordinates, "we're on autosteer now." And to show me, he took his hands off the wheel. "I thought I'd be able to retire before I had to get autosteer," he sighed. Rick is in his sixties, tan and weatherworn but still plenty fit. Most days he works sunup to sundown, especially during harvest. It wasn't the long hours that were getting to be too much, he said, but trying to keep up with the technology. "The reason for all this is inputs," he explained. *Inputs* is a kind of catchall term on the farm, a word used to cover any overhead or revolving costs —seed, fertilizer, herbicides, pesticides—as well as payments on past investments and big costs for the year, such as a new tractor or additional land. Everything hinges on keeping your inputs as low as possible without jeopardizing your yield.

The combine continued along, following the contours of the planting lines automatically recorded months earlier by GPS. As we moved, our progress was charted on the touchscreen in varying colors to show where each row or part of a row was above or below the target for bushels-per-acre for this field. All of that data is recorded and stored to plan for next year, helping farmers decide how to adjust the density of their seed populations, where to apply fertilizer, how much to water, where to add inputs, and where to save money. The sun was setting now, just south of the Platte River in eastern Nebraska, turning the browned plants a radiant gold, but onscreen the colors of our current swath shifted back and forth from green to yellow, from profit to loss.

The thin difference became especially apparent in 2014. At the end of June of that year, crop counters at the U.S. Department of Agriculture released new estimates projecting that the summer's mild weather and above-average rainfall would result in a higher-than-expected yield. It's the kind of prediction that sounds like good news, but for farmers it meant an upcoming glut of grain. One report calculated that the national soybean yield would be 3.3 million acres higher than expected at planting—not just cutting into profits but actually outstripping domestic demand. On news of such unprecedented surpluses, soybean futures, which had topped $17 per bushel, dropped below $10.

Then, in August, in the weeks just before harvest, a series of downpours moved across the middle of Nebraska, dumping two to three inches of rain at a time, pushing back the start date for bringing in the beans. While he waited anxiously for the fields to dry enough that a harvester wouldn't mire in the mud, Rick watched projections for the national yield go up and up. Every day that the crops stayed out, unharvested and undelivered to the co-op, the per-bushel prices went lower. For weeks in nearby towns, at the firehouse in Hordville and the bar in Polk, even at the Iron Skillet at the truck stop south of York, the talk had turned to the traders in Chicago making bank on the backs of farmers. Rick didn't have time for idle chatter. He moved an old grain bin in from a distant part of the farm to store as much of the harvest as possible and wait out the down market, and he tested the moisture at the edges of the fields every morning.

When he finally caught a day of clear sky and enough of a breeze to get going, the ground, after weeks of rain, was still so wet that bringing in all the equipment they'd need to work the field—the harvester, the tractor and grain cart, and the semi to haul the beans away—was going to compact the soggy soil and make it too dense to plant next year. After some thought, Rick decided to make the sacrifice. The decision might seem impulsive—why not wait just a few more days?—but "beans are weird," Rick told me. Unlike most crops, which are planted in the spring, grow all summer, and begin to mature only when the weather turns cold and the air dries, soybeans are short-day plants—meaning simply that their final stages of maturity are triggered by waning hours of sun. With every day of earlier nightfall, the beans grow riper.

This poses two major problems when you run into an unusually wet September. First, the days get shorter no matter what. Weather-dependent crops like corn slow their maturation on rainy days. You can get lucky—catch a warm spell or even a single sunny day—and get out in the field and back on track. Not so with soybeans. While you're waiting for the clouds to clear, the beans are going past maturity. Second, soybeans have to be delivered to the grain elevator at a precisely defined moisture rate: 13 percent. "We're at twelve-point-nine right now." Rick showed me on the touchscreen. "But when we get down there where the ground is a little wetter, it'll go back up." Above 14 percent, he said, the grain elevator not only charges you for drying but also docks you for the estimated shrinkage. "And you would think, well, one percent of moisture would be one percent of shrink," Rick told me, "but no. They dock you *one and a half* percent." At 15 percent moisture, they're apt to reject the whole load.

So to make your best profit on soybeans, you need a sunny day (but not too sunny) with a dry breeze (but not too dry), and you need that day to fall exactly when the plant has received the precise number of hours—yes, hours—of sunlight from the moment you planted it months earlier. To make hitting such a tight window even remotely possible, seed companies, like Rick's supplier, Du-Pont Pioneer, have hybridized soybeans for nearly a century—and genetically modified them in recent decades—according to bands of latitude called maturity groups. They number these photoregions from 0 in the northern growing zones of Canada to 7 in the light-drenched flatlands of Florida. But Nebraska is almost exactly divided between groups 2 and 3, the line bisecting the state into north and south. Most farmers here, especially in central regions like York County, plant both varieties to spread out their risk, but some daring farmers like Rick will formulate a guess as to what the weather holds for the growing season and plant more of one group, hoping for higher yields and higher returns.

In 2014, after several years of drought, Rick bet on another dry year—and planted incredibly short-season beans. While most of his neighbors were planting 3.5s, Rick planted 2.4s. And he was dead on, right up until the rains started. If he could have harvested early, ahead of farmers in other parts of the country, and caught the market at its peak, he was positioned to make up for all the other setbacks going into the harvest. But if a farmer guesses correctly on the growing season, as Rick did, and then gets an extremely wet fall, he can end up with hundreds of acres of mature soybeans and fields too wet to run the combine. With each storm that rolls up on the horizon, he could move from making a hefty profit to incurring a crippling debt.

Rick knew prices would hold for a time, on the chance of an unforeseen late-season catastrophe, a hedge against an ice storm freezing crops or a line of thunderheads dropping hail that could send prices soaring. But once grain started pouring into the elevators, prices on futures were sure to slump. With the market already in free fall, some farmers decided not to wait: they went out as soon as the mucky furrows would allow and used propane or electric dryers to deal with the high-moisture grain. This was yet another expense, and if the moisture levels were too high, the cost of drying could cancel any profit. Other farmers, like Rick, held out as long as possible, but eventually everyone had to make hard choices.

"Every day that the beans sit out there," Rick said, "you're under risk of a big storm. And beans get harder and harder to get out, because they just soak up moisture like crazy. And then, the more that happens—when they're dry, wet, dry, wet, after they're mature —they're prone to shatter. They'll split wide open in a big wind." So when the rains finally let up, he decided it was time to go, soggy fields or no. It wasn't worth risking the return on this field this year just for the promise of next year. He set up the harvester and started across the field to judge for himself whether the beans were ready.

Now halfway through another swath, Rick checked the level of the grain tank. He needed to empty it. He radioed over to his soon-to-be son-in-law, Kyle Galloway. "Can I dump on you?" Kyle pulled up alongside the combine with the tractor and grain cart, moving in perfect parallel. While the harvesting reel kept spinning and the combine inched across the field, the unloading auger arm started pouring out soybeans until the tank was empty. Kyle peeled off to unload into the trailer of the big rig, but Rick's mind was already back on the moisture levels. At the end of the swath, he took a sweeping turn and set the harvester back on autosteer.

"This here is instant yield, instant moisture," Rick said, pointing to the screen, "and this is average yield, average moisture." As we moved, he could see in real time if he was on track to hit his production targets or falling short, and whether the moisture of the entire load was within the acceptable range or inching high enough that he'd have to pay a penalty for drying. He watched the data rolling across the screen, giving the minute-to-minute condition of the crop. All the perils of modern farming seemed to crawl across the four-inch screen. But harvest, at last, was officially under way. Now Rick just had to get his crops in as soon as possible. It was going to be a race.

The overproduction of corn by the American agricultural industry has generated a lot of attention in recent years, as food activists and environmentalists have grown worried about the middle of the country turning into a vast monoculture. But that's only half the picture. The corn boom, to a remarkable extent, has been made possible by a coequal boom in alternate-year planting of millions of acres of soybeans. In many ways, corn and soybeans seem made for each other. Soybeans are a natural nitrogen-fixer, replenishing the soil for nitrogen-hungry corn hybrids, and the plants share almost none of the same pests or diseases, preventing insects, molds, and bacteria from overtaking fields. But the soybean is more than an enabler of King Corn. It is in fact far and away the most successful crop introduced to the American farm in the past century.

In 1920 there were fewer than a million acres of soybeans planted in the entire United States. But soybean production boomed beginning in the 1930s—surpassing barley production by 1940, cotton in the 1950s, oats in the 1960s, and wheat and hay in the 1970s. This year the number of acres planted to soybeans is expected to reach 90 million—virtually equal to the acreage of cornfields—

and almost all of those acres are concentrated in the Midwest and on the Great Plains. How did the soybean, a legume native to East Asia and traditionally used primarily in foods from China, come to have such a place of prominence here? The rise of the soybean in the United States is attributable to, more than to any other person, Henry Ford.

In the early twentieth century, the American farm underwent a period of unmatched innovation. The arrival of the gas-powered tractor for plowing, the combine for harvesting, and affordable trucks for hauling grain to market made it possible for farmers to plant more and more acres and to manage those acres with fewer farmhands. But by the mid-twenties the market was flooded with grain, depressing prices and endangering the very family farms that the technological revolution had promised to empower. Farmers began calling for research to develop new uses for existing agricultural supply rather than continuing to search for ways to increase yields.

In January 1927, Wheeler McMillen, an associate editor of the popular magazine *Farm and Fireside,* published a watershed article entitled "Wanted: Machines to Eat Up Our Crop Surplus." He wrote that he had been receiving panicked letters from farmers lamenting that more grain was being produced than people could possibly eat. McMillen suggested that chemical compounds in plants might be converted into industrial products, and even advocated for government backing for such research. "There is no wrong in channeling some federal funds into farmers' pockets," he wrote, considering that the American farmer "by cheap food has subsidized the growth of cities."

Among McMillen's most interested readers was the owner of the Ford Motor Company. Ford, after all, manufactured much of the equipment that had contributed to booming yields—and if the company was to maintain that market share, it had to find a way to sustain its customers. To Henry Ford's mind, it also made perfect sense to subsidize research into the uses of farm products, because he was already growing concerned about dwindling petroleum supplies. Numerous auto parts were made from petroleum-based plastics, and of course all of Ford's engines ran on diesel and gasoline refined from petroleum crude. "If we want the farmer to be our customer," he said, "we must find a way to be his customer." In early 1928 he met with McMillen to discuss this new field of research—

what was eventually dubbed *chemurgy*—and came away even more convinced that the key driver should be private industry, not the government.

Ford authorized dramatically expanding the agricultural laboratory at his headquarters in Dearborn, Michigan. Under his direct supervision, technicians experimented with a staggering range of vegetables, fruits, grasses, legumes, tubers, and roots to determine which plants might contain high levels of cellulose for plastics and which might contain sugars that could be converted to ethanol. All efforts were aimed at finding replacements for petroleum while propping up American agriculture.

The stock market crash in October 1929 exacerbated the financial crisis for farmers. Ford publicly advocated continuing full production of all crops and again urged the government to resist stepping in. "The farmer and the chemist will solve farm relief, not the politician," he told the *New York Times*. Nevertheless, the USDA sent emissaries around the world in search of new crops that could be planted on American farms—crops intended for industrial use, not food. On one such trip to China, more than 10,000 soybean varieties were gathered. Learning of this, Ford urged his staff to look at the soybean. They found that the plant had unexpected levels of usable oils and yielded high-protein soy meal after the oil was extracted. In short, it appeared that the soybean could be used to produce industrial lubricants and that the byproduct could be turned into plastics.

The results were so encouraging that in 1932 Ford approved $1 million in new research funding, and that spring had 300 varieties of soybeans planted on 8,000 acres of his own farmland in rural Michigan. The next year he expanded it to 12,000 acres, making him the single largest soybean grower in the United States. That same year he announced that he would buy any soybeans delivered to the Dearborn plant. To encourage production, he made 400 Fordson tractors available for free use to Michigan farmers and offered gas and diesel at a penny per gallon—less than a quarter of what it cost at the pump. Farmers put more than 35,000 acres of land into growing soybeans, and Ford bought their entire output, as promised. It was a daring move but good business.

Ford also put the full muscle of his publicity machine behind promoting soybeans. He hosted the national convention of the American Soybean Association, promoted blending ethanol into gasoline, and gave a series of interviews, telling one reporter that he envisioned a time when much of an automobile "could be made from by-products of agriculture." He even announced a plan to decentralize Ford production by opening a constellation of factories in rural areas to manufacture plastic parts made from local soybeans. Ford bragged that he used soybean oil in his paint and as a lubricant in his casting molds. When soybean meal was combined with formaldehyde, it could produce a thermoplastic resin, which was used to make distributor caps, gearshift knobs, and horn buttons. "There is a bushel of soya beans in every Ford car," *Fortune* declared. "He is as much interested in the soya bean as he is in the V-8."

In 1934, Ford's promotions got an unexpected boost. The first of several years of severe drought—what proved to be the worst in American history—engulfed 75 percent of the country. Corn and wheat withered in the fields. Amid rampant crop failures, farmers harvested 23 million bushels of soybeans, a better yield than most crops and far better than its oil-producing competitors, such as linseed and canola. The following spring farmers planted roughly 45 million bushels of soybeans. Selling for 50 cents a bushel during the worst years of the Great Depression, soybeans were hailed as a godsend. Soybean trading was so active and central to industry that the Chicago Board of Trade started offering soybean futures for the first time. By the end of the 1930s, the soybean harvest was exceeding 75 million bushels per year. *Time* magazine declared Henry Ford "a bean's best friend."

But no sooner had industry begun to move away from petroleum than the world's largest oil reserves were discovered in Saudi Arabia in 1938. The barrel price of crude oil fell precipitously, and the demand for petroleum substitutes waned. Ford continued to extol the virtues of soybean products, but industrial applications for soybeans were now seen as impractical. During the years when grain crops were failing, however, animal feeders had discovered that livestock fed an oil-rich soybean diet bulked up quickly. With demand from Ford and other automakers no longer elevating prices, milling companies, hoping to capitalize on their existing supply, were eager to get into the soybean trade.

In 1939, Archer Daniels Midland announced the construction of a modern soybean plant and elevator in Decatur, Illinois. Soon after, Cargill launched an aggressive bid of its own into soybean processing. By the harvest of that year, soybean mills dotted the Mississippi River, and the American Farm Bureau Federation sponsored hundreds of events to encourage farmers to plant soybeans and instruct them on how to achieve top yields. For the first time, the middle of the country was also the center of soybean production in America, and those farmers were now well positioned to take advantage when the United States was pulled into World War II.

When Hitler began his march across Europe, there were sudden scarcities of edible oils and fats, much of which had previously been imported from Mediterranean countries. After Pearl Harbor, the U.S. government pushed agricultural producers to achieve record output, and soybeans increased from 78 million bushels in 1943 to 193 million in 1945. Yet Cargill and ADM struggled to make a profit, because President Roosevelt and Congress had worked together to pass price-control legislation, creating the Office of Price Administration and thus establishing fixed prices on animal feed.

After the war, however, when the government slowly started to roll back its strictures, feed prices rose sharply. As Ford had always feared, government involvement, instituting price controls and later subsidies, made farmers subject to the whims of federal farm policy—and the agribusiness interests that controlled that policy. But by then Ford was too sick and old to keep up the fight. He turned the company over to his grandson, and just two years later died of a cerebral hemorrhage. Without his guiding vision, soybean production for industrial purposes waned sharply for several decades, but the market for feeding livestock boomed like never before.

When wartime rationing officially ended in 1947, the American public wanted French wine and a good steak. Nationwide, consumption of meat rose by more than 20 percent, and the federal government heavily subsidized corn and soybean production to keep up with the demand. Ever since, the prices of commodity grains have risen and fallen according to the demand of livestock feeders.

Rick wasn't pleased. "Not good," he said, "not good."

It was past eleven in the morning, and the sky was still overcast and threatening. With the remaining fields near the house too wet for work, Rick loaded the combine onto a flatbed and brought it to a section of dry land south of Interstate 80 where he had planted more very-short-season soybeans. The wind seemed to be picking up enough to bring the moisture down to where he could harvest. He had run a test patch just to be sure, only to find that an unusual number of the bean plants were "laid down"—that is, their stems were so flat to the ground that the spinning reel of the John Deere couldn't prop up the stalks for the cutting blades. So many beans laid flat meant a measurable loss of yield, but it also suggested the possibility of something even worse.

"We had a couple of hailstorms come through here this summer," Rick said, kneeling in a furrow next to one of the flattened plants, "but our insurance adjuster didn't expect the loss to be near this bad." He plucked one of the plants, roots and all, out of the ground and flipped open his Buck knife. Slicing longways, he split the stalk in half. "Aw, man, look at that," he said, showing the hollowed-out insides to Kyle and Meghan, Rick's daughter, who had come out to check on the field.

With one glimpse of the stem, they each set to pulling up their own plants and cutting them open. After a few tries, Rick called out. "Here we go," he said, holding up the sliced-open stem for everyone to see: a tiny larva, a narrow white caterpillar, nestled right where the stalk met the roots. "Stem borer," Rick said. "They warned us to be on the lookout for them this year, but we've never seen them here before." He turned and cursed, then flipped open his cell phone and in a minute had the insurance adjuster on the line. "Yeah, we need you to come out and have a look," he said as he wandered back toward the road.

Meghan shook her head. "You spend all fucking year trying to get these crops the best yield," she said. "It's ready to be harvested. They're done, and when they're done, you got to get them out." Meghan is the sixth generation of her family to live and farm in this area—and she and Kyle were starting to talk about a wedding within the year. Once that happened, Rick figured it would be time to give them a bigger role in the operation.

But handing over control of the operation—succession, as it's known—is one of the hardest times in the life of any family farm. The older generation struggles to let go of the reins, to trust their kids to carry on a long and fragile tradition. The younger generation bridles against meddling and second-guessing and feels the double weight of scrutiny and doubt at every misstep. Many farms don't officially change hands until the older generation dies, leaving the rising generation beholden to their parents until they're well into adulthood and often into their fifties or sixties. The peculiarities of farm succession breed resentment and too often divide generations or turn brothers and sisters against one another. The process can be so stressful and legally complex that there are psychiatrists and attorneys who build whole practices around helping families navigate it. But on the Hammond farm it was even more complicated than that.

Years ago Rick had tried raising organic corn and direct-marketing his grass-fed black Angus cattle, but those efforts had largely failed. Now he had fully committed to planting a range of genetically modified corn and soybean varieties—and to get certified organic would mean years of letting fields lie fallow. There was no going back; for better or for worse, Rick was now tied to the commodities markets. "During the era of high prices, yahoos that should have been broke were thinking, 'There's nothing to this,'" he told me. "Now we're back down to cost of production—or less. So everything matters."

For the next year Rick needed to catch a few breaks. He couldn't afford to buy new machinery, couldn't afford to replace his center-pivot irrigation system. To get the handoff to Meghan and Kyle started on the right foot, he needed to have a full year of paying down loans, not incurring new debts. He needed a year in which crops came in early and healthy, prices rebounded, equipment held out. And if he was forced to take out more loans, he needed interest rates to stay low. He needed a whole year of everything going right—and having this field infested with stem borers was a far cry from right. Now Rick would have to wait to harvest this field until the adjuster could come and assess it, which could be days or even a week, depending on how many claims were already waiting. And while Rick waited, there was the chance of suffering more losses to the field.

"Hail, wind damage, snow," Kyle explained. "Right now those crops are really vulnerable."

"Eight inches of rain," Meghan said.

"Yeah, they just got big rains in southeast Nebraska," Kyle said. "It wiped out a lot of fields. They say a two-hundred-year event."

"It's also driving the price," Meghan said.

"That's right," Kyle agreed. "In the week since those rains, beans went up a dollar. That's probably how much yield has been lost. Because the beans are really sensitive. High wind will just knock the beans right out of the pod."

Rick snapped his phone closed and started back toward the field, moving quickly. "We're not going to get it out, so bring the combine in," he said. "Let's get the head back on the trailer." He told Kyle that they would move everything over to a neighbor's property. The neighbor, Seth (we have not used his real name to protect his privacy), had gone in with them on the rental for the combine. Rick had thought that his short-season beans would be ready first, but that wasn't going to happen now. They could make the most of what remained of the day and then hope to find another field that was ready tomorrow. For now, Seth's half section was dry, so they might as well get everything over there.

Kyle went to work unhooking the head of the harvester.

"We're at least two weeks behind," Rick said in my direction but almost to himself. "And it's just killing us."

Failure is everywhere on the farm. It hides in the long shadows cast by the barn at last light. It waits amid the dark stalks shifting in the fields before dawn. It's all around, always lurking, always palpable, but just out of view.

These failures can be dramatic and sudden: the death of a patriarch, his chest rolled over while repairing a tractor or his overalls twisted into a choking knot by the auger in the grain bin. If there is no will or no clear plan for succession, the farm can go under. Just as shattering can be a divorce. Legal bills and the stress of unsettled assets can turn a farmer's attention from keeping the books or watching the markets, and somehow the business slips away. And of course failure can come from the fields—cobs stunted by drought, beans infested by cutworms.

More frequently, though, it creeps up, not one major disaster but a series of small missteps. Too little insurance in a drought year. Borrowing to build a hog barn just before the bottom drops out of the market. Buying more ground and more seed only to see commodity prices plummet. As often as not, failure comes from nothing more than a farmer overestimating his ability to service a loan.

Some would say that this is no accident. In the early 1970s, Earl Butz, the secretary of agriculture during the Nixon administration, told farmers that a new day was dawning. They had to "get big or get out." He urged those who heeded his call to acquire as much land as they could afford and plant "fencerow to fencerow." Butz wanted American farmers to produce a steady oversupply of key grains in order to manipulate commodities markets to the disadvantage of our Cold War enemies. The only way to outproduce them was to invest in every possible method of intensifying production—using chemical fertilizers and pesticides, ending crop rotation in favor of monocultures, consolidating farmland and agricultural companies, and tinkering with the genetics of row crops to make them both resistant to various herbicides and tolerant of denser planting.

Butz promised to use the emerging global economy to bolster prices. If the United States faced harvests in which supply outstripped demand, we would simply negotiate trade deals, using economic might to artificially create a market. If we could flood the global market with massive quantities of grains, pushing prices below the cost of production, then, Butz believed, the world would have no choice but to buy from us. Soon the entire Nixon administration was sold on the idea that we could make our enemies—and even our friends—dependent on us to feed themselves.

In 1972, Butz sold what amounted to our entire grain reserve to the Soviet Union. That same year Nixon went to China and brokered a deal with Chairman Mao to ease trade restrictions. The Soviets and the Chinese, who still remembered the horrible privations of Stalingrad and Nanjing, viewed these moves as a pledge not to wage war through food. But Butz saw the same deals in terms of "agripower," stating, "Food is a weapon."

The trouble, as many critics saw it, was that producing at that volume meant relying on agribusiness, making the country beholden to a handful of companies. Where family-owned farms had been numerous and diverse, the kind of small operations that had to produce a variety of high-quality products to insulate themselves against market fluctuations, multinational grain companies were centralized and large enough to capture extensive portions of critical commodities and turn a profit by doing nothing more than capitalizing on market uncertainties at strategic moments.

The most famous example came in 1973, when Cargill placed huge orders for U.S. soybeans via a Geneva-based affiliate, Tradax, making it appear that there was a pending shortage. Prices skyrocketed, eventually rising so high that Nixon ordered a halt to all soybean exports to prevent domestic scarcity. With foreign countries desperate to find new sources of soybeans, Cargill filled the canceled orders of other American companies with supply from its South American subsidiaries, commanding artificially inflated prices. When the U.S. embargo was lifted, Cargill canceled its Tradax purchases and by year's end saw its annual profits jump from less than $20 million to more than $150 million, despite an overall decrease in its production that year—and regardless of the impact on American farmers.

A few years later farmers once again saw the risks they faced. In January 1980, after Leonid Brezhnev ordered the invasion of Afghanistan, President Jimmy Carter declared a grain embargo against the Soviet Union. Ever since buying our national granary, the Soviets had been acquiring huge quantities of American grain —including 25 million metric tons of wheat and corn contracted that October for the coming year. Carter bristled at the idea that the Soviets thought they could stage an invasion when we controlled their food supply. He announced the embargo and canceled the outstanding grain orders for some 17 million metric tons of corn and wheat. He issued a temporary freeze on trading in grain futures to allow the market to stabilize, but when it reopened, prices plummeted anyway, causing grain prices to lose 20 percent of their value. Angry farmers marched on the USDA. One protest leader said, "We planted fencepost to fencepost, and now this happens."

As commodities prices fell, it became apparent that instead of making the world dependent on our grain supplies, we had grown reliant on their demand. Even after the embargo was lifted, American agricultural exports declined by more than 20 percent between 1981 and 1983, which, combined with decreased market prices, resulted in a nearly 40 percent reduction in farm income in just two years.

Some would regard this as the ultimate failure of agriculture policy, but the emergent industry of consolidated agribusiness continued to flourish. Cargill sales grew from $2.2 billion in 1971 to $28.5 billion in 1981 by turning the profits from grain shortages into a diversified portfolio. They moved into value-added operations—milling grain for animal feed, making high-fructose corn syrup for Coke and Pepsi—then expanded and vertically integrated, acquiring feed elevators and meatpacking plants. By the mid-1980s, Cargill was not only the nation's top grain exporter but also the number-one egg producer, the number-two beef packer, and the number-three miller of corn and wheat. Seeing the success of the old grain cartels, former defense contractors who had moved into agrichemicals, including Monsanto and DuPont, aggressively entered the food industry.

Meanwhile, the market free fall touched off by the failed grain embargo created a catastrophic decline in consumer confidence that led to a national recession and, as inflation began to rise, set the stage for the Farm Crisis of the 1980s. Prices on key grains stayed low, and overproduction soon drove them even lower. At the same time, the purchase of modern tractors, irrigation systems, and grain-storage bins left thousands of farmers hopelessly in debt. And this, of all the ways that failure lurks on the American farm, may be the most lethal: raised on the Protestant work ethic and a faith in the basic fairness of the system, most farmers firmly believe that the greatest success belongs to the family that works the hardest. The way out of debt is putting in longer days in the field and longer nights at the books.

But it isn't really so. In fact, at the end of the Farm Crisis, Danny Klinefelter, a professor and ag-extension economist at Texas A&M who studied and categorized farm failures during that era, found that the most common causes of bankruptcy were too much ambition, too much accrued debt, and, in Klinefelter's words, "too much wishful thinking." Farmers, he said, didn't consider the cyclical nature of farming. They took on loans for land and equipment during periods of good weather and high prices. And in hard times they expected to make up the difference with more work and more yield. It's rarely so simple.

"Many of the producers who have failed or are in trouble have been considered by the farming community to be top farmers," Klinefelter wrote, "but attaining the highest yields does not necessarily result in the highest profits." That was a lesson few farmers could accept.

In the decades since the Farm Crisis, grain production has kicked into overdrive. Big producers just got bigger. And small farmers, in an effort to keep pace with the expansion and vertically integrated models of agribusiness, began to take Butz's motto to heart. With the help of emerging technologies, everything from the GPS-mapped furrows to computer-controlled irrigation systems, they began to plant crops in places no one would have dared waste seed, much less water, a generation earlier. The more they planted, the more they stood to profit. But then all those acres and all that overhead started to become a curse.

In this case, the risk of failure was really a side effect of the good intentions of the U.S. Environmental Protection Agency. In an effort to reduce carbon emissions and improve air quality, the EPA imposed the first renewable fuel standard in 2005, requiring the production of at least 7.5 billion gallons of renewable fuels within seven years. The goal was to kick-start the biofuel industry, but the incentive, when combined with a steep increase in gas prices due to the Iraq War, instead triggered runaway demand for ethanol. The number of ethanol plants nearly doubled overnight. At first that seemed like a good thing. It created a domestic fuel source, and the higher prices profited American farmers and the American companies that supported them.

Soon, however, so much corn was being diverted to ethanol production that it created a scare on the global commodities markets. Foreign countries dependent on American grain worried that their own meat producers wouldn't be able to afford to feed their livestock, sparking a commodities run. As the price of corn reached unimaginable heights—$6 and $7 per bushel—demand increased for soybeans as a feed alternative. Soon those prices had doubled too. Then the shortage brought on by the drought of 2012 sent the price of commodities to record levels, with corn reaching as much as $8 per bushel and soybeans topping $17.

One afternoon, as we sat at a workbench in Rick's barn, he told me that the biggest pitfall a farmer faces is his own optimism. Everything starts to seem easy, and you think the good times are going to last forever. And the government, in the name of spreading the wealth and stimulating the broader economy, always provides an excuse to take on more debt. In 2010, Congress announced that it would raise short-term rapid-depreciation write-offs for farmers from 50 percent to 100 percent. So if you bought a new tractor or grain bin for $100,000, you could put that full amount against your annual farm income, instead of only half.

In 2011, across the country, farms suddenly had new trucks and tractors, new barns and outbuildings, even new houses and new equipment, that could cost as much or more than a farmhouse.

"And here's the trap that farmers fall into and we're still dealing with. Like that big sprayer," Rick said, pointing to the vehicle in the corner of the barn, its wheels taller than me. "That was a quarter-million-dollar purchase." He paused a moment, looking at the machine.

"As my banker says, people forget they have to pay the principal," he continued. "Now, during these really shitty times, everybody still has the payments. Yeah, I did benefit from all that tax write-off, and it was a hell of a deal on the interest too—but it's still an expense."

In no time the factors that had quadrupled grain prices self-corrected. Gas prices stabilized and then began to fall, lowering the market price for ethanol. Ethanol producers began idling their new plants, because they simply couldn't produce fuel cheaply enough given the high input price of grain. When the EPA tax credits expired, the agency adjusted the renewable-fuel standard downward, but the drought also broke, bringing an upsurge of production in the 2013 harvest—just as demand was leveling off. Corn and soybeans crashed, losing half their market value between the planting season and the end of that harvest year. Coming into the 2014 season, every farmer had to make his own market projection.

Rick gambled on another dry year and that the markets would remain down, so he planted mostly very-short-season hybrids, hoping to get his harvest in early, before the markets fell even further. With his crops still sitting in the fields and markets continuing to fall, I asked Rick if he was worried. He shook his head. They were more than equipped, he insisted, to weather a bad year.

"Now, if we see sub-four-dollar corn for two more years," he continued, "yeah, you'll see some people going broke, especially the young guys who started about five years ago, when it was eight-dollar corn. And they thought, 'Oh, man. There's nothing to this farming game.' They bought the twelve-thousand-dollar-an-acre ground and took out loans for the bins and the pivots and equipment . . . The Meghans and Kyles of the world," he said, "they could be in real trouble."

Kyle pulled the grain cart alongside the semi and switched on the unloading auger arm, sending soybeans cascading out of its mouth and into the cargo hold of the trailer, then he moved the semi forward to fill the second cargo hold, unloading more beans until the trailer was piled with more than a thousand bushels. Finally he drove to the grain elevator in Hordville, easing across the scale and then forward to the pit area, where he stooped to crank the gate at the bottom of the trailer until the beans rushed out, bouncing off the grating and pouring into an underground tank. For days Kyle shuttled back and forth between the field and the elevator, until all the forward contracts that Rick had negotiated months earlier had been fulfilled.

Only then, on a bright, cloudless day in early November, did Kyle and Rick shift to stocking the grain bins lining the farm's gravel driveway. Kyle hooked the tractor to the grain auger while Rick climbed the ladder up the corrugated side of the bin and then shimmied onto the slanted roof, lining up the chute directly over the opening at the top of the bin. Kyle brought a semi filled with beans and attached the hopper of the auger. Once he turned everything on, the beans dropped from the trailer into the hopper and then corkscrewed inside the auger to the opening at the top of the bin. At that open mouth, Rick turned on the electric spreader, a simple spinning plate that scattered the augered soybeans to the edge of the bin to ensure that the structure filled evenly. You can reduce the risk of rot in the bins, Rick had explained to me, by making sure that the beans are spread out, and that the roof is tight and well ventilated, that the floor is raised and perforated so an industrial blower can force through enough air to keep them dry.

This remaining stockpile would determine the income for the year. Indeed, a bin can be a farmer's best friend, making it possible to wait out a down market, but if the farmer isn't careful, it can turn into his worst enemy. The structures are expensive, forcing the farm to take on $50,000 or even $100,000 of debt. And the bins themselves can be extremely dangerous. Without a spreader, farmers have to wade into the grain at the top of the bin and shovel it to the edges. If they're not properly harnessed in, there's a chance of sliding to the center and sinking into the soybeans or corn, like quicksand. OSHA data indicates that every year an average of thirty people die that way. Even the augers can be a hazard. Little more than an Archimedes screw inside a steel tube, the spinning threads are exposed at either end, and every year there are dozens of amputations and deaths from farmers catching a hand or a piece of clothing in the turning works.

But maybe the greatest danger is the false sense of security that a row of grain bins can create. When the auger was first imagined in the early forties by Peter Pakosh, a young engineer at what is now Massey Ferguson, the idea was discounted as too treacherous. Senior engineers worried that the outer tube would warp with time and come into friction with the corkscrew, sparking fires. With all the grain dust in the air, there was even the chance of an explosion. Massey bosses advised Pakosh to give up the idea. Instead he worked on the design in his home basement until he had the kinks ironed out—and then formed his own company, Versatile, with his brother-in-law in 1947. The auger revolutionized farming, finally allowing farmers to store their crops and wait for a better price. But when grain augers were first mass-produced by Versatile in the 1950s, they were just 16 feet long and offloaded only about 1,000 bushels an hour. Today's augers, like all things in modern farming, are bigger and faster—reaching more than 100 feet high and offloading 1,000 bushels in as little as five minutes. All that height and speed has pushed grain bins to capacities of more than 100,000 bushels, making it possible to put up thousands of acres of yield in a single bin.

Now what was once a safeguard against temporary downturns has turned into a vast oversupply, with stubborn farmers hoping to stick it out until markets improve, a collective waiting game. In 2014 crop estimators expected that more than 12 percent of the soybeans harvested that season, over 475 million of the 3.91 billion bushels brought in, would still be in bins a year later. "You have some hardheaded old-timers that say, 'By God, beans were at seventeen dollars two years ago, and I'm going to leave my beans in the bin until it's seventeen dollars again,'" Rick told me. "You want to say, 'At your age? Good luck with that.'" Those prices were never coming back, he said.

In times like these, you have to be realistic, he said. You control what you can control. Make sure the bin is secure and tight, that the blowers are running, and that the grain is spread evenly. Make sure you don't lose in the bin what you're hoping to make up in the markets. But no sooner had Rick stepped back to watch the whole system working than he could hear the spreader start to wobble and scatter beans against the bin walls. Sometimes this kind of variable power to the spreader's electric motor will trip the breaker, but in this case the spinning pan continued to run, even as the noise grew louder. "You can hear the grain throwing against

the wall," Kyle said, "like sheets of rain." At this point there was no
choice: Rick switched off the broken spreader, and Kyle restarted
the auger, letting the soybeans pile up in the center of the bin.

"We're going to have to go in there with shovels," Kyle said ruefully. Rick was on edge now, and Kyle was too, but they kept quiet,
each doing his work. They still had a long day ahead.

After another day of chipping away, harvesting, filling the semi,
and unloading into the grain bins, Rick decided it was time to call
it an evening. But he wasn't quite ready for the drive back or giving
himself over to sleep. So he ducked into the empty house on the
southeastern corner of Centennial Hill Farm, the house where his
wife, Heidi, grew up. It's abandoned now, except as a guesthouse
and a place to host occasional potlucks. The refrigerator often
holds a random collection of unopened cans and jars — not much,
but enough to scavenge for a snack or a stray drink. Rick scoured
the remnants of the last get-together in search of something to take
the edge off before bed.

With no other options available, he settled on the last two cans
of Pabst Blue Ribbon, but not without a few grumbles. He cracked
one and took a long sip, then smirked. "I've raised hell about these
in the past," he said, "but, you know, it's funny how you get certain
things the right amount of cold, and they all taste pretty good."
He slid into the booth of the breakfast nook and motioned for me
to slide in across from him. He wanted to assure me that despite
everything that had been going wrong, he wasn't worried about the
current crisis.

"I don't feel like it's going to be anything like the eighties, when
everybody was going broke," Rick said, taking another deep draw
of his beer. "That was caused by Reagan and Volcker, the Fed chairman. They thought they came in with a mandate to crush inflation
— and inflation was out of control — but bankers had been pushing farmers to buy ground every year. It inflated up to about twenty-five hundred dollars an acre for good ground. The interest had
been less than the rate of inflation. So when they raised rates, to all
of a sudden have interest triple, that's what caused it. Bankers and
farmers couldn't react fast enough. They went broke, had this huge
debt. Bankers were foreclosing on farmers because your collateral
was worth a third of what it was when you took out this loan."

Everything had been different back when he met Heidi. She

was a student at the Nebraska College of Technical Agriculture, in Rick's hometown of Curtis, in the southwest corner of the state. He had been a hotshot horseman in his small town—a skilled rider with a row of purple and blue ribbons in barrel racing and pole bending at the state fair to prove it. He seemed to have the world by the tail. But college in Lincoln had been different, harder. He ended up taking a semester off and going home, but life on the farm was getting harder, especially for a family like his that didn't own the ground they farmed.

Rick found himself at loose ends as he took off another semester and then another. He was still technically enrolled at the University of Nebraska but a few credits shy of a degree in Latin American studies and in no hurry to finish up. The degree wasn't going to do him any good. He knew he wanted to be back farming and ranching, but he could see that the opportunities were drying up in Curtis. So he took odd jobs while he figured out his next move. "I'd worked on the railroad for three years, steel gangs and tie gangs," Rick told me. "They'd made me assistant foreman and wanted me to be foreman. I could see then, if I didn't quit, I never would." So he left the railroad, but he still couldn't figure out what he wanted to do. "I just wasn't finding it," he said.

That's when he met Heidi. "Oh, everybody loved her," he said. "She could drive a tractor, fix engines." She had grown up in a farming family in eastern Nebraska with a hard-driving father and three headstrong sisters. Rick's bigheaded swagger didn't fluster her a bit. "We had a few dates. I even took her to church—very honorable," Rick deadpanned, then grinned. "But I was still convinced that I could change the world." He broke off the relationship and signed up for a two-year stint in the Peace Corps. He went off to Ecuador to teach agriculture in a small village, but he soon became disillusioned with trying to apply American know-how to places with no resources or infrastructure. He came home disheartened and more lost than ever, only to find that everything that had been starting to slip away in Curtis was utterly gone. Agribusiness had swallowed up small farms. Families had moved away. "Dad had quit farming, and my sister and brother-in-law were farming that little rented place," Rick said. "I had grown up on a small rented farm. I knew there was no future there." A friend of his named Kevin had sold his farm and equipment and gone to Colorado to open a ski shop. Rick followed him out there and for a while worked a few hours a week and ski-bummed the rest of the time. At some point he'd had enough. "I said I gotta get back to school and finish my degree."

And he'd been thinking about Heidi. He called her up to see if she wanted to have Thanksgiving with his family in Curtis. After that, they could drive back to eastern Nebraska together—Rick to get himself reenrolled in school, Heidi to visit her own family. Heidi agreed and drove out to Colorado to pick him up, but by the time she arrived it was after dark, and snow was swirling.

"That night we had a hell of a storm, about two feet of snow," Rick remembered. "She was driving a little Fiat." While he packed up the last of his things, Kevin went outside to check on Heidi. She had put her farmer coveralls on and was under the Fiat putting chains on the tires. "Kevin came in and said, 'I think this one's a keeper. You better marry this gal.'" They drove across the state, all the way back to Lincoln through the storm, together. Rick went back to school, and on weekends he drove out to York County and tried to impress Heidi by pitching in on the farm. Eventually he won her over, just as her father, Tom, was getting ready to retire. Soon Rick dropped out for good and started talking about leaving Lincoln, moving in with Heidi, and getting married.

Audacious and brazen, Rick had a head full of ideas for ways to expand the operation and make way for the future. "In the eighties," he told me, "inflation was so high that everyone took out loans against their farms. Then ground went from twenty-five hundred an acre to eight hundred in two years, so farmers' equity and the value of what their loans were borrowed against went to nothing." It was a terrible time for family farms, but Rick saw the once-in-a-lifetime chance to leverage Heidi's share of the family land in order to pick up more ground at a fraction of its real value.

Tom himself had been a risk-taker in his own right, but these times had him spooked. His father had been put off the land when Tom was young, his grandfather forced to sell it off after bad decisions in the teens. His father had worked his whole life to save up enough to buy the farm back, and when he died, young and unexpectedly, Tom had had to give up his own dreams. After just one semester at the university, he dropped out and came home to save the farm from being lost again. Whatever the ambitions of the young man who wanted to marry his daughter, Tom was reluctant to make unnecessary and untested changes, and even more cautious about taking on debt in the midst of a credit crisis.

"But when Heidi and I got married, and she inherited her share of the land," Rick said, "I was fifty percent of the decision-making process on how to go forward." And he couldn't bring himself to pass up the opportunity he saw before him. Heidi had fifty cows, fifty sows, and three hundred acres of land under her control. "When I first came back from the Peace Corps, I was going to make it on forty acres, and be all holistic and symbiotic, and everything working together," Rick said, but something about having more land and livestock than he'd ever imagined possible, along with a desire to prove himself to his father-in-law, brought out his competitive side. Rick and Heidi worked it all out on paper and decided to take the risk. They upped the operation to 150 sows and 100 cows. Heidi's father thought they were being reckless. "We had a hell of a good year, that first year. We worked our backsides off, but we made a hundred thousand dollars on hogs." To free themselves from Tom's second-guessing, Rick and Heidi used their profits to buy out the remaining debt on the equipment. It took every penny, but their piece of the farm now belonged to them outright.

It didn't stop there. "After two years I got Heidi talked into taking on three more quarters." As the peak of the Farm Crisis approached, land prices were at an all-time low. Rick was eager to take on as much as possible, rolling each year's profits into renting still more land, on the assumption that an eventual recovery would set them up for life. Then, just three years after taking over their share of the farm, Rick and Heidi decided to use their equipment as collateral for a loan to make a land purchase. "I could see what a land base did," Rick told me. "Without land you cannot operate." He said he had everything nailed down for a loan from First National in York, but the day before he was supposed to sign the paperwork, he received a call from the loan officer.

"We've got a problem with our board of directors," the banker told him. "Because everyone's going broke, we want Tom to co-sign."

"By then Tom and I were just fighting like hell," Rick said, "so I told him, 'Evaluate the loan on its own merits, and if we don't qualify, we will seek assistance elsewhere.'"

Rick tipped his head back, draining the last of his beer. Then he lined up the two empty cans in front of him and shook his head.

"So arrogant. Farming just three years, and I was that brash." The bank agreed to make the loan, and the pattern was set for the rest of Rick's farming life. "Because of my aggressive ways, we have continued to stay in debt for thirty-two years, and always pushing, doing a lot more than we should. My idea was to try and build an operation that I could hand down to my children with as much land as what we were benefited when Heidi's share was handed down to her. So I did everything I could to get ahead and to turn that success into more and more contiguous land. If you can swing it, you buy it. When you're a farmer, that land means everything."

It was late now, pitch-black outside the window. Even the moon had waned to nothing but a sliver of light. The only sense of a world outside came from the distant barn light, its dim bulb always left burning and just bright enough to give shape to the shadows.

"I'm probably close to bipolar," Rick said at last. "When I'm on, everything is possible. I just go for it. But then I'll get really down, thinking, *God, how are we going to get out of this?* And I put it on my kids—that I was doing it for them. That was my excuse in my head."

He sighed deeply. Months before, Meghan had warned me that one of Rick's defining characteristics is self-doubt. "He worries every decision to death," she said, "and then, no matter what he decides, he always thinks there could have been a better way." It's a common trait among farmers. The neighbors' corn always looks taller, their cattle fatter. Every farmer kicks himself for not doing enough to capitalize when the markets are up and for being too exposed when the markets are down.

"I just get comfortable, to where the wolf's away from the door," Rick said, "and what do I do? I go and remortgage everything and do dumb things—buy more land, more equipment, build a barn or a new house."

He tapped the empty cans on the table in front of him.

"And it's caused a hell of a lot of stress on my family," Rick said. "Was that worth it? I don't know. That will be for them to decide."

Kyle drove the pickup south across the interstate and then east toward what all the maps label as Lushton, Nebraska, though it's barely more than a wide spot in the road anymore. We were still several miles outside of town, making our way toward Seth's farm. Kyle told me that he didn't know how exactly to explain why Rick and Seth had started harvesting together, but it had something to do with a kind of shared stubbornness.

A few years back, for example, Seth had taken a load of high-moisture corn to the grain elevator and been charged a drying fee. But the elevator simply blended his corn with a load of overly dry corn, so the dryer didn't actually have to be turned on. "I was there," Seth told the operator. "The dryer was not running. I am not going to pay a drying fee." Rick had told me earlier that he'd admired Seth for telling the co-op that it wasn't right.

As we hit the rise and the acreage appeared, we could see a field of ready soybeans and then a shelterbelt of tall trees, a farmhouse, and a cluster of outbuildings tucked behind. The beans, brown and mature, seemed almost to glow in the autumn light. "Wow," Kyle said, surveying the field. "It's ready to go." But then he turned along the south edge of the property and drove slowly, so he could count rows and divide them to figure out the number of rounds to complete the field. As he went, I could see the shimmy and drift of Seth's rows.

"He just hasn't invested in autosteer yet," Kyle said, and laughed. "He just put this pivot up last year. Before that it was flood-irrigated with the pipes and all." It was a system that most farmers, especially in eastern Nebraska, where center-pivot irrigation was invented in the 1950s, had abandoned long ago.

But Rick and Kyle were going to have to harvest the old-fashioned way—keeping an eye on the outside furrow, following the wobble and drift of rows planted by the human eye rather than computer-drawn straight lines. Every turn of the combine required lining up with where Seth had tried to match row spacing between each pass at planting. Farmers call these "guess rows." The sixteen rows laid out by the planter are perfectly spaced, but the furrow between passes can be slightly narrower or slightly wider than the machine-spaced rows. Because the harvester is twelve rows wide, it's impossible to split each planting swath. Instead you have some passes within the planted pattern and some where the harvester is straddling the places where two planting rows come together. But as the light failed and the shadows grew longer, it was getting harder and harder for Kyle to keep track of the guess rows. He leaned forward, peering down over the steering wheel to be sure that the spinning reel of the harvester was standing up the rows and cutting everything cleanly.

To make things even more challenging, Seth, back in the spring, had planted around the concrete platform of his new center pivot for the first time. And rather than setting his row spacing starting from that platform, he'd started from the edge of the field and worked in. Ordinarily, farmers won't plant closer than 30 inches from their pivot, but Seth, hoping to get a little extra from the field, had allowed just 5 inches. So as they neared the platform, Kyle had to figure out where to set the floating bar on the outside of the harvester head, what they call the snout, in order to stay aligned but without having to take multiple passes to get around the pivot.

"We try to put the outside of that head on the guess row," Kyle explained. "But the eye-planted rows can sometimes run together. And if you don't guess right, you're taking half a swath trying to fix it—which takes fuel and time." And if you get off by too much —you miss a guess row and don't notice or just try to keep going —you can start to run over rows, breaking the pods or treading the plants into the muddy soil and making them impossible to harvest. Seeing the trouble it was causing, Seth told them not to worry about the rows right around the pivot, but even in a neighbor's field, Rick and Kyle wanted to capture every bit of the yield. So between passes Kyle would come down from the cab, study the rows with Rick, and then hustle back behind the wheel.

At dinnertime Meghan drove to pick up food Heidi had waiting for them at the house and returned with tacos wrapped in aluminum foil and a cooler full of Coke. Everyone sat on the tailgate of the pickup or leaned against the bed, eating quickly. Rick kept eyeing the sun, now sinking into the line of trees that stood between the edge of the field and Seth's house.

"I think we should call it a night," Rick said finally.

"It's all right," Kyle said. "There's just a few more swaths."

Kyle was hoping to finish this field before it was fully dark, so that they could load up the head and the combine for another field for tomorrow. If they could get done in the next hour, they would have a jump in the morning. Together Rick and Kyle walked over to the remaining rows, getting a read on how many rounds were left to complete the field but also going back and forth about whether to continue or stop. Finally Kyle won out. He took the combine down to the north edge of the field, then turned back toward the pivot, watching the spinning reel below him and steadying the wheel.

As he neared the southern edge of the field, Meghan, waiting in the grain cart, came on the radio. "You're driving crooked," she said. "You're knocking over rows." Kyle looked down at the reel. Everything seemed in line. So he stopped the harvester and climbed down to see what was going on. Right away he could see: the snout was bent in, and the plastic body of the soybean head was broken. He'd hit the pad of the pivot and never even felt it.

"Goddamn it," Kyle rasped under his breath. This could be thousands of dollars of damage. Worse still, if it was more than he could fix himself, it could be days of waiting for a Deere-certified mechanic. He pulled back the plastic body and stuck his head inside. He could see that the snout had been pushed in and bent up the hydraulic arm on which it floats. That arm was rubbing on a pulley belt that runs the cutting sickles, putting slack in the system and creating friction. "It was still cutting," he said, "but it was already getting really, really hot." He reached in to see if he could straighten the bent arm by hand. No dice.

"I should have just left that row," Kyle said, still tugging hard on that arm. "It was planted *right* up against the pad."

"That's what Seth said," Rick snapped. "You *cannot* harvest something that's planted that close."

"Yeah, I probably should have just left that little bit."

"If Meghan hadn't seen it, it could have started a fire," Rick said. He couldn't hide his anger, but Kyle was already thinking about what they needed to do. He said he could straighten the arm if he could just heat it up, but he couldn't afford to wait until morning to fix it. If they were going to finish this field in the morning and still stand a chance of loading up and getting some beans out of their own fields, he was going to have to make the repairs right then, in the dark. He asked Seth if he had a cutting torch and a wrench he could borrow. Seth told them to pull around to his shop, and he set off across the field.

By the time Kyle and Rick drove over in the pickup, Seth had already rolled out a portable light and the tank and hose and a rosebud heating tip for the torch. He grabbed a couple of wrenches. Kyle asked if he had any fender washers. Seth pulled out a box and shook several into Kyle's hand.

Hoping to get out of the way, I went with Meghan back to the house, where we waited, saying little. It was close to an hour before Rick and Kyle came rolling into the driveway. They stomped into the mudroom, laughing and kicking off their boots. "You asked for that fender washer, and Seth just said, 'How many you need?'" Rick said, slapping Kyle on the back. "Why can't I have a shop like *that?*"

"I assume everything's working," Meghan called from across the kitchen.

"Yeah," Kyle said with a long sigh. "We had to drill out some rivets and get the plastic bent so we could get the torch in without burning everything up. And then we had to heat that arm to get it straightened out so it quit rubbing. It was really hard steel and we couldn't get it bent by hand. And then a little piece on the back side broke. So we had to weld that back together."

Rick interrupted. "I want you guys to know: the combine is better than it's ever been."

"Better than before?" Meghan asked skeptically.

"At least," Rick said. "We should hit every center-pivot pad."

Before long they were seated together around the dinner table, recounting stories of all the near disasters of past years. The time they'd taken out a power line with the unloading auger. The time Meghan had swung wide to make a turn on a country road with the bean head strapped onto the flatbed trailer and clipped a stop sign. They laughed until the tension and worry of the accident, the adrenaline from what could have happened, had been shaken off and disappeared.

In 2014 American farmers harvested more than 14 billion bushels of corn and nearly 4 billion bushels of soybeans—setting new records, as they had the year before and would in the year to come. With so much production, roughly three quarters of the harvest nationwide went directly into bins, as every farmer waited and prayed for rebounding prices. They never came. Instead prices continued to slump as yields continued to grow, and whispers spread about the possibility of another Farm Crisis.

That fall Rick had warned that the American farm might be in trouble if we saw two more years of record harvests. That's exactly what has happened. The harvest of 2016, another record-setting year of production of core commodity grains like corn and soybeans, pushed prices down again. Corn, in particular, has plummeted to less than half its market value of five years ago. Livestock prices have fallen simultaneously and at a rate that made it impossible to capture profits on that end. This downward spiral is already having broader effects. Cash-poor farmers aren't updating equipment or buying new trucks or even going to town to spend money on food and entertainment. The rural economy is stalling.

Worse still, farmers who took out loans for land or equipment at the peak of prices are starting to worry about their ability to service their debts—and banks are growing nervous too. Lending institutions are starting to call on big farmers to liquidate landholdings used as collateral, in order to reduce their risk. But this trend is already dragging down property prices, forcing still more liquidation —the exact cycle that led to rapid devaluation in the 1980s. Today the potential dangers of a rural bank panic to the broader economy are even greater. Half of all farmers have quit the business in the past thirty years, so now every failure carries twice the weight.

To break this downtrend, the American Farm Bureau Federation had been counting on President Obama's Trans-Pacific Partnership, which promised to expand markets for beef, pork, and soybeans. But the rural areas that were depending on this new deal, as well as standing agreements such as NAFTA, voted overwhelmingly for Donald Trump and his protectionist, antiglobalist policies. Trump is threatening to cancel manufacturing trade deals with China, and China is responding by threatening to cancel its purchases of American grains. At the same time Mexico is threatening to suspend its imports of American corn. If such a thing were to happen, it would make the Farm Crisis seem like a ripple.

For now the Hammonds are waiting and hoping for the best. In November 2015, Meghan and Kyle were married, and less than a year later Meghan found out she was pregnant. "The hardest part of my job is working with family," she told me. "But that's also the best part of my job, because family can be pretty hard on each other, but at the end of the day, they're the ones that will be there for you in the hardest times. We've been through some hard times on the farm, and we're still here, still going—and hopefully on to the next generation."

Is Dinner for Two Worth $1,000?

FROM *The Los Angeles Times*

IF YOU WERE looking for the oddest dish being served in an American restaurant right now, you should probably start with the fish course at Jordan Kahn's new Vespertine, a dish that nudges the idea of culinary abstraction dangerously close to the singularity. It doesn't look like fish, for one thing—it looks rather like an empty bowl, coarse and pebbly inside and out, of a blackness deep enough to suck up all light, your dreams, and your soul.

If this were Coi or Alinea, to name two modernist temples, your server would instruct you on how to eat the dish, or at least on where you might direct your spoon. At Vespertine the server, wearing a severe frock like something out of *The Handmaid's Tale*, does not. If you prompt her, she may whisper the word *hirame*, which in a sushi bar can mean either flounder or halibut. She will leave before you discover that the flounder has been pounded thin, crusted with charred-onion powder, and pressed into the bowl over a kind of porridge studded with minced shallot, perfumy bits of pickled Japanese plum, and bright, crunchy bursts of acid that could be either finger-lime vesicles or chopped stems of the wildflower oxalis. You are not sure exactly what you are eating. You are not meant to know. You have traveled from darkness into light, and that is enough.

Los Angeles has recently become known as one of the best places in the world to eat, renowned for its diversity, splendid produce, and receptivity to the ideas of young chefs, although perhaps lacking in restaurants of the very top tier. Vespertine, a wavy, waffle-skinned structure in Culver City's Hayden Tract, is among the area's first leaps into the international avant-garde — the sort of dining rooms that tend to do better on the World's Top 50 Restaurants list than they do in the Michelin guide; the kitchens where the artistic imperatives of the chef tend to outweigh any questions of what a customer might want to eat; the meals after which a cynical diner, confronted with twenty-plus courses of kelp, hemp, and tree shoots, makes jokes about stopping for tacos on the way home.

As at Trois Mec and Alinea, you buy your table in advance through Tock, as if you were buying tickets for a show. As at Noma, you choose between wine and elaborate juice pairings. As at Eleven Madison Park, each course is part of a narrative, although here you are never quite sure what the narrative is supposed to be. I still have no idea whether Vespertine was designed to function as a restaurant or as an architectural folly by Eric Owen Moss; a dining room or an art installation; a showcase for the ceramics of Ryota Aoki or a stage for an extremely ambient soundtrack by the Texas post-rock band This Will Destroy You, three or four thrumming notes that will follow you around for hours.

(The tickets are expensive — $250 plus tax, obligatory tip, and supplements for wine pairings and after-dinner coffee and liqueurs in the garden — more than $1,000 for two, all told.)

It May Be a Must for You

I would say that a meal at Vespertine is mandatory for a certain kind of diner, but mandatory in the way that the James Turrell show at LACMA a couple of years ago was mandatory, or Berg's *Wozzeck*, or the current season of *Twin Peaks*. It's not dinner; it's *Gesamtkunstwerk*.

"Checking in with valet before dinner is required," says an email sent to you before your dinner, "as this member of our team is integral to your experience."

You hand off your keys. You walk past a watery ditch lined with shattered rock whose cracks ooze green light. You are led to an elevator in the rust-colored steel structure, and are let off in the kitchen and a bowing Kahn. You climb stairs to an aerie at the top, settle into low couches, sip at a concoction of white vermouth garnished with a purple passionfruit flower. This is the first of many flowers you will see tonight. You will recognize none of them.

There will be white Asiatic dayflower petals arranged into a torch blossom shape atop a sliver of ripe Japanese melon atop one of Aoki's black ceramic vessels, and when you finish, a waitress flips it and you find tannic, velvety bougainvillea leaves glued with a gel of beets and Concord grapes to a cavity underneath. An inverted pottery arch holds a black hoop inside which another hoop fashioned of toasted kelp is glued with a salty yuzu cream that has the smack of party onion-soup dip. A slab of cured mango, laminated with sunflower petals, fits into what looks like the monolith from *2001: A Space Odyssey*. What looks like a model rocket's nose cone appears at the table, and it takes a moment or two to discover how to take it apart to get at the jet-black burnt-onion cookie inside it, which itself hides a wisp of crisp fruit leather, a berry or two, and more cream.

The sun is setting. You can see the mountains behind Malibu, the Hollywood Hills, and the lights of downtown. A Metro train skitters across the skyline like something from the set of the Spike Jonze movie *Her*. It is time to go down into the dining room. The minimalist soundtrack, which all sounds like the part where the icebergs float by in a National Geographic film, has seared itself into your brain.

Welcome to Jordanworld

Is the main room different? It is, kind of, more like a regular dining room anyway, with tacky acrylic tables—tacky in the slightly sticky sense—and lighting that seems dominated by the wineglasses reflected onto the ceiling. Is the music different? Yes, in the sense that it is made up of a different set of four notes.

You go through the fish, a composition of pea ice, candied peas, and tendrils that resembles what Kahn was doing at Red Medicine a few years ago, and an arresting composition of smoked bone marrow with braised leek hearts in plum broth sprinkled with deathly bitter wormwood leaves. (Was the orange smear puréed mussels, chicken liver, or foie gras? I'll never know.) Did you know yucca blossom petals were edible? Apparently they are—Kahn affixes them to a bowl's interior with smoked cheese, and they look a bit like spiky Komodo dragon scales.

Some nights there is shaved white asparagus arranged into something that resembles Frank Gehry's hockey stick chairs. Some nights the shaved white asparagus appears as thin coins garnishing a plate of raw scallops, almond, wild fennel fronds, and what tastes like raw oats. Once there are baby turnips the size of chickpeas, served with onion-powder-blackened balls of banana, chewy rice dumplings, and tiny flowers that looked as if they had escaped from a Watteau painting. The more you eat of the turnips, the more vinegary the dish becomes, until by the end you are practically coughing at the fumes.

If by this point in the evening you are ill at ease, that is probably the point. When you escape to use the restroom, you may be baffled by the sink, flanked by vials of essential oils on one side and what looks like a bowl of white sand on the other. (The sand is apparently powdered soap.) If you step outside for a breather, you will discover that the air is thick with frankincense. When you try to swirl your glass of orange-hued Central Coast Viognier blend, you will find that the sticky tabletop has bonded the delicate Zalto stemware to the table.

Almost all good Los Angeles restaurants have a sense of place and time, fashioned from local produce, a sense of season, and a nod to the diversity of the area. At Vespertine you may as well be on Jupiter—I kept humming Sun Ra's "Space Is the Place" to myself as I ate.

So it wasn't altogether surprising to encounter Thanksgiving in the heat of summer, a credible thumb of roast turkey breast, wrapped in sheets of shaved, braised rhubarb that had the tang of cranberry sauce, and garnished with slivered raw rhubarb tossed in turkey fat, which tasted even more like the holiday than the bird.

There was Dungeness crab wrapped in cabbage after that, and blossom-encrusted warm avocado with yeast butter and roasted strawberry paste, and smoked, dried lamb hearts shaved over a bowl of marionberries bleeding into pale yogurt. We could talk about the Muscat grapes mounded over horseradish ice cream, the sour puck of black sorrel ice in a marshmallow-coated bowl, or the almond fudge with cucumbers and redwood ice. I could probably go on for a while just about the silverware, some of which looks as if it was hammered out by elves and some of which resembles prison shivs rather too closely. But by the end of the meal you're going to be pretty exhausted. And that cup of osha tea in the humming garden, the currants and elderberries served on a rock, are going to seem pretty good.

At Mugaritz, the revered modernist restaurant near San Sebastián, Spain, diners used to be presented with two envelopes before dinner, one of which read: "150 mins . . . submit," the other "150 mins . . . rebel." The meals were identical. The experiences, not so much. At Vespertine, you should probably submit to Jordanworld. You will be back on Earth soon enough.

How Driscoll's Reinvented the Strawberry

FROM *The New Yorker*

ONE FOGGY MAY morning, the Joy Makers, a team of scientists employed by Driscoll's, the world's largest berry company, gathered at its research-and-development campus, which is known as Cassin Ranch, in the small agricultural town of Watsonville, on California's Central Coast. Before them was a table laden with plastic clamshells: red, white, and pink strawberries for the pipeline. Phil Stewart, an affably geeky, sandy-haired strawberry geneticist, offered me a yellowish white specimen with rosy stains, like a skinned knee when the blood starts seeping through. The Joy Makers watched expectantly as I tasted it. The fruit, an unpatented variety referred to as 21AA176, was juicy and soft, mildly astringent but tropical, reminiscent of white tea. "It goes back to a variety called White Carolina, which is maybe the oldest strawberry variety still in existence," Stewart said. "It dates back to the seventeen hundreds."

In some Asian markets, white fruit is coveted, and Driscoll's has conducted commercial trials in Hong Kong. But although the company has been breeding whites for fifteen years, it has yet to introduce any to U.S. grocery stores; Americans, accustomed to an aggressive cold chain, typically fear underripe fruit. "I brought these to a wedding, and all the parents were telling their kids not to eat the white ones," a Joy Maker remarked. Lately, however, Driscoll's focus groups have shown that millennials, adventurous and open-minded in their eating habits and easily seduced by novelty, may embrace pale berries. With these consumers, unburdened by preconceived notions of what a white berry should look or taste like,

Driscoll's has a priceless opportunity: the definitional power that comes with first contact. Before that can happen, though, the berries must conform to Driscoll's aesthetic standards. Stewart held a 21AA176 up to his face and inspected it carefully. "Microcracking," he said, pointing out some barely perceptible brown spots, caused by moisture on the plastic packaging, that were marring the surface. "This is not going to go forward."

Driscoll's, a fourth-generation family business, says that it controls roughly a third of the $6 billion U.S. berry market, including 60 percent of organic strawberries, 46 percent of blackberries, 14 percent of blueberries, and just about every raspberry you don't pick yourself. Miles Reiter is the chairman; his family owns some 70 percent of the company, which develops proprietary breeds, licenses them exclusively to approved Driscoll's growers, and sells the fruit under one of the few widely recognizable brand names in the fresh section of the grocery store. Though the farming is technically outsourced, the Reiters also own a farming company, run by Miles's brother Garland, which grows about a third of Driscoll's fruit. "We're commonly referred to as the Evil Empire," Allison Reiter Kambic, one of Miles's daughters, told me ruefully. "They're the leaders," Herb Baum, who for decades led the berry cooperative Naturipe, said. "I regret to say, as I worked for a competitor." At ninety, Baum is retired, but when he tells people that he worked in strawberries and they say, "Oh, Driscoll's?" he knows just how Salieri felt.

Produce is war, and it is won by having something beautiful-looking to sell at Costco when the competition has only cat-faced uglies. In the eighties, beset by takeover ambitions from Chiquita, Del Monte, and Dole, Driscoll's embarked on a new vision: all four berries, all year round. Otherwise, Miles told me, "we could be outflanked." Driscoll's berries are grown in twenty-one countries and sold in forty-eight; since the nineties, the company has invested heavily in Mexico. Driscoll's sells more than a billion clamshells every year; it was Driscoll's idea to put berries into clamshells in the first place. At the corporate offices, in a business park a few miles from Cassin Ranch, interactive maps mounted on the walls monitor every truck carrying Driscoll's fruit in North America, some 250 at any given time. An alarm goes off if a truck's temperature deviates from an accepted range, if a truck stops for too long (in Las Vegas, for instance), or if security is breached. A full load of strawberries is worth about $50,000; blueberries garner twice as much. The maps resemble battle plans, with armies of trucks fanning out across the continent.

Strawberries can be orange or white, the size of a pinkie tip, oblong, conjoined or bloblike, ecstatic, defiant, ungainly, unique. But you don't think of them that way. What you picture is a Driscoll's berry: glossy, red, and heart-shaped, and firm enough to ship to the East Coast or to the Middle East and eat two weeks past the harvest date. Driscoll's berries tend to lack the sugar rush and perfumed oomph of a tiny sun-warmed heirloom discovered on a country lane. Since the company's inception, it has placed an emphasis on appearance. "We have helped shape what a strawberry looks like with our relentless focus," Soren Bjorn, the company's president, said. Its cultivars—the genetically distinct new varieties it creates through breeding—and the germplasm, the genetic library of plants its breeders can draw on as parents for future cultivars, constitute the company's intellectual property. Speaking with a legal newspaper, Driscoll's senior vice president and general counsel compared the company to its neighbors in Silicon Valley. "Growers are sort of like our manufacturing plants," he said. "We make the inventions, they assemble it, and then we market it, so it's not that dissimilar from Apple using someone else to do the manufacturing but they've made the invention and marketed the end product." Like Apple, Driscoll's guards its IP jealously.

Berries are the top-grossing produce in the supermarket. ("I remember when we were little and berries surpassed bananas in revenue," Brie Reiter Smith, Miles's oldest daughter, who is the general manager of North American production, said.) According to Frances Dillard, Driscoll's global brand strategist and a veteran of Disney's consumer-products division, berries are the produce category most associated with happiness. (Kale, in contrast, has a health-control, "me" focus.) On a slide that Dillard prepared, mapping psychographic associations with various fruits, strawberries floated between Freedom and Harmony, in a zone marked Extrovert, above a word cloud that read "Social, pleasure, joy, balance, conviviality, friendship, warmth, soft, natural, sharing." (Blueberries vibed as status-oriented, demanding, and high-tech.) As I studied the slide over Dillard's shoulder in her office, she smiled tightly and said, "This is proprietary."

In apples, varieties are obvious—Fuji, Braeburn, Honeycrisp

—and at farmers' markets and certain specialty stores strawberries too are sold by name. (In early summer, Bi-Rite, a fancy grocer in San Francisco, announced the much-anticipated arrival of Seascapes and Chandlers with cardboard strawberries dangling from the ceiling.) But most strawberries meet our mouths anonymously. Compared with tree fruits, which take a decade or two and a small fortune to produce, strawberries are quick and cheap; plants, hardiest in their first year, are ripped out after a single harvest. Growing in microseasons and microclimates and easily falling victim to mildew, weather, and pests, strawberries are sensitive and fleeting. The contents of a clamshell in April are likely to be Marquis berries from Oxnard, where Driscoll's has a large operation; by June they're probably Del Reys out of Watsonville. It takes about six years to develop and test a cultivar, but Driscoll's releases several in North America each year; in addition, it maintains breeding programs around the world to furnish its various geographies with berries tailored to the local conditions. (Varieties are made obsolete based on the decisions of an internal group called the Dead Variety Society.) For the shopper, the only impression that matters is the Driscoll's name and the red berries, as uniform as soldiers or paper valentines.

For decades Driscoll's most forbidding competition has come from an unexpected direction: a thriving strawberry-breeding program at the University of California, Davis, which for nearly thirty years was led by Doug Shaw and his colleague Kirk Larson. The program is Driscoll's antithesis—public, open, nonexclusive—supplying, for a nominal royalty fee, any grower wishing to use its plants and sharing crucial information about horticulture derived from its research. University berries are not labeled as such, but they account for the vast majority of strawberries grown in California, and in the world. During their time, Shaw and Larson worked assiduously to advance the university's germplasm, creating crosses that would result in commercial cultivars that farmers deemed worthy of planting; every farm the university supplied was another acre not given over to Driscoll's.

During the taste-testing at Cassin Ranch, the Joy Makers encouraged me to try Albion, a university berry invented by Shaw, only to deride its physique and criticize its crunchiness. (Two weeks earlier, in Oxnard, I had preferred a university variety in a blind tasting, unleashing a cascade of explanations; this time there would be no chance of embarrassment for either party.) According to Driscoll's employees, university varieties tended to be dull-hued, malformed, seedy at the tip. I mentioned that my favorite variety was Gaviota, another Shaw berry, which I get from Harry's Berries at the Friday farmers' market in my neighborhood and which to me seems exceptionally complex and flavorful. They quickly disabused me. "There's nothing special in the genetics," Michael Schwieterman, a biochemist, said. What I was enjoying was overripe, he said pityingly, and wouldn't survive the weekend.

Behind the animosity lies a desperation that everyone in the business feels. Even as demand from consumers remains strong, the strawberry industry has been contracting rapidly; there are now 30 percent fewer acres under cultivation than there were in 2013. (With a sharp decline in migration from Mexico and Central America, the primary sources of agricultural labor for half a century, "stoop work"—jobs requiring harvesters to crouch doubled over for hours a day—has become difficult to hire for. Nearly every farm I passed in Watsonville in May and June had a sign by the road saying, SE SOLICITAN PISCADORES. At the same time, changing minimum-wage and overtime laws have made labor more expensive.) A suite of troublesome diseases has emerged as long-standing soil fumigants are being banned. This past winter a five-year drought was followed by a biblical deluge. New varieties are the only way forward, and it is the savviest breeder with access to the best germplasm who will prevail.

According to scholars of medieval art, the strawberry is a symbol of perfect righteousness. But the story of Driscoll's long dominion begins with what might be perceived as an original sin: in the midst of the Second World War, the group of growers that eventually became Driscoll's got hold of the university's germplasm, hired its chief breeders, and created a strawberry leviathan.

By then the Reiters were established berry growers, alongside their relatives the Driscolls. The first Reiter, a butcher who eventually farmed near Watsonville, where there was a nascent strawberry industry, came to California from Alsace in 1849. Wild strawberries grew abundantly in the sandy soils along the Central Coast; in *A History of the Strawberry,* Stephen Wilhelm and James Sagen write that in peak season, Native Americans would camp beside the patches and eat for a week. The conditions were ideal: cold fog in the morning, mild sun in the afternoon. The butcher's son, J. E. (Ed) Reiter, started growing with his brother-in-law, R. F. (Dick) Driscoll. One summer Ed's sister, visiting friends at a guest ranch in Shasta County, was served some especially sweet and shapely berries for breakfast; when she got back to Watsonville, she told her brother, setting in motion what family members thereafter referred to as "the California strawberry gold rush."

In 1904, at Cassin Ranch, Reiter and Driscoll planted the berry that came to be called Banner. Other berries at the time were awkward and irregular; Banners were very consistent. Already shrewd marketers, the brothers-in-law began an energetic promotional campaign, declaring Banner "A Wonder: The talk of the Pacific Coast. People write about it to their Eastern Friends." For more than a decade Driscoll and Reiter maintained exclusive access to Banner, but eventually most farmers on the Pacific Coast had it. "There were no plant-patent laws," Miles Reiter, a gentlemanly, white-haired man in his sixties who studied history at Princeton, told me. "Ultimately, there was no way to keep it to yourself."

The pursuit of new strawberry breeds was a hotly competitive area of agriculture — *The Small Fruits of New York,* published in 1925, lists more than a thousand varieties — but Mendel's theory of genetics had only recently been rediscovered, and many promising varieties were created by chance pollination or dimly understood laws of reproduction. (One Cincinnati strawberry farmer briefly controlled 90 percent of the market in his city because he had grasped that the variety he was planting required a particular approach to pollination, a sexual secret that the Cincinnati Horticultural Society devoted two years to investigating; its subsequent report drove down the price of berries and forced the farmer out of business.) An oddity of strawberry reproductive life made the fruit ideal for commercialization, and prone to theft. Strawberries are self-cloning; "mothers" send out runners, creating genetically identical "daughters." This was also a problem in the fruit-tree business, where clones can be created by grafting, and in the first decades of the twentieth century nurserymen began to agitate for protection from copiers. One large Missouri nursery, the exclusive carrier of the Red Delicious apple, built a fence around its mother tree and asked buyers to sign contracts promising not to propagate. When that didn't work, the nursery appealed to Congress. Thomas Edison sent a telegram supporting legislation, saying, "Nothing that Congress could do to help farming would be of greater value and permanence than to give to the plant breeder the same status as the mechanical and chemical inventors now have through the patent law." The Plant Patent Act, which described breeders as inventors, passed in 1930 and became a cornerstone of intellectual-property law.

The Driscolls and the Reiters had enjoyed the advantages of controlling a breed, but after a twenty-year run, Banner fell victim to "the yellows," a viral infection spread by strawberry aphids. Looking for disease-resistant plants to cross into the Banner line, the plant-pathology department at the University of California at Berkeley began to collect germplasm. Under the guidance of Harold Thomas, a brilliant pathologist, and his talented field manager, Earl Goldsmith, the department established a breeding program, systematically inventing and releasing new strawberry varieties. The primary objective, according to a history by Henry Wallace, who served as the secretary of agriculture in the 1930s, was "a large, firm berry which could be picked one-fourth green and which could stand shipping to the east coast."

The strawberry industry in the early twentieth century was dominated by Japanese immigrants, who represented not only the labor force but also some of the most experienced growers. In 1942, when the Japanese were forced into internment camps, the business effectively collapsed. According to the Reiters, Ned Driscoll, Dick's son, was one of the few farmers still planting strawberries during the war, testing crosses invented by Thomas and Goldsmith. By the mid-forties the university was making plans to suspend its strawberry-breeding program. Rather than accept reassignment, Thomas and Goldsmith quit the university and went to work for Ned.

Family lore has it that in 1944 Ned Driscoll and some grower friends pooled their gas rations and drove to the university plots to rescue the life's work of Thomas and Goldsmith: untold thousands of strawberry seedlings, representing precious university germplasm. "We usually say that the launch of Driscoll's was in 1944," Miles Reiter told me. "That was initiated by the abandonment of the UC Berkeley breeding program. Which would have been lost otherwise." Ned Driscoll appointed Goldsmith his breeder and Thomas the director of a new research institute, which later merged with an exclusive growers' collective that Ned and his cousin Joe

Reiter formed—the precursor to the modern Driscoll's. (Family records indicate that the institute paid $1,000 for the germplasm, which was made available to other growers too, but those other growers hadn't hired Thomas and Goldsmith.) Herb Baum, the former Naturipe director, told me that the Reiter and Driscoll families were "smart enough to know, If we can get this material and have a monopoly, we're going to make a fortune."

In spite of what Thomas and Goldsmith, and the Driscolls and the Reiters, believed in 1944, the university did not abandon its breeding program. In 1945 the university, which presumably retained copies of plants that left the collection, released five new varieties, designed by Thomas and Goldsmith and named for the mountains and lakes of California. It moved its laboratories north from Berkeley to Davis and hired breeders to take up where the others had left off. Under the new breeders, strawberries grew to be one of California's most significant and lucrative crops. But in the meantime, Driscoll's had begun its ascent.

Developing successful cultivars from a set of potential parents depends on intuition, experience, sensibility, and luck as much as it does on systematic data collection and dogged trial and error. With the university's plants, the Driscolls and the Reiters gained access both to a rich and diverse source of genetic traits and to the expertise of the two men who had studied that source for decades. In 1946, Thomas and Goldsmith crossed two university varieties, only one of which was widely available, yielding what at first appeared to be an unimpressive plant of uncertain commercial value. In an account provided by Driscoll's, Thomas writes that nevertheless Goldsmith "did recognize it as having a fruit character of excellent quality." He and Goldsmith kept at it, testing and adjusting the growing regimen until they had "perhaps the finest commercial strawberry ever developed." In 1958 they released it as Z5A, Driscoll's first proprietary cultivar, a blockbuster berry that would prove momentous for the company. Z5A could withstand shipping; equally important, it fruited in the late summer and early fall, giving Driscoll's berries in the months when other growers had none. With that, the company was on its way to becoming a grocery-store staple, a nationwide brand that markets could rely on enough to build display cases around.

*

The strapping, broad-shouldered modern strawberry that Driscoll's exemplifies is the product of a cross between a Virginian male and a Chilean female that took place in France in the eighteenth century. The female was imported by a French Army intelligence officer, who, on a reconnaissance mission to South America, spotted the berry growing along the coast near Concepción; he described it as being as "big as a walnut, and sometimes as a hen's egg, of a whitish red, and somewhat less delicious of taste than our Wood strawberries." The Virginian was bright scarlet and, according to an apothecary at Nuremberg who published a treatise on the medicinal garden there, "consistently large, the size of a plum, fleshy, and of an excellent flavor and fragrance." The cross resulted in *Fragaria x ananassa*, whose pineapple-scented fruit an early taxonomist declared to be "monstrous," in a good way.

As the cost of growing berries rises, Driscoll's must find ways of enticing people to pay more for them. Recently the company built a consumer lab equipped with a gas chromatograph and a gene-sequencing machine so that the Joy Makers could begin to pick apart the scientific components of flavor and figure out how best to appeal to a public whose idea of "strawberry" is influenced by strawberry syrup and red Popsicles. Dillard, the brand strategist, dreams of a $10 clamshell filled with splurge-worthy super-premium berries. Bjorn, the company's president, says, "Consumers have to be more satisfied, or what we call more delighted, all the time." Produce companies tend to be driven by supply: what they grow, they try to sell. Driscoll's, conversely, sees itself as a consumer-products company. According to Bjorn, "We create the demand. It's more like a Procter & Gamble." Through the efforts of the Joy Makers, Driscoll's is trying to do the equivalent of adding body-butter-enhanced shave-gel bars between razor blades.

One day at Cassin Ranch, Phil Stewart, the strawberry geneticist, took me into his greenhouse. Germplasm was everywhere: geriatric university stock; plants from a public seed bank maintained by the USDA; others foraged by Driscoll's employees on backpacking trips. In one corner Stewart was running hydroponic tests on a cross between a Driscoll's variety and *Fragaria chiloensis*, which was picked up on a beach in Santa Cruz. "The beach species is exceptionally tolerant of salt, because it evolved on sand dunes," Stewart said—a compelling quality, because drought and fertilizers cause salts to accumulate in soil. To explore the limits of this capacity, he was growing a leathery dark-green plant in a tub of heavily salted water. (An oversized jar of Morton salt sat nearby.) Half the plant's leaves looked like potato chips, and its roots were a brown mess.

Deeper in the greenhouse we came upon a droopy little berry that looked like a gnome hat felted by a Waldorf mom. It was a *moschata*, or musk strawberry, possibly the kind that Bosch supersized in *The Garden of Earthly Delights*. This particular variety, Mr. Zuks, was thought to have been grown by Thomas Jefferson; Stewart ordered it from a nursery that works with Monticello. (Based on Jefferson's writings, Stewart believes that Jefferson got it from an Italian friend, who got it from a Pole.) The shelf life is pathetic— berries picked in the morning are trash by the afternoon—but it is strongly resistant to mildew. Even more interesting to the Joy Makers is its aromatic profile, which reflects an abundance of methyl anthranilate, an ester that is rarely found in cultivated varieties and that calls to mind grape Jolly Ranchers (though it can also have a whiff of Gorgonzola).

Like much of what I saw in the greenhouse, Mr. Zuks was part of an intensive effort under way at Driscoll's to recast the parameters of *Fragaria x ananassa*, established some three centuries ago. "You have a random event that happened in France that defined what we think of as the strawberry," Judson Ward, a molecular biologist at Driscoll's, said. "We're going back to the wild and picking up new traits. We have people just as capable of identifying good flavors as whoever it was in France who happened upon that strawberry." In the revision process, the company is deliberately reversing some of its own breeding biases, as mainstream consumers become increasingly interested in dainty shapes and offbeat tastes. Ward mentioned that Stewart had made a cross with a wild berry from Alaska. "It was like a fantasy of what people imagine picking wild strawberries is like," Ward said. "They were all cute little things. Each one has a different flavor, so it is like that experience that people want to have in the wild." Dillard added, "I think we have some packaging on that!"

The next day I visited the consumer lab. It was spacious, consisting of two rooms, and had a determined-to-be-cheerful air, with an orange-painted wall and a whiteboard on which someone had doodled a picture of a raspberry plant over a diagram of a chemical compound. Michael Schwieterman, the biochemist, sat at a computer looking at an array of data from the gas chromatograph comparing commercially available Driscoll's varieties with two old European *Fragaria vescas,* or wood strawberries: a *moschata* and a tiny, elegant French variety, Mara des Bois, popular among epicures.

"We can look at methyl anthranilate," Schwieterman said, clicking onto a screen that described the aromatic as "sweet and fruity, Concord grapes, with musty and berry nuance." He pointed to a graph that resembled a staircase. "In a commercial strawberry, there is practically none," he said of the methyl anthranilate. (Only the Mara des Bois exhibited its presence.) "In those *vescas,* there's a twenty- to fifty-fold increase. In those *moschatas,* it's through the roof." Methyl anthranilate, he said, is "what potentially is different about wild strawberries and commercial strawberries. That's why we have a lot of focus on it. French consumers really like Mara des Bois, and people like wild strawberries."

On the next screen, Schwieterman showed me concentrations of gamma-Decalactone, which suggests "fruity, creamy, peach and apricot with a syrupy, fatty nuance." In contrast to methyl anthranilate, it was highly prevalent in commercial varieties and scarce in wild ones. He explained that Driscoll's and other breeders, liking the flavor yet oblivious of the chemistry, had crossed it in. "It's potentially an anthropomorphic artifact," he said. Another compound, cinnamyl acetate, showed up in some of the berries. "Would that be good, if we planted a variety that had a cinnamon kind of flavor?" Schwieterman went on, "What about reconstructing a basil flavor in a strawberry? This species has one component that's pretty important to basil, and one of our commercial species has another. What would happen if we introgressed that and got multiple compounds in a strawberry? You'd have a strawberry that's going to taste great with your salad and balsamic dressing, because it has a nice basil undertone." Driscoll's hopes that its breeders can use this information to create new cultivars, producing strawberries as you would a track, dialing down the greasy peach and laying in some cinnamon and must over a bass line of drought tolerance.

As the head of the strawberry-breeding program at Davis, Doug Shaw—effectively Driscoll's chief rival—took a traditional approach, advancing the germplasm by stalking the fields to find the highest-yielding, best-looking, tastiest berries. Looking to the wild for exotic traits—that would be absurd. A formidable if cantankerous and territorial breeder, Shaw was loyal to the growers who depended on his cultivars and uninterested in working with proprietary companies like Driscoll's. The program's patented plants, grown by farmers in California and around the world, generated some $100 million in revenue for the university. (As inventors, Shaw and Larson earned as much as $2 million a year in royalties.) But in 2011, as Shaw prepared for retirement, he began to worry that the university was shifting its focus from fieldwork to the well-funded area of genomics. Where would the cultivars come from?

Like Thomas and Goldsmith before them, Shaw and Larson decided to leave the university for the private sector. Working with their superiors in the Department of Plant Sciences, they proposed "spinning out" a breeding company "based in UC germplasm." If the university was no longer interested in commercializing the germplasm, Shaw and Larson would be happy to make use of it. In particular, Shaw wanted access to the varieties that he had developed but had not yet released. "My motivation?" Shaw said. "I'd say it's more ego than anything else. I want my cultivars to be used." After his retirement Shaw joined California Berry Cultivars, a new proprietary company that hopes to compete with Driscoll's in the race to invent a superior berry. But in May, while the Joy Makers were eating berries in the sun, he stood accused in federal court in San Francisco of having stolen the university's germplasm.

Shaw is sixty-three, with a rust-colored boot-brush mustache and a high bloom in his cheeks. His eyes, which he squints warily, are the color of gingerbread. He's red-green color-blind and tends to pick his berries by their sheen. "You're looking at maybe the best place on earth for strawberries," he told me in June, as we surveyed a field of strawberry plants at the headquarters of California Berry Cultivars, in Watsonville. Monterey cypresses stooped witchily, wind-bent; in the near distance, the Pacific Ocean was visible behind fog. "The soil is ninety-six percent sand, and we get this fog that you're seeing right here every day in the summer." He dug his shoe into the soil, kicking up a flint-knapped arrowhead—he has a collection—and nodded toward a nearby building with a porch. "One of my favorite things to do is sit there and look out," he said. Interestingly, CBC had arranged to lease the same piece of land the university had once leased for its breeding program. Shaw knew it well, as did most of the people CBC had hired to manage the fields and collect data; they were former Davis employees.

Shaw's troubles began in 2013, when a strawberry research-and-marketing commission filed a lawsuit against the university, claiming that giving Shaw access to the germplasm would be "a classic case of the fox guarding the henhouse." In May, Jane Fujishige Yada, a farmer who is a partner in CBC, testified that the commission's lawyer had said that the lawsuit was intended to "prevent Doug Shaw from breeding again." She went on, "At that point, I think I got my first inkling that our little CBC company might be going up against a pretty big—pretty big five-hundred-pound gorilla in the industry." In the months leading up to Shaw's retirement, the university tried to get him to submit a patent for the unreleased cultivars, in order to assert its right to make use of Shaw's intimate knowledge of the plants. Shaw refused.

A. G. Kawamura, a former state secretary of food and agriculture and a major grower who serves as the president of CBC, believes that the commission's lawsuit originated with what he has described as "competitive angst" on the part of the proprietary companies. He told me, "The proprietary companies have an opportunity to benefit from no more competition from new and improved varieties." When I broached the subject, the commission denied that Driscoll's had influenced the lawsuit. Miles Reiter called the suggestion "totally fabricated."

In 2016, frustrated that Shaw couldn't get a license to breed with the cultivars, CBC decided to sue the university, claiming that it had "risked the loss and destruction of the varieties, and has put them in a 'black hole,'" suppressing competition and denying Shaw the benefit of his own inventions. What was at stake, CBC said, was nothing less than the future of the strawberry industry. Without new cultivars, growers dependent on the university could not continue. Only Driscoll's and a few other proprietary companies would survive. Fujishige Yada testified, "If anybody's ever had a strawberry in California, it was probably created by Doug or Kirk . . . My concern was that we wouldn't have those new varieties in the pipeline to grow, as farmers." To others it just looked like history repeating itself. Baum, the retired strawberry executive, said, "If you make any kind of deal letting Shaw and that group have those materials,

you are going to be doing the same thing that happened with the
university and Driscoll's, giving them the same kind of a hold that
Driscoll's had for fifty years. They could easily eclipse Driscoll's."

The university, in a countersuit, accused Shaw of illegally breeding with the pipeline cultivars on behalf of his new company while
still employed by Davis. Entrusted with the "crown jewels," the
university contended, Shaw had attempted to destroy the public breeding program in order to enrich himself and his friends.
Steven Knapp is a genomics expert, formerly of Monsanto, who
was hired as Davis's new breeder. When I talked to him by phone
not long ago, he was apoplectic at what he perceived to be Shaw's
breach of loyalty. "It's one of the worst conspiracies I've ever seen
by a faculty member," he said. "They did it while they had the keys
to the castle! They had the plants in their own hands." Contrary to
what CBC had claimed, he said, the program was not dead. Knapp
had sequenced the strawberry genome and secured a multimillion-dollar grant and would be releasing new cultivars in the fall.

I was in the courtroom when the jury's verdict came back, siding
decisively with the university. A DNA expert from Yale had found
that seedlings in CBC's field, crossed in Spain in 2014, had university parentage. After the verdict I drove a couple of hours down
to Watsonville to see Kyle VandenLangenberg, a young breeder at
CBC, and Lucky Westwood, who works for a large shipper called
California Giant Berry Farm, which is also a partner in the business. Whatever happened next in the legal battle with the university, Westwood said, "we don't intend to stop." (Settlement talks are
under way.)

We walked around the field, filled with hybrids that Shaw had
designed, including the contentious 2014 Spanish crosses. Those
were in a legal limbo and might need to be destroyed. The rulings
and decisions, Shaw later wrote me, had created obstacles, but they
were not insurmountable. "Long-term success will depend on what
you know, not what you have," he wrote. IP, he seemed to be insisting, lives in the inventor's head.

Westwood, however, wasn't thinking about the Spanish crosses;
he was looking for something else. "Is this the one?" he said.

"The one they can't take away!" VandenLangenberg crowed
when he came upon the right row. Like Shaw, who trained him,
VandenLangenberg is color-blind. With help, he found a ripe

berry, red and plump and nicely shaped. It looked like a commercial fruit—with luck, it would be available in five years—and, best of all, it had no UC parentage. I asked where it had come from. "We're not going to talk about it," VandenLangenberg said. The information was proprietary.

Temples of the Seasons

FROM *Saveur*

ENJOYING A TRANSCENDENT meal is a little like having a wedding or a car accident—time slows to a crawl. That's the sensation I had in Kyoto while I negotiated biting into an *umeboshi* plum sheathed in translucent tempura batter, a dish so lovely that I nearly couldn't bring myself to eat it. So many others arrived as part of this unforgettable three-hour lunch that I began to lose track: a perfect sphere of seafoam shiso sorbet; a clay teapot filled with a dark broth of shiitake mushrooms, gingko nuts, and custard-like tofu; pearly squares of wheat gluten fragrant with the aroma of yuzu. More memorable still was a cube with the color and consistency of the freshest buffalo-milk burrata. I pointed at it and the server spoke the words *ebi imo*. After fumbling with a translation app, I learned that I'd eaten a taro native to the Kansai Plain called a shrimp potato. Count me among its fans.

This, one of the most ravishing meals in my recent memory, didn't take place in some hushed fine-dining pavilion but at Izusen, a chairless, bustling restaurant inside the Daitoku-ji temple complex. I could hear shouting from the kitchen. Behind me a busload of visiting retirees noisily enjoyed their meal. I was unaccustomed to sitting on the floor and kept sliding off a growing stack of cushions. One of the women caught a glimpse of my ordeal and let out a delighted peal. She pointed at me and soon two dozen elderly tourists in sun visors and bucket hats were holding themselves with laughter.

Shojin ryori is Japan's oldest codified cuisine but is seldom encountered outside temples, religious festivals, and funerals. In accordance with the Buddhist prohibition against killing, *shojin* (which means "earnest effort") eschews animal products and in retrospect appears to be eerily prophetic, having presaged a whole slew of contemporary food trends—by about a millennium. It insists on produce that's both local and in season, requires that it be prepared with simple hand tools, and allows no waste—instead of "nose to tail" you could call it "root to leaf." And as I was discovering, despite a fairly limited ingredient list, *shojin* can produce textures and flavors limited only by the cook's ability and imagination.

Another thing I was discovering: writing about the food of Japanese monks and nuns for a magazine like this one presented several difficulties. From the Buddhist perspective, cooking is a form of spiritual practice that produces nourishment to prepare the body for hard work and meditation. Unlike, say, Memphis barbecue or the louche cuisine of Lyonnaise bouchons, *shojin* doesn't have a whole lot to say on the subject of pleasure. *Shojin* has bigger fish to fry. Its goals are nothing less than permanent enlightenment, nirvana, the fundamental transformation of the human mind and society. It does not yield easily to an outsider's explanation.

I chanced upon my salvation, journalistically speaking, in the person of Toshio Tanahashi. He'd practiced the art of *shojin* as a Zen monk in a rural temple near Kyoto and then did something unprecedented—he opened a restaurant in Tokyo's chic Omotesando neighborhood that presented vegan monastic cuisine in a fine-dining context. The restaurant, Gesshin Kyo, became both successful and influential. Reviewing it for the *New York Times,* author and culinary authority Elizabeth Andoh described it as a "secular space imbued with a spiritual respect for food." It was a spiritual respect that nonetheless made room for distinctly un-Japanese elements like tomatoes, mangoes, and white Bordeaux. Freed from temple kitchens and its role as nourishment, *shojin* dazzled Tanahashi's diners with its unfamiliar and subtle beauty. The Zen monk had become a famous chef by reimagining monk food.

Tanahashi closed Gesshin Kyo after fifteen years, in 2006. Along the way he wrote two books about *shojin ryori* and came to see it as a corrective to the world's restaurant culture, which he believes to be addled with costly, scarce, and unhealthy ingredients. "In the long term, gastronomy is unsustainable," he wrote me in an email, an odd sentiment from a chef who'd recently spent a month in Paris delving into the finer points of vegetables with the staff at Alain Ducasse's restaurant at the Plaza Athénée. "It's crucial that good nutrition and sustainability become a part of restaurant culture," he continued, "and the Michelin Guide should award a fourth star for the food's healthfulness." As Tanahashi sees it, *shojin* is not merely the nourishment of monastics but the would-be lifeline and future of global food culture—the vegan blueprint of how we will one day eat.

"Come to Kyoto," he wrote me, offering to lead me on a tour through the world of *shojin* in its hometown, a world that he assured me was closed to outsiders. He also promised to cook for me the "modern" version of *shojin* that he had developed over the course of his career—to demonstrate that health, spirituality, and sensory pleasure could coexist on the same plate. During our correspondence, I was beginning to sense that Tanahashi didn't put much stock in the Japanese penchant for self-effacement nor in the Buddhist ethic of humility. "Who else in Japan is making modern versions of *shojin*?" I asked him. "No one," he replied.

When we finally met at my hotel in Kyoto, Tanahashi turned out to be an intense, slight, unsmiling man in his fifties. He wore an expensive-looking blazer and fedora by the designer Yohji Yamamoto that, in contrast with his rather glum mien, danced with just about every color in the visible spectrum. He greeted me by brusquely clasping my hand in his. Noticing my surprise at his costume, he remarked, "I bought these when I was rich." Our acquaintance was off to a peculiar start.

Shojin ryori was brought to Japan from China in the sixth century, and by the thirteenth—when the Zen patriarch Dogen wrote a manual titled *Instructions for the Cook*—it had become thoroughly Japanese. In the fifteenth century it was reimagined again by Sen no Rikyu, the great popularizer of the tea ceremony and the aesthetic of exquisite shabbiness known as *wabi-sabi*. The simple *shojin* dishes and powdered green tea that Rikyu served in his rustic teahouses eventually gave rise to *kaiseki*, the elaborate, time-consuming, and often stunningly costly multicourse dining experience one encounters in Japan today. The word *kaiseki* comes from the warm stone that mendicant monks once pressed to their stomachs to dull hunger pains. That it came to describe dozens of laboriously plated courses served on museum-grade ceramics and lacquerware in hushed dining rooms and gardens is a distinctly Japanese paradox.

This paradox colors the world of *shojin* too—a world poised between the rigorous simplicity of spiritual practice and its often exquisite trappings. Consider the tools found in a *shojin* kitchen. On the day we met, Tanahashi took me to Aritsugu, renowned as a shrine among the international brotherhood of knife fetishists. The family-owned shop has been in continuous operation since 1560 and once supplied swords to the Imperial House of Japan. At the modern-day shop in Kyoto's enclosed Nishiki Market, we shimmied past vitrines of eye-wateringly expensive sashimi blades to a back room, where a soft-spoken manager showed us the principal tools of the *shojin* chef. There was an adorably petite vegetable cleaver called a *nakiri-bocho,* a one-sided grater of tinned copper trimmed in magnolia wood and deer antler used for working with lotus root and wasabi, and a strainer-ricer made of the braided hairs of a horse's tail bound with a band of cherry bark. These utensils, made by hand, were remarkably beautiful. "Things that are made by humans for humans are good for the spirit," Tanahashi declared. He explained that *shojin* kitchens forbid plastic and machinery. Taking care of one's tools, he added, turning the cleaver in his hand, was in itself a form of Buddhist meditation.

Over the next several days Tanahashi led me on a breakneck tour of *shojin*—not the grand theory behind it, but the myriad building blocks. He referred to it as my "education." At an antique lacquerware shop called Uruwashiya, behind one of those dimly lit Kyoto storefronts that always look closed, Akemi Horiuchi, the elegant proprietor, showed us the most important dishes used in serving *shojin*—several attractively worn red bowls and a matching tray. Red is the auspicious color of the temples, she explained, and the tray's raised edge indicates that it encloses a sacred space. *Shojin* must be served in handmade vessels, and few are as painstakingly handmade as these—delicately carved wood covered with layer upon layer of *urushi* lacquer, making the dishes supple, lightweight, and resilient. The lacquer on the bowls Horiuchi showed us had faded in places—a prized quality, she said—because they were made nearly five hundred years ago, in Sen no Rikyu's lifetime.

Afterward Tanahashi and I sat at a tea merchant's counter, sipping from handmade lilliputian cups. *Shojin*'s spiritual twin is tea, and we sampled savory, piney *sencha;* grassy, pleasantly bitter *matcha* whipped to a neon-green froth with a bamboo whisk; and a Kyoto specialty, *hojicha,* a roasted reddish brown tea that smelled like a campfire.

Our next stops on Tanahashi's excursion were for three savory *shojin* staples—tasted in their best guises. No ingredient turns up in *shojin* dishes as frequently as tofu, and I'd never tasted tofu like they make it at Hirano, a homely, closetlike institution on Fuyacho Street. The crisp fried rectangles were tasty enough, but Hirano's reputation rests on the snowy, disconcertingly creamy fresh stuff, which had a complexity I'd never expected from soybeans.

At the posh Fuka—which resembled a Ginza boutique more than a food supplier—Tanahashi and I sampled the oddly versatile wheat gluten called *fu.* It's made by washing wheat flour dough until the starch granules are gone, then cooking and sometimes drying the remaining sticky gluten. We tasted velvety *fu* in soup, a crisp, meaty version in a stir-fry, and a *fu* confection filled with sweet red bean paste called *fu-manju.*

My favorite of the three actually turned out to be tofu skin, or *yuba,* a gossamer, paper-thin delicacy that in its basic form tastes a little like good homemade pasta. The version Tanahashi chose came from Senmaruya; being less than two hundred years old, the shop is a relative newcomer to the Kyoto food scene. Its youthful proprietor, Ochi-san, pointed to a well near the counter that dated to the nineteenth century. Kyoto's aquifers give water renowned for its low mineral content and subtle sweetness, which makes the city's tofu and *yuba* sought after throughout Japan.

Later Ochi-san drove us to Senmaruya's production facility at the city's edge, where we watched *yuba* firming up on trays of steaming soy milk. Collecting it is a task too delicate for machines, and workers in blue smocks and face masks walked quickly along the rows of trays, lifting the tofu skin with a bamboo stick and hanging it on steel rods. Tanahashi stood by the door, glancing impatiently at a tablet with our itinerary; we were scheduled to visit a daikon farmer across town. My education was not yet complete.

That evening Tanahashi and I visited a casual restaurant near Shijo Street named Ki Haru. It didn't serve *shojin* but was shaped by it nonetheless. Because Kyoto is the country's Buddhist capital, its cuisine remains hugely influenced by temple fare: sesame tofu, which kicks off many meals here, is a *shojin* classic. Even neighborhood joints like Ki Haru rely on vegetables and grains more than they do elsewhere in Japan.

Our interpreter was close friends with the restaurant's loud, excitable, vividly bald chef-owner. His name was Ichiro Tanaka, but everyone called him Taisho, which means "General." His face was so animated that it looked painted with a brush. He kept a collection of old and rare sakes behind the bar and poured them for everyone so relentlessly that three courses into our stupendous meal, everyone — most of all Taisho himself — became undeniably drunk.

In honor of Tanahashi's visit, Taisho prepared a meal of mostly vegetables. After an appetizer of mizuna, chrysanthemum, and *shimeji* mushrooms, Taisho ladled out a soy-milk-based soup with broccoli, daikon, zucchini, and lightly grilled leek whites. In the meantime he'd dropped several large onions on the grill. They turned so smoky and soft that I wondered why more people back home didn't grill whole onions. Taisho followed this with wedges of tempura of shredded carrot and gingko nuts that had been boiled with rice. Like everything else he served, he claimed to have invented the dish on the spot — a playful *shojin* improvised with the ingredients at hand.

The counter seating area at Ki Haru was filled entirely with regulars who'd exchanged loud friendly greetings with Taisho; a visitor showing up without an introduction was liable to be politely but firmly turned away. (Elizabeth Andoh explained to me that this policy is actually quite common in Japan. "The Japanese prize harmony over a level playing field," she said. "Restaurants strive to make sure that every diner wants to be there and will appreciate what it does.")

Amid chopping, grilling, and pouring, Taisho told us that he adored his children but strongly disliked his wife and that the restaurant served as a refuge from his marriage. A regular who sat beside us at the bar — a badgerlike man in a sweater vest who smoked cheap cigarettes and guffawed loudly during the meal — chimed in with unflattering comments about *his* wife, and I wondered whether spousal disparagement was a leitmotif of Kyoto nightlife.

During the meal Tanahashi told me about finding *shojin*, or rather having it find him. His leap into the unknown came when he was twenty-seven and working for an advertising agency in To-kyo. Something about his life felt empty. "I was born in Japan but didn't know what it meant to be Japanese," he told me. He thought he might have glimpsed an answer in a documentary film about Myodo Murase, a sixty-year-old Zen nun. She was renowned for her wry sense of humor and the *shojin* meals she prepared at a minus-cule temple in Otsu, a town in Shiga Prefecture, meals made all the more remarkable by the fact that Murase had lost an arm and the use of a leg in an auto accident.

Shortly after watching the film, Tanahashi gave notice at his job, moved to Otsu, and became Murase's disciple. He called his teacher a "character" but added, "I was very lucky." Sitting medi-tation, called *zazen,* is the heart of Buddhist practice, but Murase taught that this was unnecessary. Her radical teaching was that the profound mindfulness required to cook with all of one's being was enough to attain enlightenment. For her disciple, this meant cooking from morning till night. "No one made sesame paste from scratch," Tanahashi told me, but every week he spent hours in a lotus position on the floor of Murase's temple, grinding sesame in a mortar. He seeded eggplants (picture for a moment the number of seeds in an eggplant), peeled daikon, grated mountains of lotus root. The whole time Murase's promise stirred at the back of his mind — cooking could make you a Buddha.

Several hundred feet from Izusen, Tanahashi and I knelt on the terrace of one of Daitoku-ji's most scenic subtemples, facing a pond and a garden bathed in late-afternoon sunlight. Sen no Rikyu was buried a few buildings away. The subtemple was closed to the public, but Tanahashi had wangled us an invitation because the head monk had, in a former life, worked at his Tokyo restaurant as a busboy.

The monk, Jobun Haruta, was dressed in a patched indigo robe and appeared to be in his mid-twenties. He was improbably beauti-ful, and there was something about his manner that suggested ease and unflappable kindness. I'm as skeptical as anyone of spiritual men, but he looked as if a lamp glowed inside him. "A person who walks the path," our interpreter muttered. Haruta began to seem even more remarkable when I learned that he was forty years old.

Haruta agreed to demonstrate for us the ritual of a midday mon-astery meal. We watched as he knelt on the terrace and unwrapped several lacquered bowls and a pair of absurdly large chopsticks. He showed us the chopsticks' secondary function—announcing the periods of a monastic meal—by clacking them together. Before eating, monks recite five reflections, which instill mindfulness, gratitude, and joy. Afterward Haruta closed his eyes and chanted the Heart Sutra, one of Buddhism's most inscrutable texts. "All things are empty: nothing is born, nothing dies, nothing is pure, nothing is stained," Haruta sang, lit by the setting sun. Then he ladled miso soup and plain white rice into the bowls and proceeded to eat with deep concentration. We sat nearby, watching him a little self-consciously. When he was done, Haruta cleaned the bowls with a piece of pickled daikon, stacked, and wrapped them. Then he looked up at us and grinned.

Later, while we slurped warm *matcha* from lopsided clay bowls, Tanahashi sat beside Haruta, put his arm around him, and posed for a photo. I couldn't decide whether the look on Tanahashi's face was envy, admiration, or pride. Earlier he'd told me that he was living alone in rural Okinawa and mulling his next career move. "I'm in a slump," he admitted. In the meantime his former busboy had become an important figure in the Buddhist world, and I wondered what Tanahashi was thinking about, having traded the unbending routines of monastic life for the inconstant promises of worldly success. I never worked up the nerve to ask him.

I've been to my share of memorable places, but none quite like Mugino-ie. Below a thatch-covered farmhouse, terraces of vegetable rows cascaded down a mountainside all the way to Lake Biwa, which was covered in morning mist and glowed the color of old silverware. We were twenty-five minutes from Kyoto but wouldn't know it. A blue-black crow pecking the ground beside me let out an inquisitive caw.

We were greeted by a farmer, a smiling man in his sixties named Takashi Yamazaki, who held his two-year-old granddaughter, Yuki. Yamazaki said his grandfather had come here from Kyoto shortly after the bombing of Hiroshima and Nagasaki, when Japan's cities were devastated by war. He'd given up on urban living and decided to become self-reliant, eating only what he could grow. Five generations of his family had sustained this organic permaculture experiment. The eggs came from their henhouse, and everything they ate grew on this land. After speaking about the war, Yamazaki asked about America. I grimaced and said that the recent presidential election had left me shaken and scared. The farmer looked me in the eye and said, "Sometimes terrible things happen to great countries."

We'd come to Mugino-ie because it's where Tanahashi wanted to cook us a meal that demonstrated his modern *shojin* and summed up everything he'd shown me. Tanahashi said he first came here when he was a monk. I could see why he'd chosen it—besides its staggering beauty, everything about the place spoke to these venerable and vulnerable culinary traditions and their meaning. Just below us, Yamazaki's son harvested sweet potatoes. Yuki and her older sister helped by hugging the dirt-covered tubers, running around and giggling madly.

Tanahashi spent part of the morning grinding sesame; he sat on the floor, slowly moving the pepperwood pestle in a heavy ridged mortar, his back still and his eyes shut in concentration. Later, in the farmhouse kitchen, he cooked beside an assistant, a slim thirty-something Londoner named Neil. Tanahashi darted amid steaming pots and mixing bowls—simmering seaweed, slicing chestnuts, measuring out spices—and conferred with Neil in Japanese. The serenity of the sesame-grinding session had evaporated. He looked harried and quite possibly nervous—in other words, like a chef preparing a big meal in an unfamiliar kitchen.

Though he was preparing lunch, the meal wasn't ready until three. Someone had opened the screens in the farmhouse, and we gathered around a low table with a view of the mountain and the lake and all the glorious particulars. I was feeling impatient and hungry, but the dishes Tanahashi finally brought from the kitchen made everyone fall silent.

After ambrosial sesame tofu there was a rich broth of mushrooms and grated turnip, garnished with mizuna stems, a lotus-root croquette, and two colors of chrysanthemum. Fried bundles of paper-thin *yuba* were filled with *nameko* mushrooms, shiso, and, unexpectedly, cinnamon. An oddly unified cool salad of tofu, Fuyu persimmon, apple, mustard, and hand-ground sesame paste was followed by the centerpiece—a dish Tanahashi named Fuki-Yose, or Autumn Leaves. On a huge red-spotted persimmon leaf he'd arranged roasted chestnuts, gingko nuts, *fu*, shiitake mushrooms, lotus root, Kyoto carrot, burdock, and the caramelized, slightly garlicky bulb of the lily plant. Tanahashi finished the meal with sliced figs and grapes encased in transparent cubes of sweetened agar-agar, an elegant dish that nonetheless got indexed in my mind as Buddha's Jell-O.

All of it looked arresting, with flavor and texture combinations that somehow managed to taste harmonious yet consistently surprise. More important, Tanahashi had prepared a meal worthy of a fine-dining restaurant kitchen, and he did it using no animal products, no scarce or expensive ingredients, nothing unhealthy or from far away. The lunch was everything he'd promised—a traditional hymn to autumn presented in a resolutely modern style. As we took in the meal, it seemed entirely possible that at a time of rapidly dwindling resources, *shojin* might come to shape the way we eat, and sooner than we expect.

After we cleared the dishes, Tanahashi sat down at the table, looking relieved and proud. For the first time since we'd met, he smiled with his whole face. A breeze came off the lake and blew through the farmhouse. It was getting dark. On a two-lane road somewhere below us, a stream of buses and trucks headed for Kyoto and Osaka, but all we could hear was the wind in the cedars and, farther off, the cawing of a crow.

The Struggle of "Eating Well" When You're Poor

FROM *Catapult*

I UNFURL A bag of chips, barefoot and alone. I keep the lights out. I drop my shoulders, bend my neck forward, and allow my mouth to be happy when it meets the salt and the grease. I eat one chip, then two, then the entire bag. Eating satiates nothing: not my hunger nor my sadness. I close cupboards quietly, open the microwave before it beeps. When I am done, my stomach is distended with bloat. The next day, I know, my fingers will be swollen from all of the salt. With enough sugar, a patch of bright acne will sprout around my mouth and chin. At first I cover it with concealer. Before long, I leave my skin how I feel: angry, red-hot with loneliness. In the months following my grandmother's death, I repeat this process: I try cookies, spoonfuls of peanut butter, an entire sleeve of crackers, rum balls with too much liquor, frozen pizzas that melt and burn in my microwave. Nothing works.

For the first time, I want food to bring me home: not to her kitchen, where we rarely turned on the oven to cook, but to our small town's greasy diner, where once every summer—because that's how often we could afford it—we shared a plate of fried clams and french fries. I want food to bring me home to the gas station where I walked most afternoons after school and bought a slushie and stained my tongue blue.

I search my cupboards, then the fridge, then the freezer. In the morning I will drink black coffee and eat the tartest tangerine I can find. Later it will be vegan pad Thai, farm-to-table tacos, or a wood-fired pizza that costs four times as much as the one in my freezer. I've spent my adult life hungering for these foods, not just for their taste but for their status. In the months following my grandmother's death, these meals make me feel like an imposter.

Now, more than a year after her passing, I continue to search for her in food. There are no family recipes, no favorite casseroles or signature birthday cakes. When I eat the food that reminds me of her, it comes wrapped in plastic or spills out of a can. A first-generation Italian-American, she defied stereotypes when it came to kitchen life. We ate microwaved TV dinners in front of the tiny television in our living room, watching talk shows on local stations. It's hard to have pride when you're poor. Finding joy in food that comes from a bag or a box feels like a sin in a society that demonizes it. Now it's hard for me to honor that happiness while grieving. Food brings me home, but it also makes me face my shame.

In Riddle's, my grandmother hands me her shopping list. We are in the only grocery store in Hull, the 7-mile-long town she raised me in, nestled on the coast just south of Boston. I know the lists from memory, but because I am five and eager to prove I can read, I read it out loud anyway. Canned vegetables first: spinach, green beans, corn. Canned soup too: tomato, minestrone, Italian wedding. Condensed milk, to later be diluted with water and poured into cereal.

Frozen broccoli makes the cut, as does cauliflower, when it is on sale. We toss in a few boxes of candy that cost just shy of a dollar each, then make our way to the produce. That day only tomatoes are on the list. We live off of her fixed income — I know, already, how important it is that we follow the list.

In line at the register, my grandmother makes small talk with the woman in front of us. As the cashier scans the woman's items, the woman squats down and talks to me directly. She tells me that I am a nice girl, very well behaved, and that I need to be good for my grandmother. At this age, a lot of adults tell me this, because our town is small and everyone knows my parents are in and out of the picture.

The bagger puts the woman's bags in her cart and she puts her change in her wallet. She smiles at my grandmother, then at me, then at our food on the belt: canned, boxed, frozen. "You really do a lot," the woman repeats. "I mean, it's really great that you do what you can, considering what you have to work with."

*

Jacqueline was the first person to call me poor directly. We were assigned partners on a class field trip to the aquarium. Her family moved to Hull from Quebec, where her parents left behind corporate jobs for the softer, slower kind of life business people imagine you can live by the ocean. She was long and lanky with red hair, a slew of acne on the curve of her cheeks, and signed the notes she wrote me in class with greetings and goodbyes in French, a touch I found incredibly sophisticated. The closest I ever got to kissing her was when she asked me to check her braces for specks of food.

I slid beside Jacqueline on the bus. At twelve, our thighs had just started to flesh out and jiggle, and they spread out onto the sticky seats, unyielding wills of their own from beneath our denim cutoffs.

Jacqueline hesitated. "I'm not supposed to share with you," she said, eyes still on my fluffernutter sandwich. "But it tastes really good, so I want it." She grinned and took one of the sandwich halves, then gave me her yogurt and some orange slices.

I stared down at my lap: my peanut butter and marshmallow creme sandwich on white bread stared back at me. I asked her what she meant.

"My mom said the food you bring is bad for me," Jacqueline said, dipping a carrot stick into her tub of hummus. "But it's okay. She said it's not your fault that you're poor."

I thought about Jacqueline coming to my house after school, sitting beside me on the living room floor while we ate microwaved meals in front of the TV—a treat, my grandmother said, because I had a guest—for dinner. The bus started moving. I crumbled my half of the sandwich and put it back into the paper bag. The sandwich oozed peanut butter and marshmallow onto my hands. I wiped it on my shorts, where it stayed the rest of the day.

I was quiet for long enough that Jacqueline stopped asking me what was wrong. Finally she squeezed my hand hard, and I pulled it back; she didn't leave a bruise, but the mark lingered for years. She'd move by the end of the school year, and we would lose touch entirely. Until then we spent as much time together as her parents would allow, but it was never the same.

Hull is home to one Dunkin' Donuts. The national chain originated in Quincy, a small city just a twenty-minute drive from where

I grew up. The chain is prolific enough to have penetrated even my small, sleepy town, which mostly fishermen and retirees call home.

My grandmother loved it all: the apple crullers, the croissants, the cake doughnuts, the Munchkins filled with jelly. She ate Boston creams without irony. When I went to school, she occasionally went there and ordered a baked good and drank coffee by herself. I don't know if my grandmother considered herself a feminist; I have no idea if she saw eating alone as an act of quiet revolution. Eating alone and eating processed food, high in fat and coated with sugar and grease, at that. We shared such intimate things: food, money, a home. But I can't know if she shared my shame in any of it, if she ever struggled with feeling that her happiness was undeserved. The funny part about grief is that it feels revisionist —so many questions I waited too long to ask.

When I visited my grandmother in the nursing home she lived in for the years before her death, she mostly asked me about food. I knew it was voyeurism; she was missing almost all of her teeth by then, so hard foods were out of the question. She ate mostly applesauce, pudding, and spaghetti with a marinara sauce she did not like. "It doesn't taste like home," she said to me during one visit.

The nurse's aide smiled at me as she changed my grandmother's sheets. "A family recipe?"

I looked at my grandmother, who was looking out the window into the courtyard that sometimes brought her happiness and sometimes scared her. When she wasn't asking me about food, she was asking me where she was. She remembered almost nothing; most days, not even me. She wore a light-blue dress with small, small flowers on it and a big, bulky white cardigan on top. She loved to be warm.

"No," I said. "Not from scratch. Just a favorite kind."

When the aide leaves, my grandmother goes back to asking me about what I eat. "French fries?" she asks. "Hamburgers?" I switched from beef burgers to black bean, from french fries to roasted sweet potatoes. Now greasy food is falafel or pizza with cheese made from cashews.

"You still eat well, don't you?" she asks. Our definitions of eating well have changed, and I feel too guilty to correct her.

"Yes," I say, "I do."

*

In health class our teacher talks about the benefits of eating fresh food. We are in the fifth grade, and this is the week after the boys and girls are separated to learn about puberty. I haven't started my period yet, but I am already worried about gaining weight when I do. She passes around copies of the food pyramid. She stresses the importance of words like *fresh, whole grain,* and *organic.* We separate into small groups to write out menus of what we eat, then match them on the pyramid. I am naive enough not to lie. She writes a note for me to take home to my grandmother, on the importance of eating healthy. I am smart enough to tear up the note and throw it away before my grandmother sees it.

I struggle with the equation of food with love, of effort with love. Women especially are held to a standard that equates cooking with a way to express love and care. How often does society equate the time spent at the stove with how much love went into the meal? When we hear that a baked good is homemade, we imagine the delicate steps: mixing the dry ingredients, then the wet. Cracking eggs without dropping in a sliver of shell. Monitoring the rise before pulling the bake. We understand domestic labor, from the time it takes to cook an elaborate recipe to the neatness of folded laundry, as a tangible representation of love.

My grandmother's love was in opening a can of soup and heating it over a stove burner. She didn't make a broth from scratch. She didn't dice vegetables or braise meat. We were poor and she was tired. There is no other way to say it.

A woman stands behind me in line at the drugstore. We're in the Lower East Side of Manhattan and just about everybody has the flu. I'm holding Gatorade and ramen noodles. At the last minute I pick up a chocolate bar. This is an indulgence: I am twenty-three, less than a year out of college, and making $11 an hour working in a high-rise office in midtown.

"You're lucky," the woman says. "If I ate like that, I'd blow up." We are the same size, and I don't know what to say. I chuckle until she adds, "All that processed stuff can catch up with you, you know."

At the register I forget to ask for a bag, and my purse is too small to carry my purchases. I hold them in my hands for the walk home, and when I get inside, the chocolate bar is mostly melted in my hands. I peel back the wrapper and eat it before I remove my jacket.

That night my grandmother is not dead yet, but it had been close to a year since I had seen her. When I go home to Massachusetts, she will no longer live in the house I grew up in and will have already transitioned to the nursing home where she will die.

On the phone that night, she struggles to hear me. I use this as an excuse to keep many things from her: that I am exhausted from my job, that I feel terrified of New York, that I am in love with a woman, that I am ashamed and unsure of how to eat in front of my coworkers.

"Are you eating well?" she asks.

"Oh yes," I say. "Oh, yes."

These are some of the last conversations we have on the phone. By the time she moves to the nursing home, she has forgotten how to speak into the receiver. When I do call her and someone holds the phone up to her ear, I say hello over and over, and her voice is a disembodied giggle at whoever is in the room with her, not hearing me at all.

Once a week I eat a doughnut. Sometimes I eat the doughnuts in the morning, when they are fresh and soft, and sometimes I eat them at night, when they are flaked over and stiff. Every time, I go to the same diner and survey the case: these doughnuts are filled with marshmallow, whipped chocolate, matcha green tea creme. The muffins are gluten-free, sprinkled with almond slivers. There are breakfast sandwiches with tofu-based eggs and sausages made from seitan.

It's a Tuesday morning, and I am working from home. I establish my usual space: a narrow table in the corner, against the wall, with just enough room for my laptop and a small plate. It is the first of her birthdays to pass since her death, and I challenge myself to bring my grief outside with me.

The doughnut I choose is filled with vegan marshmallow, topped with peanut butter. In the center of the doughnut, a second marshmallow is brûléed. The cashier hands me the doughnut on a plate.

The man in line after me orders a vegan sausage biscuit and an espresso, to go.

"Wish I was eating that," he says, nodding at my plate. I smile at him until he says, "Sure a whole lot of sugar, though."

"Yeah," I say. "I know." He watches me sit. I bite the doughnut in half. Marshmallow oozes onto my chin and nose. I can feel peanut butter on my right cheek. The dough feels thick, and my cheeks puff to hold it all inside. He doesn't answer, then his order is ready, and he goes out the front door. I watch him leave and new people come inside, and I eat. I eat.

The NBA's Secret Sandwich Addiction

FROM *ESPN The Magazine*

THE LEGEND HAS been passed down by NBA generations, chronicled like a Homeric odyssey. The tale they tell is of Kevin Garnett and the 2007–08 Celtics, and the seminal moment of a revolution. Bryan Doo, Celtics strength and conditioning coach, recalls it as if it were yesterday, how before a game in December of that season, an unnamed Celtic—his identity lost to history, like the other horsemen on Paul Revere's midnight ride—complained to Doo of incipient hunger pangs.

"Man, I could go for a PB&J," the player said.

And then Garnett, in an act with historical reverberations, uttered the now-fabled words: "Yeah, let's get on that."

Garnett had not, to that point, made the PB&J a part of his pregame routine. But on that night in Boston, as Doo recalls, Garnett partook, then played . . . and played well. Afterward, from his perch as the Celtics' fiery leader, Garnett issued the following commandment: "We're going to need PB&J in here every game now."

And so a sandwich revolution was born.

At the time, Doo notes, the Celtics not only didn't provide lavish pregame spreads, they didn't offer much food at all. But he soon found himself slapping together twenty PB&J's about three hours before every tip-off, the finished products placed in bags and labeled with Sharpie in a secret code: *S* for strawberry, *G* for grape, *C* for crunchy. Of vital import: Garnett was an *S* man, and woe unto he who did not deliver him two *S*'s before every game. "If Kevin didn't get his routine down, he'd be pissed," Doo says. "Even if he didn't eat them, he needed them to be there."

From Doo's perspective, PB&J's were a far better option than players seeking out, say, greasy junk food from arena concessions. "It was a win-win for everybody," he says. But as the Garnett/Paul Pierce/Ray Allen Celtics steamrolled to a sixty-six-win season and an NBA title, the secret to their success, so cleverly disguised between two pieces of white bread, was eventually leaked. "Boston was doing it at a mass-produced level earlier on than I noticed other people doing it, for sure," says Tim DiFrancesco, the Lakers' strength and conditioning coach since 2011. "They were really on the forefront of this revolution." In time, as visiting teams swung through Boston, opposing players caught wind that a new day had dawned. DiFrancesco recalls hearing from his troops during a visit, "Wait a minute, there's PB&J's in the Celtics' locker room? Can we get some?" Doo's colleagues around the league were less effusive. "B-Doo, I can't believe you did this for the guys," one told him. "Now you got me making them."

There was no putting the jelly back in the jar. Over the course of the following seasons, as that Celtics championship run ran its course, the pieces of that team would be spread far and wide: Pierce and Garnett migrating the PB&J down I-95 to Brooklyn; Glen "Big Baby" Davis converting the Orlando Magic; Tony Allen spreading the bug to Memphis; coach Doc Rivers bringing the virus across the country to infect the Clippers.

And nothing would ever be the same.

The Trail Blazers offer twenty crustless, halved PB&J's pregame—ten of them toasted, a mandate ever since an opposing arena prepared them as such and Blazers guard Damian Lillard approved. They're composed of organic fixings, save for white bread, which Portland's assistant performance coach Ben Kenyon notes is a high-glycemic carb that easily digests to provide a quick energy jolt. Typically all twenty vanish well before tip-off; sometimes the Blazers double their order.

The Rockets make sure the PB&J is available in their kitchen at all times, in all varieties—white and wheat bread, toasted, untoasted, Smucker's strawberry and grape, Jif creamy and chunky—and offer twelve to fifteen sandwiches pregame, with PB&J reinforcements provided at halftime and on postgame flights.

The secretive Spurs, it has been confirmed, indulge in their own pregame PB&J's. The Clippers, at home and on the road, go through two loaves of bread, almond and peanut butters, and assorted jellies from Whole Foods. The Pelicans offer PB&J everywhere: hotel rooms, flights, locker rooms. The Wizards had some "minor uprisings" from players, one source says, when management tried to upgrade team PB&J's with organic peanut butter on whole-grain bread—but peace was restored when each side compromised to include all options.

The Bucks might boast the NBA's most elaborate PB&J operation: a pregame buffet featuring smooth, crunchy, and almond butters, an assortment of jellies (raspberry, strawberry, grape, blueberry, apricot), three breads from a local bakery (white, wheat, and gluten-free), and Nutella. The team scarfs twenty to thirty PB&J's per game and travels with the ingredients, which rookies prepare on the plane and in visiting locker rooms. They've even offered their players PB&J-flavored oatmeal, PB&J recovery shakes, PB&J waffles, and PB&J pancakes. Bucks team chef/dietitian Shawn Zell won't rule out one day making a PB&J burger.

It's a tale of two diets in Cleveland's Quicken Loans Arena, where the Cavs, courtesy of a partnership with fellow Ohio-based outfit Smucker's, foist about a dozen of the company's prepackaged Uncrustables PB&J's on opposing teams every game night. (Both the Lakers' and the Celtics' strength and conditioning coaches tell their players to avoid those processed, once-frozen snacks.) But the Cavs fare far better with their fare, serving themselves twenty artisanal PB&J's prior to tip-off, with homemade grape and raspberry jelly, as well as almond butter and banana and peanut butter and banana sandwiches—the power of the PB&J being wielded as a form of asymmetric nutritional warfare.

No matter how you slice it, it's hard to swallow: the NBA is covered in experts, obsessed with peak performance, and still this pillar of grade-school cafeteria lunches is the staple snack of the league. An exorbitantly wealthy microclique, backed by an army of personal chefs, swears by a sandwich whose standard ingredients boast a street value of roughly 69 cents.

It was winter of 2013, and those in Dwight Howard's inner orbit begged the All-Star center to kick his addiction, but he denied he had one. Why, he'd dominated for years as the NBA's best big man, carrying the Magic to the finals in 2009. Then came surgery on a herniated disk in April 2012, followed by an August trade to the Lakers, who had paraded him around like their next Wilt, Kareem, or Shaq—an unstoppable center who would deliver titles in droves. But his back just wasn't healing. Howard was twenty-seven, sculpted like a statue in the Louvre, but he labored down the court like a retired fullback. The Lakers plummeted below .500 in January, with Kobe Bryant barking at Howard to man up, though in terms a tad more colorful. But the team's chef and its strength and conditioning coach stressed a different message: "Man up—and get off this *sugar.*"

By February's All-Star break, it was time for a full-blown intervention, and Dr. Cate Shanahan, the Lakers' nutritionist, led the charge, speaking to Howard by phone from her office in Napa, California. Howard's legs tingled, he complained, but she noticed he was having trouble catching passes too, as if his hands were wrapped in oven mitts. Well, he quietly admitted, his fingers also tingled. Shanahan, with two decades of experience in the field, knew Howard possessed a legendary sweet tooth, and she suspected his consumption of sugar was causing a nerve dysfunction called dysesthesia, which she'd seen in patients with prediabetes. She urged him to cut back on sugar for two weeks. If that didn't help, she said, she vowed to resign.

To alter Howard's diet, though, Shanahan first had to understand it. After calls with his bodyguard, chef, and a personal assistant, she uncovered a startling fact: Howard had been scarfing down about two dozen chocolate bars' worth of sugar *every single day* for years, possibly as long as a decade. "You name it, he ate it," she says. Skittles, Starbursts, Rolos, Snickers, Mars bars, Twizzlers, Almond Joys, Kit Kats, and oh, how he loved Reese's Pieces. He'd eat them before lunch, after lunch, before dinner, after dinner, and like any junkie, he had stashes all over—in his kitchen, his bedroom, his car, a fix always within reach. She told his assistants to empty his house, and they hauled out his monstrous candy stash in boxes—yes, boxes, plural. Howard ultimately vowed to go clean all at once, but before he committed to cutting the junk in his diet, he asked Shanahan one question. It was about one food he wasn't willing to surrender, one snack at which he had to draw the line.

He wanted to know whether he could still eat peanut butter and jelly sandwiches.

DiFrancesco was hardly surprised. When he'd joined the Lakers in 2011 and begun traveling around the league, he'd already seen it: four years after KG's PB&J epiphany, virtually every players' lounge and practice site was stocked with jumbo-sized jars of peanut butter and jelly, bookended by a loaf or two of bread. DiFrancesco had had his eye on improving player diets, but Mount PB&J was clearly not the hill to die upon. "You pick your battles," he says.

Which is exactly what DiFrancesco told Shanahan as they began working with Howard, in 2013, to overhaul his sugary diet. Their demands weren't onerous: he didn't have to quit cold turkey, they only wanted Howard to try a healthier approach, with soft sourdough, organic peanut butter, and low-sugar jelly. Tensions were high when they presented Howard with the healthier version. But as he sank his teeth in, Howard grinned: "Yeah, this will work." Howard, as requested, cut out sugars from his diet. The tingling in his fingers and legs ceased. After the All-Star break, he tallied 1.8 more rebounds, 2.1 more points, and 2.5 more minutes per game.

Today Shanahan accepts what DiFrancesco realized years ago: "The peanut butter and jelly sandwich is absolutely never going to not be in the NBA. And I feel confident saying *never*."

But why? What is it, exactly, about a PB&J?

In dozens of interviews with players, coaches, executives, nutritionists, trainers, and others in and around the NBA, the most common explanation offered was the most obvious: PB&J is comfort food, and countless players, like countless other humans, grew up on it. "It's a soothing memory from childhood," Shanahan says. It's "peace of mind," says Brett Singer, a dietitian at the Memorial Hermann Ironman Sports Medicine Institute, who adds, "You feel good, you play well." Brian St. Pierre, director of performance nutrition at Precision Nutrition, who's consulted with the Spurs, says it's not so much a placebo effect but "almost more than that. They just simply believe." Lakers coach Luke Walton has a theory: NBA players are superstitious nuts, especially when it comes to routines. "Athletes are strange people," he says. "We've got weird habits." Walton, now thirty-six and in his first season leading the Lakers, still downs a PB&J before every game.

Factor in the NBA schedule—teams flying constantly, red-eyes, bad traffic, rotten night's sleeps—and on a night-to-night basis, so much is outside a player's control. It's all the more natural to cling all the tighter to something quick, cheap, and all but impossible to foul up.

Cute theory. But now let's engage in a little evolutionary anthropology and travel back millennia to when humans began to walk upright and our ancestors developed cravings for certain qualities in hard-to-find calorie-dense foods: fats, sugars, starches, proteins, and salts. Today the smell of these—even the mere awareness of their proximity—still triggers a release in humans of the neurotransmitter dopamine, which once provided our ancestors with an energy boost for the hunt, along with serotonin, the "happiness hormone." At first bite of a PB&J, receptors detect the food's chemical composition and report back to the brain—fats! sugars! starches! proteins! salts!—where reward centers release opioids and, after a few minutes, endorphins, which briefly reduce stress. It's an effect, St. Pierre notes, that's similar to sex. They also lower the body's heart rate, a bonus for an anxious hunter or a player just before tip-off. "These are the exact same pathways that make heroin addicts chase their next fix," says Dr. Trevor Cottrell, director of human performance for the Memorial Hermann Ironman Sports Medicine Institute.

Heroin, sex . . . peanut butter and jelly. You can see why players might revolt if someone tried to take away their PB&J. So are they actually good for you—or good enough for the physical demands of the most physically taxed athletes on the planet? Perhaps you've seen articles in your Facebook feed about the horrors of sugar and carbs. Within that framework, no, PB&J's aren't great. The typical PB&J contains roughly 400 to 500 calories, 50 grams of carbohydrates, 20 grams of fat, and 10 grams of protein. As Jill Lane, a Dallas-based sports nutritionist who has worked with NBA players, says, "It's not the best, but it's not bad."

But nutrition may be beside the point. "Even if we argue that physiologically a PB&J isn't the 'best' pregame meal," St. Pierre says, "that's only true if you think psychology doesn't impact physiology, and we know it does. Your thoughts about a food will actually help to shape how your body reacts to that food." As Stephan J. Guyenet, author of *The Hungry Brain,* notes, "The brain mostly cares about calories, so plain celery sticks and kale don't release much dopamine and we don't develop cravings for them." Or as Cottrell says, "The brain is a complex organ system that we know very little about. But what we know [about food cravings] alludes to some important neural pathways that are often associated with crack cocaine addiction, believe it or not."

Make that heroin, sex . . . and crack cocaine.

The mutinous undertones for the Warriors appeared in October 2015, on the team's first flight of the season. In the prior off-season, the Warriors had hired Lachlan Penfold, former head of physical preparation for an Australian men's rugby squad, to man a newly created position: head of physical performance and sports medicine. Penfold arrived in the Bay Area with a simple vision: less sugar, healthier food. The Warriors in turn had willingly parted with candy, cookies, and soda. But now, on this charter flight, they found nary a PB&J. Concerned glances were exchanged. "Just the fact that it wasn't there shook me a little bit," Stephen Curry told ESPN at the time. Clearly Penfold had made a mistake, yes? No. "Sorry, mate," Penfold explained then. "We're not doing sugar." History records this sinister act as the first shot fired in the Great PB&J War of 2015.

Walton, at the time the interim coach for an injured Steve Kerr, decided to lead the revolt. Perhaps in an effort to ingratiate himself with his new charges, whenever Walton was asked by flight attendants in the coming weeks, "Coach, what can we get you?" he'd reply, without fail, in a voice loud enough that Penfold and his players could all hear, *"Peanut butter and jelly!"* Walton would be duly informed that no such option was available. But his message was clear. This would not stand. Said Penfold at the time, "I haven't heard [complaining] like that since my youngest daughter was about three years of age."

As the Warriors' PB&J ban persisted, Walton upped the stakes: he began telling flight attendants he wanted PB&J . . . or nothing. Then on December 11, after the Warriors beat the Celtics in double overtime to improve to an NBA-record 24–0, players again asked for PB&J for the flight to Milwaukee on the second night of a back-to-back. Again Penfold said no. "Who needs peanut butter and jelly when you've got Vegemite?" Penfold joked at the time, referencing a famously distasteful Australian food spread. The following night the Warriors lost to the Bucks. "I have to believe we lost a game because of it," Warriors GM Bob Myers said then, tongue firmly in cheek—perhaps stuck to the roof of his mouth. "I think you can trace it to the peanut butter."

Finally Walton called in the heavy artillery: Curry, the MVP guard. The sharpshooter had become a PB&J devotee during the 2014–15 season, when, during one halftime, Curry complained of hunger and the team's strength and conditioning coach whipped one up. From then on Curry's PB&J (for the record: Smucker's strawberry, Skippy creamy) became his go-to pregame meal. "If you look at Steph's warmup, some of it is sensical, some of it doesn't make sense," Myers said. "But if peanut butter and jelly are part of our routine, to take that away from him, it was actually an irresponsible thing to do from the outset." It was time for Walton to fire back. He explained to Curry that if the guard entered the fray, they'd win this war. "Once Steph got on board," Walton says, "we got them back pretty quickly after that."

Penfold relented. "A peanut butter and jelly sandwich every now and again wouldn't kill them. I wouldn't eat it, but you know, whatever turns you on, you know?"

"Catastrophe avoided," Myers said.

Today Penfold is no longer employed by the Warriors. Last October it was reported that he'd joined the Melbourne Storm, an Australian rugby league team, as the new director of performance. No formal announcement ever appears to have been made explaining what led to his departure from the Warriors, after their seventy-three-win season. One can assume it was not because of sandwiches. But last February, Walton was quoted by the *Wall Street Journal,* defending his battle and proclaiming victory for the common man over the forces of anti-PB&J tyranny: "You gotta fight for your rights. If you believe in something, you gotta fight for it."

In the aftermath, when Walton was named coach of the Lakers last summer, he was approached by DiFrancesco, who also helps shape the Lakers' pregame and postgame meals. DiFrancesco asked Walton whether there was any specific item that Walton wanted on the team plane after games.

"Nope, your call," Walton told him. "I'm sure you do a great job. But . . . there better be PB&J's."

It's late January, midday, at a shared workspace along Sunset Boulevard in Hollywood, and NBA commissioner Adam Silver has a plane to catch. He's leaving a panel discussion at the second annual Total Health Forum, hosted by the league and its partner, health giant Kaiser Permanente, and there's a crowd waiting.

Silver, in a red tie and black suit, shakes a slew of hands, smiles for a few selfies, and, as the minutes become precious, disappears through a doorway into the back. He removes a microphone affixed to his jacket, then meets a reporter, who warns Silver that what's coming next are serious questions for a serious story. Silver agrees to be grilled, and the two walk and talk. And then Silver is asked, *What is the league's official stance on the very obvious peanut butter and jelly epidemic in NBA locker rooms?*

"Our official stance," Silver says, "is that it is a healthy snack."

And then he stops. Clearly Silver recognizes that this subject is not one to be discussed in passing. These questions must be given his full attention, even if he's on a tight schedule, with a plane to catch.

"Let's talk," he says.

In Golden State last year, the reporter notes, a sports scientist wanted to do away with the snack, sugars and all that—and the players revolted. The players won. So you have the health community vs. the players. Whose side are you on? "Well, so where I fall is I listen to Chris Paul, our first speaker this morning," Silver says. "He talked about balance. So I'm an advocate of balance. So people need to eat nutritious meals, but a little bit of sugar . . . okay."

But is allowing a little bit a slippery slope?

"No, because my response to any slippery slope is you draw lines."

Finally the crucial query is broached: *How do you take yours, Adam Silver? And where do you fall in the grape vs. strawberry debate?*

"I'm clearly on the strawberry side of the debate," Silver says, with some measure of emphasis, as if selecting grape is indefensible. "And I take, usually, my peanut butter with toast in the morning. I've been going light on the jelly. I do peanut butter virtually every day. I don't always add the jelly."

Growing up in Latvia, Knicks sensation Kristaps Porzingis had never heard of a PB&J. Then he joined the NBA. "I fell in love," he told the *Wall Street Journal.* Pacers nutritionist Lindsay Langford says rookie Georges Niang begs—yes, begs—for her PB&J recovery-shake recipe (frozen blueberries, vanilla whey protein, creamy peanut butter, and milk), which she makes once a week, to his delight. Warriors forward Kevin Durant is such a fan that he worked with Nike to unveil a PB&J-colored sneaker. His ex-team-mate Russell Westbrook prefers a pregame marriage of Skippy and strawberry jelly between toasted wheat bread, halved sometimes, depending on his mood, with butter slathered on the inside.

Then there's Lakers nineteen-year-old rookie forward Brandon Ingram, who, before road games, carefully inspects his team's PB&J's, each made with organic ingredients, to make sure they're up to his standards. Ingram, a jelly-come-lately, says he began eating pregame PB&J's only about two years ago. But when he arrived in the NBA and found the habit leaguewide, he knew he'd found a home. "Brandon has the highest requisites," DiFrancesco says, "on what constitutes a perfect PB&J for any player I've ever come across."

Ingram, the number-two overall pick in the 2016 draft, self-identifies as a "big grape jelly lover" and demands a healthy spread of peanut butter on the inside of *both* slices of bread, and if he doesn't see jelly poking out on at least two sides of the sandwich, he's got serious concerns. Ask him to name a place where the PB&J was lacking and he doesn't hesitate. "Utah," he says. "Not enough jelly."

Brandon Ingram might not realize that he's inherited a legacy. He might not know that he's but one soldier in a decadelong war. But Celtics trainer Doo knows. He knows that the legend they speak of is real. He knows there is a Johnny Appleseed of the PB&J revolution.

And he knows where to find him.

And so it was that during a January visit to Atlanta, when Doo stopped by the TNT studios, he saw, as part of a skit for TNT's new *Area 21* show, several NBA greats sitting together to dine. There was Shaquille O'Neal, feasting on barbecued chicken. There was Celtics guard Isaiah Thomas, enjoying a steak.

And Kevin Garnett? Well, come on, you know what was on his plate.

LAUREN MICHELE JACKSON

The White Lies of Craft Culture

FROM *Eater*

LAST FALL THE chef Sean Brock and brewmaster Ryan Coker of Revelry Brewing unveiled a collaboration called Amber Waves, a malt liquor made with locally sourced ingredients and grains reflective "of the 19th-century South." The "historically accurate heritage grain" malt liquor, whose name derives from the lyric in "America the Beautiful," comes in a bottle that's wrapped in the iconic brown paper bag, which is stamped with a blue corn logo and comes tastefully pre-unrolled. Sold in a modest 22-ounce portion rather than the 40-ounce size that the malt liquor is known for, a bottle runs $29, or more than $1.30 an ounce.

Outlets like *Modern Farmer* have praised Brock and Coker for "successfully elevating this bottom-shelf booze to small-batch status," a rhetorical sleight of hand that both conceals and dramatizes its racial subtext: "bottom shelf" is code for corner store and drunk on a dime, for poverty and homelessness, and for the black and brown communities who've made the beverage a part of hip-hop and hood culture; "small-batch status" and "heritage grain" signify the antithesis of the former—something artful and refined. By evoking the nineteenth-century South—an era when slavery and indentured servitude thrived—Amber Waves transforms hood to urbane.

Amber Waves and its act of historical transfiguration are typical products of what might be loosely labeled as "craft culture," which has, over the past two decades, radically reshaped how the richer swaths of America think about what they eat and drink and how those things were produced. Craft culture has seeped into cities and spread throughout the country, bearing the fruits of bean-to-bar chocolate and traditional butchery and single-barrel whiskey; ancient-grain breads and heritage-breed pigs and heirloom corn and $8 mayo and $12 ice cream; local honey and local beer and local pickles. Craft culture fetishizes the authentic, the traditionally produced, and the specific; it loathes the engineered, the mass-produced, and the originless.

Craft culture looks like white people. The founders, so many former lawyers or bankers or advertising execs, tend to be white, the front-facing staff in their custom denim aprons tend to be white, the clientele sipping $10 beers tends to be white. Craft culture tells mostly white stories for mostly white consumers, and they nearly always sound the same: it begins somewhere remote-sounding like the mountains of Cottonwood, Idaho, or someplace quirky like a basement in Fort Collins, Colorado, or a loft in Brooklyn, where a (white) artisan, who has a vision of back in the day, when the food was *real* and the labor that produced it neither alienated nor obscured, discovers a long-forgotten technique, plucked from an ur-knowledge as old as thought and a truth as pure as the soul.

These techniques and the goods they produce do have origins, specific ones rooted in history and in people. The character of craft culture, a special blend of bohemianism and capitalism, is not merely overwhelmingly white—a function of who generally has the wealth to start those microbreweries and old-school butcher shops, and to patronize them—it consistently engages in the erasure or exploitation of people of color whose intellectual and manual labor is often the foundation of the practices that transform so many of these small pleasures into something artful. A lie by omission may be a small one, but for a movement so vocally concerned with where things come from, the proprietors of craft culture often seem strangely uninterested in learning or conveying the stories of the people who first mastered those crafts.

In the U.S., historical memory considers slave labor in relation to one crop: cotton. From common images depicting enslaved black people in fields to phrases like "wait just a cotton-picking minute," there is a persistent notion that American slavery was limited to performing a single unskilled chore. But antebellum society depended on a diverse set of skills transported and developed by enslaved and indigenous peoples and immigrants.

Southern architecture alone, of both luxe and modest scale, evinces not only the aesthetic influences of African-descended cultures—classic "southern" shotgun house design has origins in early African and Haitian communities formed in New Orleans—but as structures, they exist as living testimony to learned hands and specialized building techniques. Besides field laborers, planter and urban communities both depended on proficient carpenters, blacksmiths, gardeners, stable hands, seamstresses, and cooks; the America of the 1700s and 1800s was literally crafted by people of color.

Part of this hidden history includes the revelation that six slaves were critical to the operation of George Washington's distillery, and that the eponymous Jack Daniel learned to make whiskey from an enslaved black man named Nathan "Nearest" Green. As Clay Risen reported for the *New York Times* last year, contrary to the predominant narrative that views whiskey as an ever "lily-white affair," black men were the minds and hands behind American whiskey production. "In the same way that white cookbook authors often appropriated recipes from their black cooks, white distillery owners took credit for the whiskey," he writes. Described as "the best whiskey maker that I know of" by his master, Dan Call, Green taught young Jack Daniel how to run a whiskey still. When Daniel later opened his own distillery, he hired two of Green's sons.

Over time that legacy was forgotten, creating a gap in knowledge about American distilling traditions—while English, German, Scottish, and Irish influences exist, that combination alone cannot explain the entirety of American distilling. As bourbon historian Michael Veach suggests, slave culture pieces together an otherwise puzzling intellectual history. It wouldn't be a stretch at all to assume a period of history when alcohol production was largely undergirded by enslaved men and women; Risen notes in a recent update on Green's story that "in all likelihood, there were many other men like Green, scattered around the South," who were "the brains as well as the brawn" behind distilling operations.

Inspired by last year's *Times* piece, real estate investor and author Fawn Weaver has done extensive archival research on Green, collecting "10,000 documents and artifacts," and has begun working on a book. Because of Weaver's research and advocacy, this past May, Brown-Forman, Jack Daniel's' parent company, named Green as its first master distiller, ahead of Daniel himself. (The company told the *Times* that it intended to more formally recognize Green's contributions last year but didn't want to look like it was profiting from the political climate that surrounded the election.)

For now, the public image of what distilling looks like in America remains white, even in the face of more recent history. Moonshine, experiencing a craft renaissance of its own, almost exclusively conjures a certain image of backwoods whiteness and Prohibition-era bootlegging—a product in part of the white cultural monopoly on all things "country," while black people are endlessly "urban"—an image that continues to be burnished by vested interests. "We as a society have created its value and meaning, bound up in images of mountains and overalls and shotguns and the way a man wears his hat. I played my part in this fiction," admits the writer Matt Bondurant in an essay about his family's moonshining legacy and his efforts to tell their story.

The rural is as much a domain of black life, and moonshining was a part of it. "I lived in a totally black world," the artist Jonathan Green said in a recent conversation with the poet Kevin Young about his family's moonshine production. That world was not an urban jungle but a southern, rural community of landholders, farmers, hunters, and store owners. "Moonshine was also called a happy drink, it was also a medicinal drink," Green said. "I only knew of moonshine as a sort of miracle liquid, if you will." As a child, Green's grandparents allowed him peeks into moonshining; he recalls the long early-morning walks with his grandfather to stills that "were always hidden" deep in the woods, and how family visiting from out of town always left with crates full of moonshine. "I only saw moonshining as a major part of my family history and culture."

But now that moonshine is a part of craft culture, what's ultimately left to do is "package the story, feed the legend, make some money," as Bondurant writes. Only white stories seem to have made it into the package.

The history of barbecue in America is, unlike whiskey or moonshine, so inescapably black that it has been impossible to completely whitewash that legacy, one succinctly encapsulated by Lauren Collins in *The New Yorker*:

> Before the Civil War, enslaved men often cooked these civic meals. They prepared their own feasts, too, either sanctioned by their owners or organized on the quiet. Much of the planning for the rebellions organized by Gabriel Prosser and Nat Turner took place at barbecues. After emancipation, black men continued to be some of the country's leading pit masters, catering enormous spreads that featured everything from barbecued hogs, shoats, chickens, and lambs to stuffed potatoes, stewed corn, cheese relish, puddings, coffee, and cigars. In 1909, the *Times* noted the death of a man born around 1865, on a plantation in Edgefield County, South Carolina. "Pickens Wells, one of the most famous barbecue cooks in the South, dropped dead today while preparing a barbecue," the item read. "Pickens prepared the famous barbecue at which President Taft was the guest of honor last Winter. White men here are raising a fund to erect a monument to the negro as a tribute to his fidelity and character."

And yet, in the new wave of craft barbecue, or what *Texas Monthly*'s Daniel Vaughn calls "big-city barbecue," marked by a "focus on premium quality meats," uncannily tender cuts, higher prices, and interminable lines, it is often distanced from black people and black culture. In 2015 the BBC reported that black pit masters are being left out of the U.S.'s current "barbecue boom." This is partly a matter of who has access to capital—Daryle Brantley, the owner of C&K Barbecue in St. Louis County, told the BBC that he could not get a loan to support his barbecue empire because of "structured racism" (the number of Small Business Administration loans that went to black-owned businesses dropped significantly and disproportionately between 2008 and 2014)—and partly a matter of representation. "The national press would have you believe barbecue is dominated by white hipster males," the food writer Robb Walsh has noted, pointing to coverage that leaves out or diminishes the work and visibility of black pit masters.

One glaring example, a compilation of "America's most influential BBQ pitmasters and personalities" published by Fox News, rather conspicuously included zero black people. Another, more recent list by Zagat, of "12 Pitmasters You Need to Know Around the U.S.," names just two black pit masters, Ed Mitchell and Rodney Scott, who frequently appear in such lists as lonesome bulwarks against all-white casts of barbecue mavens. (Scott and Mitchell, two of the most accomplished pit masters in the country, also make the cut in a *Southern Living* video about the South's best pit masters, for instance.)

The enormous power of craft culture to omit and obscure is in some ways rendered most clearly by the case of barbecue: even though its roots in pit-style cooking on plantations are well known, its transmutation from a staple to a product of true craft is a feat largely attributed to the exceptional taste and unique skill of the white pit masters who have claimed it as their own. In the process, the people and cultures most instrumental to the development of barbecue are effectively barred from participating in the genre at its highest and most exalted levels. Instead they're left to continue developing it in their own communities and establishments — waiting for their innovations to inevitably be taken and elevated so that they can be distributed to a wider, whiter audience always hungry for the next carefully packaged piece of another culture's cuisine.

Within craft culture, coffee seems like an exception to narratives of white authorship. In the 1990s the coffee industry experienced something of an ethical crisis as avid drinkers became aware of the inhumane costs of their daily cup. This led to the rise of socially responsible roasters, widely known as the "third wave of coffee," and most visibly associated with Intelligentsia, Stumptown, and Counter Culture. These roasters and their ilk were and are, in theory, a curative to the ills of Big Coffees: unlike large corporate entities who abuse the land and labor of the Latin American, West Indian, African, and Asian communities where coffee is exclusively grown, small-batch roasters claim an intimate and amicable relationship with farmers who are fairly compensated, as evinced by posters and pamphlets of lovingly profiled and photographed farmers that blanket their websites and cafés.

But craft coffee readily displays the black and brown bodies of the people who farm it only because it doesn't have much of a story to sell without them. While many artisanal products derive a portion of their premium from the perception that they are ethically produced — the heritage hog that gave its life for this pork shoulder died happy; the heirloom grains in this beer weren't sprayed with planet-killing pesticide; the butcher's apprentice is fairly compensated — it is the core value proposition for craft coffee, which cannot be produced locally. The sociologist Nicki Lisa Cole has found, as a result, that the movement toward a socially conscious cup of coffee is heavily invested in making "interaction with racialized bodies safe for white consumers."

In a survey of imagery used by coffee companies, Cole found that they leaned on "racially and culturally essentialized depictions of the coffee farmer, their lives, and communities, which facilitate knowledge of coffee farmers as distinctly different from consumers in the United States," neatly distancing the farmer from the consumer.

Further, Cole writes, "coffee farmers, their families, and communities are described as helpless against the exploitative forces of the capitalist market that undervalues their labor by setting a low price for coffee. The discourse tells consumers that by purchasing socially responsible coffee they can improve lives and communities in coffee growing regions, thus consumers too are able to help steward coffee farmers toward a better way of life." Every $5 cup is dosed with a whiff of philanthropy, satiating the coffee drinker's desire to be an ethical consumer with good taste, even though farmers get just pennies on the dollar.

A white-savior narrative is also neatly embedded within the typical story of how craft coffee gets from the farm to the consumer: the pristine crop lies deep in a primitive land, waiting to be discovered by oracle-like coffee buyers; the benevolent coffee company shows the farmer how to grow his own crop to meet its high standards; finally, the beans' essential flavors are unlocked with masterful roasting on vintage equipment and the skillful techniques of tattooed baristas.

Beyond the farms, like most other realms of craft culture, there are few visible people of color in coffee. Michelle Johnson, known as the Chocolate Barista, writes in a blog post, "I can comfortably claim that specialty coffee is a white man's world. All of my bosses have been white men; at competition, most of the judges and baristas are white men, and so are a majority of my guests when I'm working behind the bar." As Johnson concludes, "I recognize that for now specialty coffee is mostly a white man's game, but it doesn't have to be a racist one."

Instead of living up to the vibrant, unique histories that food and drink have to offer, craft culture's commitment to lifting itself away from its origins has made it monotonous and predictable. From product to product and industry to industry, artisanal quality seems to generate the same set of descriptions—small-batch, local, sustainable, vintage, heritage, farm-to-table, nose-to-tail, crop-to-cup—even though the point of consuming craft products is to enjoy something unique. The signifiers of craft have become so diluted that now even McDonald's proudly advertises its "signature crafted recipes." It's not so surprising then that the public is rediscovering its appreciation for and even pride in fast food, the common, and the gluttonous.

For craft culture to survive as more than an artful label or meaningless slogan, as something not synonymous with the Panera Breads and Blue Moons, it will need to take its own objectives seriously and embrace the stories behind the façade, the ones about individual people and specific histories and ongoing traditions. Otherwise it will succumb to the same cycle of alienation as the mass-produced culture it once stood against. Rather than look for the next picture-perfect face to head the trend, food culture would do well to look around and pass the mic to the people of color. Craft is only as white as the lies it tells itself.

BETH KOWITT

Where's the Beef?

FROM *Fortune*

IN AUGUST, ONE of Silicon Valley's hottest startups closed a $17 million round of funding. The Series A had attracted some of the biggest names in tech. "I got closed out because of Richard Branson and Bill Gates," bemoaned Jody Rasch, the managing trustee of an angel fund that wasn't able to buy in. Venture capital firm DFJ—which has backed the likes of Tesla and SpaceX—led the round, with one of its then partners calling the nascent company's work an "enormous technological shift."

The cutting-edge product the startup was trying to develop? Meat—the food whose more than $200 billion in U.S. sales has come to be the defining element of the Western diet. But what made this company's work so revolutionary was not what it was trying to make so much as how it was attempting to do it. Memphis Meats, the brainchild that had the startup-investor class salivating, was aiming to remove animals from the process of meat production altogether.

It's the type of world-saving vision that has oft captured the imagination of Silicon Valley—the kind of entrenched problem that technologists believe *only* technology can solve: feeding a fast-growing, protein-hungry global population in a way that doesn't blow up the planet. Conjuring up meat without livestock—whose emissions are responsible for 14.5 percent of global greenhouse gases —is core to that effort. Just listen to how the progenitor of Googleyness itself describes the prospect of animal-free meat: "It has the capability to transform how we view our world," Google cofounder Sergey Brin has said. "I like to look at technology opportunities where the technology seems like it's on the cusp of viability, and if it succeeds there, it can be really transformative."

Indeed, in the eyes of many Silicon Valley engineers, meat-making is a process that's so inefficient it's ripe for disruption. Animals, it seems, are lousy tools for converting matter into muscle tissue. Cows require a whopping 26 pounds of feed for every one pound of edible meat produced. In a culture obsessed with high performance, that is maddeningly wasteful.

So why not take them out of the equation? That's precisely what Memphis Meats and a cohort of other startups are trying to do. Memphis represents one possible path, called cellular agriculture, in which scientists are trying to grow what has become known as "cultured" or "clean" meat from animal cells. Others are trying to make plants taste like meat. The goal here is not to create your vegan cousin's Boca Burger of yore but instead a veggie patty that a hardcore carnivore wouldn't be ashamed to bring to a neighborhood barbecue. (In principle, anyway.) Companies in this camp include Beyond Meat and its rival Impossible Foods—which has raised an eye-popping $275 million from the likes of Gates and Khosla Ventures. These more convincing plant burgers can already be found in the meat aisle of mainstream grocery stores like Kroger and are on the menus of restaurants ranging from famed chef David Chang's Momofuku Nishi to TGI Fridays starting in January.

Both cellular ag and plant-based meat companies have the same goal—but their paths to get there couldn't be more different. The plant-burger boosters don't believe cultured meat will ever be able to scale; Memphis Meats and its brethren counter that plants—no matter what you do to them—will always taste like plants. But both groups share the same ultimate vision: to create the post-animal economy—a world free of consumer sacrifice, guilt, and compromise.

As a sign of the market's potential, alternative-meat producers point to the explosive growth plant-based milk has made in the dairy aisle, now capturing almost 10 percent of U.S. retail sales by volume. "I want to be able to say you don't have to make a choice in what you're eating," Memphis CEO and cofounder Uma Valeti says, "but you can make a choice on the process of how it goes to the table."

Hoping to make that choice easier, the new agripreneurs are tackling semantics first—redefining what *meat* means. Beyond

Meat CEO Ethan Brown says he'd like to get people to think about meat "in terms of its composition" rather than its origin. The reframing isn't just an epistemological one but also a scientific one, reducing meat to its molecules.

That won't be an easy sell, and the movement has its detractors —some of whom seem miffed by the notion that anyone would try to mess with Mother Nature. "They want to make up their own dictionary version of what meat is, and these are people who do not eat meat," says Suzanne Strassburger, whose family has been in the meat business for more than 150 years. "The real question is, are they feeding people or are they feeding egos?"

The $2,400 Meatball

Growing cells in petri dishes sounds like the stuff of science fiction, but the basic elements of the science are actually decades old. It's essentially the same process used in medicine to cultivate human cells and tissues. Memphis Meats' Valeti started thinking about growing meat when he was training as a cardiologist at the Mayo Clinic. Later, at his own practice in the Twin Cities, he began injecting stem cells into patients' hearts to regrow muscle after a heart attack.

The trouble is getting the economics to work for a hamburger, not a human heart. Memphis Meats created a cultured meatball that costs about $2,400 a pound to produce, and that was notable progress. The cost last year was $18,000 a pound—down from the more than $300,000 spent on the first cultured burger, made in 2013 by Dutch scientist Mark Post.

The biggest hurdle to lowering the cost is the cellular medium, the stuff the cells feed on. Mike Selden, CEO of Finless Foods, told me that this substrate contributed 99 percent of the cost of growing the company's first fish croquettes (price tag: $19,000 per pound). A critical part of the standard medium that works across animal cell types is fetal bovine serum (FBS), which is extracted from the heart of a calf fetus when its mother is pregnant at slaughter. One does not have to be an animal rights activist to see why this is not an acceptable option for the industry. As a result, much of the R&D focus right now is on finding an alternative. Selden says Finless has cut its FBS use down by half by reproducing the essential components of the serum through fermentation, and Memphis says it has come up with an FBS-free medium but won't reveal what it's using instead because it's proprietary.

But even if scientists forswear FBS, cultured meat may not be wholly acceptable to one group of potential customers—vegans —because the animal can never be completely removed from the process. Cultured-meat producers still have to source the first set of cells from an animal—even if it's just a small biopsy that doesn't require slaughter.

Post, however, says he's not trying to turn vegetarians and vegans into cultured-meat consumers anyway. In fact, he believes it would be counterproductive. "Eating a plant-based diet is always going to be more efficient," says the sixty-year-old entrepreneur.

Then why not forget the cell-culture route and try to make better burgers from the likes of peas and carrots? "We've seen plant-based products for forty years," he says, "but they are basically still substitutes that are very different from the real thing. We believe plant-based options alone are not going to make a big difference."

I never got to taste a meat product made from cellular agriculture—very few people ever have—because none are on the market. For one thing, there are significant regulatory challenges to getting them to grocery store shelves, and it's unclear how a manufacturer seeking approval would even proceed in this uncharted area of science. The FDA oversees products made through fermentation—a key process used in the biotech sector—but the USDA is responsible for regulating meat quality and safety. Vincent Sewalt, who works in regulatory compliance at DuPont, has said that if a company started the approval process today, it would take two years to get through in the very-best-case scenario.

Post has been working on cultured meat since 2008, now through his company MosaMeat, and his experiences over the past nine years have made him somewhat cynical about the hurdles to scaling. The challenges of finding an alternative to FBS, bringing costs down massively, speeding up cell growth, and finding an appropriate regulatory pathway have compounded one another. And there's another scientific roadblock too: getting the cells to adhere to a certain fixed structure—assuming, that is, that the aim is to produce more than ground chuck. Want your petri-dish animal cells to end up shaped like a porterhouse? Not so easy.

Post won't put a timeline on how long the quest to get to market will take, but during my reporting I heard people throw out dates ranging from next year to more than a decade hence. "Most of the companies are overly optimistic," Post says ruefully. "They're very idealistic." A few sources even spoke of cultured meat in the context of space exploration; we need this technology to colonize Mars, they contend. For nearly all of these scientists it has been hard not to get sucked into the grand notion that science can solve the world's big problems. "I wouldn't call myself an idealist," says Post, "but I'm driven by the societal impact this can have. I guess that is idealism."

There Will Be Blood

If scaling up is the limiting factor for cellular ag, the key challenge in making viable plant-based meat is more rudimentary: getting ingredients like sorghum to taste like sirloin. "There's no black-and-white path to creating the perfect plant-based burger," says Selden. Even if you can get a garden emulsion to look like meat, and even feel like meat in your mouth, it's a whole different animal, so to speak, to get it to taste like the real thing.

Beyond Meat's research takes place at a lab dubbed the Manhattan Beach Project, down the street from its headquarters in El Segundo, CA. "I wanted people to understand the global significance," says CEO Ethan Brown. "We have the brightest scientists and we're going to fund them at a level that this work deserves," he adds. "This is a global problem, not a culinary choice."

Beyond Meat is taking the proteins from plant matter and resetting their bonds using heating, cooling, and pressure, so they mimic animal muscle. "Why go through all the trouble of using the animal or any organism if you don't need to?" says Brown. "The animal is just taking all of that material from the plant and organizing it in a certain way."

Brown admits that his team still has a ways to go. "I'm more critical than others," he says, "and I say we're pretty far away." As a constant reminder of the work that still needs to be done, Brown has a poster hanging in his office that reads "Slightly better Tofurky"—a harsh line from a critic in 2015.

For anyone working on alternative meat, the first step is fully understanding what it is you are trying to replace—not just its taste and texture but why it makes that certain sound and changes color when it cooks, what one scientist described to me as the "theater of meat."

"We started out by basically asking how does meat do what it does —how does meat work," explains Pat Brown, CEO and founder of Impossible Foods (and no relation to plant-based-meat rival Ethan Brown). Pat Brown, a professor emeritus of biochemistry at Stanford, started by studying meat in the way a researcher would study disease. "You don't just say, I want to cure this cancer," he says. "You have to understand how normal cells work." He adds, "That's the way you solve a problem in biomedical research. And really that is not the mindset in the food world at all."

Impossible's breakthrough was in discovering that meat's essence comes from heme—the iron-rich molecule in blood that carries oxygen and is responsible for the deep-red color. Heme also exists in the roots of plants like legumes that turn nitrogen into fertilizer. Brown spent a little over a year thinking, incorrectly, that he could source heme by harvesting the root nodules of soybeans. But using the dirt-covered plants would be a food-safety disaster —and turning the soil to harvest them would release carbon into the atmosphere, creating the kind of negative impact on the environment Brown is trying to offset.

He again went back to his roots for an answer. Thirty years ago he engineered a bacterial strain to produce an HIV enzyme so he could study how it enables HIV to infect human cells. "That's the go-to move of a molecular biologist," he says. So several years ago he tried the same approach for producing heme. He took the plant gene for the protein and inserted it into yeast, then fed the modified yeast sugars and nutrients to stimulate fermentation. In that process, most of the yeast is filtered out, leaving behind heme.

At Impossible's lab just outside San Francisco I try heme in its pure form. It was far from delicious, with a metallic quality that tastes like the aftermath of biting down hard on your lip. Its flavors lingered for a long time in my mouth and oddly reminded me of soy sauce. A team of engineers was sorting out a production problem the day I visited, and their white lab coats, splattered with plant blood, made it appear like an especially horrific crime had just taken place. "This is not normal," apologizes Chris Davis, Impossible's director of R&D. Davis had been working on biofuels at a company in the same office park when he got a call from Brown five years ago. "I said, 'You do know what I do, right?'" Davis recalls telling him. Brown, says Davis, simply explained the "idea that the cow was just a technology to turn plants into something you want to eat."

Much of the work the R&D team focuses on is developing meat flavor, a minor fraction of which we perceive by way of our tongues and the rest via aroma. No single molecule makes up the smell of meat, so Impossible's scientists are trying to identify the hundreds of compounds involved. Davis walks me by its gas chromatography mass spectrometry system, which separates out those molecules as a slab of real meat is cooking. A young researcher sits by the machine marking down notes about the varying aromas. One recent tester, for example, had identified the scents of cilantro, Cheerios, plastic, and raw potato. (Yum.)

If heme is the Impossible Burger's blood, then coconut oil is its fat. Wheat protein and potato protein gel make up the meat's "muscle"—its sinewy fiber—and then gum gel is added to make the whole concoction moldable. The R&D team constantly plays with those ingredients to adjust smell and texture. A couple of times a day the team comes around with samples for employees to taste. That can sometimes hit a snag when they come around to Brown. The startup's founder is a notoriously slow taste tester. "He's been a vegan for so long that he doesn't actually do a very good job," Davis says. "He doesn't know what meat tastes like."

Davis says the best description of the company's first successful meat analog was rancid polenta. "It was still terrible," he says. "And yet it was so much better than anything we'd made to that point." The rule of the lab, explains Davis, is that "it's very bad manners to poison your friends, but you're allowed to make it taste bad."

In the food industry, companies traditionally don't launch a product until they think it's ready for prime time. But the likes of Impossible Foods and Beyond Meat are emulating the tech world by constantly rolling out improved versions—or, in Valleyspeak, "iterations."

Every major reformulation of the Impossible Burger gets named after a bird—anhinga, blue-footed booby, condor, dodo. The updates represent Brown's ultimate goal of making something superior to a cow rather than something identical to one. The effort is about far more than making a great burger, says Brown. "Our mission is to develop the technology that makes animals obsolete as a food-production technology," he tells me as we each chow down on an Impossible Burger—the version known internally as Oriole 2.0 —at New York's sleek Saxon + Parole restaurant.

But as it turns out, there's one rather important player who has some questions about the company's technology. And that's the FDA. While Impossible Foods doesn't need the agency's approval to market its burgers in the U.S., the company voluntarily asked the regulator to confirm the designation of the protein it uses to carry heme as something "generally recognized as safe," or GRAS. But the FDA responded with some follow-up questions instead. (In November 2015, Impossible withdrew its GRAS submission, but re-filed it this October with additional safety data.)

More troubling to some is that studies have shown that heme found in red meat facilitates the production of chemicals called N-nitroso-compounds, or NOCs, which have been shown to be carcinogenic. Davis, for his part, is not convinced by the science. "Right now there's good epidemiological data that eating meat is bad for you," he says. "That's pretty much clear. But which part of meat is causing that—the data just isn't there."

The Vegan Mafia

For some animal rights groups, the alt-meat effort marks a chance to finally make some progress on their ultimate aim. Or as Paul Shapiro, vice president of policy at the Humane Society of the United States and author of the forthcoming book *Clean Meat,* sums up: "It's possible that folks in this field might end up doing more good for animals than what I've done with my life."

While the movement may have persuaded industry to free some pigs from gestation crates and hens from cages, it has so far pretty much failed in the goal many view as paramount: getting people to stop killing and consuming animals. The percentage of people who identify as vegetarians in the U.S. has remained essentially unchanged over the past three decades. If mainstream Americans won't stop eating animal flesh for ethical reasons, suggest many animal rights advocates, then perhaps they will if they're given a tastier alternative. "Rather than presenting people with tradeoffs, we should focus on making new products that are better than the status quo in every way," says Kyle Vogt.

Vogt is part of what several people jokingly refer to as the Vegan Mafia, a group of wealthy investors whose main motivation is to remove animals from the food system. Like a surprisingly large number of millennials, it seems, Vogt in part got interested in animal welfare after binge-watching a series of Netflix documentaries on the topic. But unlike many others in his age cohort, Vogt sold his self-driving-car startup Cruise to General Motors for $1 billion in 2016—and therefore has the money to do something about it. He and his wife, Tracy Vogt, who opened a farm animal sanctuary, subsequently became vegan and invested in Memphis Meats. For him it's a straightforward thought experiment: for people living one hundred years from now, "what are they going to see that seems barbaric or abhorrent or just completely wrong?"

With Silicon Valley's dollars has also come impatience, say some. Post, of MosaMeat, who created the first hamburger from cultured animal cells in 2013 with backing from Google billionaire Brin, believes that some of his competitors have set unrealistic timelines to market in part because that's what tech investors want to hear. "The whole Silicon Valley rhythm is imposed on this development," Post tells me. "That may not be realistic, but part of the charm and myth of Silicon Valley is that nobody cares."

Its influence can also be seen in the language of the enterprise —one that casually refers to living creatures as protein conversion technologies. In the months I spent reporting this story, I heard those kinds of descriptions regularly. It was always jarring—and at times came across as a bit soulless.

"In most realms of human endeavor, technology is a positive thing," says Andras Forgacs, the forty-one-year-old cofounder and CEO of Modern Meadow, which operates on a nondescript campus in Nutley, NJ. "Food is the one realm where we're very suspicious about it." Early on, Modern Meadow decided to focus on leather materials rather than meat, because that's where it thought it could have the most impact. Forgacs also had some concerns about how long it would take a food product to get to market as well as consumer acceptance. All food involves technology, he explains, but the most established food companies don't want to call it that— they want to call it the art of cooking. Still, "if you want to attract investors and seem like you're the revolutionary new thing, you have to robe yourself in the language of technology," he says. "That doesn't necessarily appeal to consumers."

In one of the stranger ironies, what has given real credence to the alt-meat realm is Big Food's arrival on the scene. It's an odd turn of events. When legacy packaged food companies began gobbling up natural-food startups, the latter lost much of their street cred. But the opposite has happened with meat nouveau: Big Food's backing has helped validate the burgeoning industry.

The executives I spoke with at Tyson and Cargill, which have invested in Beyond Meat and Memphis Meats, respectively, laid out a future in which meat from animals, cultured meat, and plant-based meat all sit side by side in the supermarket. "To feed nine billion people we're going to need everybody," says Sonya McCullum Roberts, president of growth ventures at Cargill. "It's not a threat to us, it's an opportunity."

Not everybody in the alt-meat crowd is willing to partner with the big guys. Pat Brown, Impossible's CEO, can't imagine how his interests could possibly align with those of a meat producer. "Let's put it this way," he says. "I don't have any illusions about what would happen if one of those companies had any measure of control over us. They would not want us to completely replace their industry in fifteen years."

Says Cargill's Roberts, "I have heard some of those comments. And they hurt a little bit."

Passing the Smell Test

In October some three hundred people gather in a converted warehouse in Red Hook, Brooklyn, for the second annual New Harvest conference on cellular agriculture. As is typical of alt-meat confabs, the lunch is vegan. (And good luck finding any real milk for your coffee.)

Despite the niceties that come in an industry where everyone knows everyone else, there are still plenty of moments of discord. One clear point of angst is how candid the various startups are being with one another about the advancements of their technology. Scandal-plagued vegan mayo maker Hampton Creek had recently said it would have a cultured-meat product on the market next year, and questions abound about how realistic the pronouncement really is. Not very, seems to be the consensus. ("We aim to make our first commercial sale of a clean meat product by the end of 2018," the company said in a statement.)

One can sense another underlying tension in the way companies are describing their products in the first place. The battle lines seem drawn between the joys of weird science (which the techies cherish) and those who fear consumers will run from that.

Jesse Wolff of International Flavors and Fragrances is clearly in the first camp. He kicks off Day Two with a presentation that includes show and smell: He instructs us to open a vial that's been placed on the back of every chair and then take a whiff. Inside are sixty-two components that make up organic vegan roast chicken aroma, he says. There's a lot of science behind the flavor, he tells the crowd. (When I take the vial back to my office, most of my colleagues think it smells like Doritos.)

Two hours later, during a session called "Getting Cellular Agriculture into the Real World," Mary Haderlein, principal of Chicago consulting firm Hyde Park Group Food Innovation, alludes to the strangeness of an additive with more than five dozen ingredients in an era when shoppers say they want simplicity. There's a big push for fewer ingredients, unprocessed foods, and clean labels, she tells the same conference-goers. "And then on the other hand we have lab meat. Those are conflicting thoughts that have to come into focus."

Embodying this issue is the debate over what to even call meat made from cellular ag. The industry has landed on *clean meat,* after deciding that terms like *lab-grown meat, in vitro meat,* and *cultured meat* all have too much of an ick factor. But *clean meat* has its own baggage. For one thing, it has a different meaning to consumers who think of clean food as something free of artificial ingredients. "It seems like a weird term to attach to a bioengineered meat product," Haderlein tells me. But even more problematic is that *clean meat* suggests that the alternative—plain old regular meat—is dirty and wrong. "The term is offensive and insensitive to farmers," says Danielle Gould, founder and CEO of Food + Tech Connect, a resource hub and community for food entrepreneurs and investors. And making potential consumers feel demonized, judged, or guilty is unlikely to be an effective marketing strategy.

The veggie meat cohort is not immune to the tension. This summer the University of California at Berkeley launched an alt-meat lab for students to do plant-based food research. The program was so popular, it was expanded to accommodate about a dozen extra people. But the students rebelled after the first semester, disheartened by how many of the products had the same heavy formulation as processed foods. They wanted to change the current food system, not replicate it, says Ricardo San Martin, cochair for the new lab. Somehow making a burger, even one made of plants, didn't seem quite so innovative. "They were not convinced that this was the route they want to take," San Martin says. "They feel it fulfills their ethical concerns with animals, but it doesn't fulfill the kind of food they want to eat."

Over the course of reporting this story I asked pretty much everyone I talked to whether they were vegetarian or vegan. It was surprising to me how many of those engaged in this movement weren't. Post, of MosaMeat, said that he should be but that he wasn't. "There is something in us that makes it inherently difficult to take that step to a plant-based diet," he admits. "It feels like a step back. And something in me resists that." San Martin of the alt-meat lab offered that he feels horrible whenever he sees any information on the mistreatment of animals, "but when I go to the supermarket and eat ham, I don't see the connection. I just can't make it."

I felt their confusion. Most days I eat vegetarian, and I rarely eat any red meat at all. In fact, for months, as I've reported this story, I've been acutely aware of all the reasons why we probably shouldn't eat beef, chicken, or pork.

But in early November, as I was driving on the highway in Northern California, I saw an In-N-Out Burger up ahead. I pulled off the highway and gave in to the cognitive dissonance. It was the best hamburger I can remember.

In Good Hands

FROM *Afar*

MAYBE THE OIL STICK man had been here for twenty-five years, maybe thirty. The street vendors of Penang lose count after a while. That morning, every morning, the man kneaded and cut strips of dough, slipped them into roiling oil. They drifted for a moment, then puffed, floated, and bobbed golden brown. It was dark still, hours before people would come to this market for their vegetables or their live-but-not-for-long chickens.

Azalina Eusope was a little girl, five, six, or seven, watching the oil sticks pile up under a string of lights. She would ask her father, Muhammed, to buy her one of the fritters, chewy and soft and smelling deliciously of hot grease. Her parents had given her up to be raised by her grandparents, but her father tried to visit her every day. And so he would smile, buy her the oil stick, then shop for ingredients to stock his little noodle stall, a mile or so from here. Most of Air Itam Market is Chinese, which is to say not halal, and Azalina and her father are Muslims. They are Tamil-speaking Mamaks, Malaysians with roots in India. But Muhammed grew up in this neighborhood, spoke Hokkien Chinese, and always felt at home here. His specialty, *mamak mee*, is a stir-fried metaphor for his culture—Chinese noodles yellowed with turmeric common in Indian cooking, tossed with tofu, coconut fritters, and deliciously dank braised squid, then fired in a hot wok to absorb a sweet potato curry.

Like many Mamaks, Azalina came from a family of street vendors, four generations of them. But she was not going to be the fifth. No, she was going to be a doctor or a lawyer or a teacher, and have a title and respect. So she studied hard. She got A's in school, got into college, and got her hands on a scholarship application. It asked for her ethnicity. "You're a Mamak. You're not going to get anything," someone told her. She learned, though, that she *could* qualify for a scholarship if she did well in her first eighteen months of college, provided she could pay for them. She went to her family, all her aunts and uncles, to ask for money. No one offered.

"Nobody believed I could do it," Azalina told me. So, at fifteen, Azalina decided to leave behind mornings with her father, take a job as a cook in a hotel chain, and escape Malaysia, the home that didn't seem to want her.

She cooked her way around Asia in high-end pastry kitchens, sculpting desserts that were a world away from the street food her family made. After a few years she married an American and settled in San Francisco. Finally she was secure, had two darling children, and was miserable. "I didn't really speak English," Azalina says. "People saw me with my kids and thought I was their nanny. I was so lonely." So she stayed home, learned English by watching *Cheers, Friends,* and *The Jerry Springer Show,* and comforted herself by cooking the foods she remembered eating as a girl. It was odd, feeling homesick for the place she had worked so hard to leave, but the scents of pandan and star anise brought back memories of riding on her father's bicycle, of playing with her pets, of going to her family's spice farm, climbing into the trees when she wanted to cry by herself and be calmed by the taste of young peppercorns.

Then she and her husband separated and, unsure of how to support her children, she panicked. Again she went back to cooking. She drizzled turmeric batter out of perforated cups onto hot pans to make gorgeous, yolk-yellow nets called *roti jala.* She simmered curries to go with them. She packed it all in her car, set up a stall in a San Francisco farmers' market, and, fifteen years after leaving Malaysia, became the street vendor she had promised herself she would never be.

I met Azalina in the Bay Area in 2012. I remember a tiny woman smiling at me as she offered me a turnover. She turned away, hustling to fry more orders as the dish implanted itself in my brain. Crisp, curry-filled, and topped with blueberries, it was like nothing I'd ever tasted—she was marrying the flavors of her Malaysian youth with a California sensibility, creating a hand pie from local ingredients and memories formed halfway around the world, half her lifetime ago.

She told me her story, told me about her father, and we kept in touch; she always asked after my wife, and later my daughter, before regaling me with stories of Mamak culture. "Ten thousand, Francis. Ten thousand people came to my brother's wedding," I remember her saying. The weddings last for weeks, guests coming and going. That's how you learn to cook, in massive pots every family keeps for the occasion, she told me, eyes softening the way they do when you offer a friend a gift. Every wedding has a special color, and people, by the hundreds or thousands, descend on your village in waves of blue or green or pink or red. I imagined the sight, in love with just the thought of it. She told me these stories of the place she is from in a tone that never betrayed why she left it.

Then, a few years ago, her father passed. Azalina was heartbroken but couldn't bring herself to go back for his funeral. The ache was too intense: the sense of regret over leaving in the first place, the fear that she'd failed as a daughter. And yet the moment also awakened her. She realized, finally, that the distance from her life now to the life she once lived had grown too great. She wanted to reconnect to her past, to her heritage and to its flavors and dishes. "My grandmother is a hundred and nine years old, Francis," she told me. "Can you imagine how many stories she knows? Who will remember them? I want to remember them." It took her three years to finally face down her feelings of guilt, to know that she was ready to visit her father at his burial site. In that time, as she built her business and opened her restaurant, she heard stories from Penang, how it was changing, how street vendors were moving away, displaced by new shopping malls, how their kids didn't follow in their footsteps. She knew she needed to return to Penang, to taste the food again as it tastes there, to live for a while among those flavors, to remember and help preserve them before they went away. And so in 2016 she decided to go back to Malaysia, for the first time since she had started selling food on the street, since her memories of home had started to keep her afloat.

Azalina arrived in Penang a few days before I did and planned a trip full of visits with family and farmers, makers and markets, to take in the heat of coal-fired woks and the wisdom of elders. As soon as I walked out of the airport I smelled a sweet, tropical smell in the oil-thick air, smoky and fruity and rich. "Coconut husks," Azalina told me. She waved her hand toward the hills, where the sun was about to finish its set. "People in the villages burn them to keep the mosquitos away."

I filled my lungs with it. "It's amazing," I said, smiling, grateful to be here.

"Well, I'm glad *you* think it's amazing," Azalina said.

Azalina and her jolly-faced brother, Daus, wanted to make sure I had something to eat right away. We got in Daus's car, and soon I felt the terrible thrill of buzzing by men, women, and children on motorcycles to play kiss-kiss with oncoming traffic. He pulled into a roadside restaurant—really three walls and a roof—radiating fluorescent light and spicy smells to the world. It was just dark, but the buffet was already nearly empty after a throng of Ramadan fast-breakers had their way with the food. The curries were delicious, humming with cinnamon and lemongrass, reminding me how vibrant spices are when you're eating in the places that grow them. On the way out we walked past a booth of women in electric-red headscarves, their plates covering both the table and the empty seats between them as they laughed their way into the night.

The next morning Daus drove us up into the hills of Penang to see a durian farm; the owner, Song Hai, had been their father's best friend. In his mid-eighties, silver hair immaculately coiffed high on his forehead, he could have been the president of a small nation retired to the country. He greeted us warmly and took us up the steep slopes of his farm, pointing at nearly ripe rambutans, like sweet sea anemones on trees. As he talked, I looked over the property. It wasn't a farm in the way I'd imagined. There were no ordered rows, no carefully rotated crops, no obvious signs of people making the earth do their bidding. Instead Song Hai calls himself a mother to his trees and knows each one of them; he pointed to one, hundreds of feet away, and told us the year it started bearing fruit. Azalina marveled at his knowledge, and he smiled.

"My father used to take us up here on his bike," Azalina said. "We had to wear helmets in case the durians fell on our heads." She'd never thought much more of this than as a pleasant place to get away from the heat of the lowlands, but this visit felt full of metaphor and meaning. A durian tree grows for thirty years before it gives fruit; Song Hai is the fourth generation of his family to care for these trees. It's not clear if there will be a fifth.

Song Hai opened a durian for us. He apologized that it wasn't quite what he wanted it to be, insisting on opening another one, even as Azalina called out to him, "Uncle! Uncle!" to assure him it was perfectly delicious. Its flesh was so soft, like holding a banana pudding in your hands, a banana pudding that was hung over, possibly still drunk, and running with a rough crowd. Durians are famously pungent—you might say stinky—and I understood in that moment that they're not to be nibbled on. To really taste the creaminess, the sweetness, the mix of every tropical fruit you can think of rolled into one, you have to dive in, get it all under your nails, and commit to it. That's how it becomes a pleasure.

As we left, Song Hai told Azalina and Daus that it had been so good to see them, and they exchanged warm looks. Then he said to Azalina, directly, that she was missed when her father passed. He looked at his feet, avoiding her eyes, then turned and walked back up the slope.

Driving back to town, Azalina spotted some tables of fish, splayed open and drying in the sun. We stopped. The shopkeeper took us around back, where he and his wife shower salt onto small fish in massive primary-color tubs. "I love this work," the shopkeeper said, and when Azalina asked how his wife felt about it, he replied, "Well, she loves me, so she likes it too." The man was ninety years old, and the third generation of his family to preserve fish. There won't be a fourth, but you probably already guessed that. Azalina walked back to the car slowly. "Seeing these people doing this makes my heart bloom," she said. "But it makes me sad to know these things are going away."

I wondered, though, if there was another source of sadness. Back in San Francisco, Azalina's energy and smile were constant and kinetic, but here I could sense a distance, an interiority in her being. I thought back to that odd goodbye at Song Hai's farm. It turned out that her return to Penang hadn't been easy. As she told me stories about her father, as she revisited market stalls, she relived the memory of the last phone call she had with him, when they both realized that they would never see each other again. She described to me how her sense of guilt swelled. She struggled to explain to her family why there had been times when she couldn't send money back home to help, and they didn't understand why she didn't come back for her father's funeral. Her grandmother—

the grandmother she so wanted to see, whose stories she came back to hear and to commit to memory—was so upset she would barely speak to her, even as Azalina sat dutifully at her feet. When she and Daus took me to lunch one day, she didn't want to eat, nervous that people might see her and whisper that they saw her cheating during the daylight fast. Daus marched into the restaurant, scoped out the place, and gave an all-clear, but Azalina was still uncomfortable, feeling unsure and judged and watched. It's always hard to leave the place you call home. Sometimes it's harder to come back.

Still, with Ramadan drawing to a close, there was also much beauty as family drew nearer. A couple of nights before Hari Raya, the celebration that ends the month of fasting and repentance, Azalina invited over some aunts and uncles to memorialize her father in a ceremony of atonement and, she hoped, of closure. One, two, then eight and nine people came to Daus's house. There were so many salaams, so many hands kissed, foreheads touched, and suddenly twenty-five people were in the room. Some of the uncles began chanting, and soon the sound of four voices on four intertwining paths, praying for mercy and for those who've passed, met in harmony as they recited a long passage of the Koran.

And on Hari Raya, I followed Azalina as she paid visits to Auntie with the Coffee Cart, and then Spice Farm Caretaker Uncle, and then Uber Driver Uncle, and then and then and then, in a day of feasting and family. One of these uncles, Hamid, talked to me about the tradition of going from house to house, how this day is about letting bygones be bygones and starting a new year together. "If your family is broken up, you have nothing, *lah*," he said.

But bygones don't just go away. One night Azalina excused herself from the family. We went to the Gurney Drive hawker center, 12,000 square feet of food stalls lighting the night like a pinball machine. Azalina sighed, barely picking at the food. "Maybe it was my father that was the glue to tie me to this place," she said. "I try to cook the food that reminds me of my childhood. But I'm not a child, and I don't know who I am here anymore." She was thinking about cutting her trip short. It was a shock. Not just that the indefatigable Azalina suddenly seemed tired, but that it seemed she might be giving up on her own story, on capturing and saving the collective memory of this place.

Another night, at a different market, we got in line for a *char kway teow* vendor working a wok over a barrel of flaming coals. He sizzled rice noodles in lard, tossing in chili pastes, sweet Chinese sausage, and shrimp, adjusting the fire with a little electric fan clipped to his coal vent. The scent of pork fat bloomed with every order, mingling with the smoke, and I was tantalized. Azalina wasn't going to eat it, so she walked up and talked to the cook.

His name was Poon, he looked to be in his sixties, and he had been here for twenty years. But for nineteen and a quarter of them he was an assistant, chopping sausage and taking money. He got his big break on the wok only eight months ago, and he was trying to make good on his training, making this one dish over and over.

"Wait, he stood there for nineteen years to *get ready* to cook noodles?" I asked Azalina. She laughed, wryly. "This is why I can't be a cook here," she said. It was a joke, but she was right. Her father, Song Hai, the fish-drying man, Poon—they created this cuisine by putting the time in, generations' worth of time; by being situated and rooted; by always being the same person in the same place. She could never be that person.

But. That same night another auntie and uncle had taken us to dinner. There was a wait at the restaurant, so we went for a walk, coming to a rice paddy, the intense green pulsating, like breathing, in the breeze. We smelled that coconut-husk smoke, and Azalina's curiosity took over. How is this harvested? What varieties are for flour or for table rice? Her uncle showed her a sheaf of grass, and she pinched at the husk to reveal a tiny drop of milk and a speck of white. She tasted it and her uncle laughed. It was barely there, a half-formed grain of rice, but it was sweet, announcing the presence of calories, food, life.

Back at the restaurant, we ate a tripe salad—"village food," Azalina called it—warm and chewy, punchy with hot chilis, lemongrass, tomato, onion, salt, and tart *calamansi* juice. Azalina took a bite, then another, growing excited. She smiled, then looked into the distance, her cook's brain working. "I would skip the tomatoes. But add roasted peanuts, some ginger buds, and lots of herbs," she said, imagining the taste of this new dish as she spoke. "Yeah, that's how I would do it."

Listening to her describe this creation, I realized that Azalina may be cooking the food that reminds her of her childhood, but her food is of her present, of her imagination, and of the memories she chooses, not the memories she is saddled with. If, as the cliché goes, cooking is love, then some part of it must be about showing love for yourself, and the story about yourself that you want to tell. And the story of her food is not that she stayed in Malaysia and preserved the place through constancy and muscle memory, but that she left Malaysia and preserves its spirit, taking it with her across the world.

On the morning of my departure, so early it was still dark, Azalina took me to Air Itam Market. Uncle Hamid came as well, insisting he help see me off, even though he was visibly uncomfortable as we walked by several stalls where pigs hung, about to become pork. But that oil stick vendor was there. Maybe he'd been here for fifty-five years, maybe sixty. He was kneading and cutting strips of dough, slipping them into roiling oil. I watched the oil sticks pile up under a string of lights. I offered to buy one for Azalina. She looked at her purse-lipped uncle and demurred. But as we walked away, she turned to me and said, "It's okay, Francis. I'll come back for it later."

To Wash or Not to Wash?

FROM *Lucky Peach*

DID YOU GET a whiff of the chicken shitstorm of August 2013? It was a brief but intense controversy (complete with the #chicken-shitstorm hashtag, bestowed by Michael Ruhlman) over a USDA-funded public-relations campaign that warned against washing raw chicken before cooking. According to the Don't Wash Your Chicken! crusade, most of the raw poultry we buy is contaminated with infectious bacteria from the animals' guts, and washing splashes those bacteria all over the kitchen, where they can contaminate other foods and utensils and end up making us sick. In other words, raw chicken is too dirty to clean safely, so we should just slide it right from package to pan with whatever stale fluids and smells come with it, kill the bacteria with the heat of cooking —and enjoy!

The initial PR blast included a press release, a YouTube "Germ-Vision Animation" that simulated toxic chicken splatter in ghoulish fluorescent green, and four short Don't Wash Your Chicken! videos and photo novellas, in which unwitting cooks were schooled and saved from washing just before they made their roast or oven-fry or stir-fry or mole. The blast had its intended effect and kicked up plenty of media gusts. NPR: "Julia Child Was Wrong: Don't Wash Your Raw Chicken, Folks." *Slate:* "Don't Wash Your Chicken! No Matter What Your Cookbook Says." *Gizmodo:* "Science Says Not to Wash Your Chicken Before You Cook It."

These feature stories then provoked social-media winds of apocalyptic force—but in the opposite direction. Alton Brown tweeted to his (at the time) 625,000 Twitter followers a series of Post-it instructions for safe chicken preparation: after washing gently, "douse house with accelerant," "burn down house to kill germs," and "take off and nuke the entire site from orbit." On Ruhlman's website there was a post called "Bacteria! Run Away! Run Away!"

Then an eerie calm set in. There was a follow-up "Don't Panic!" blog post from NPR and some backpedaling from the chief campaigner. As the post paraphrased Drexel University nutrition-sciences professor Dr. Jennifer Quinlan, "If you rinse your chicken out of safety concerns, just stop," she says, "because you are making it less safe. If you are doing it to enhance flavor, that's fine, but use proper precautions." This clarification, that the real problem with washing chicken is the cook's misconceived motivation for washing, suggested that the campaign motto should have been Don't Wash Your Chicken for the Wrong Reasons!

The storm passed, but without really clearing the air. Many cooks, myself included, continue to rinse chickens of old fluids and smells, to soak them in flavorful brines, massage them with butter, stuff them with herbs, and otherwise brave their bacterial load in the pursuit of deliciousness. Food-safety professionals continue to publish reports that categorize poultry washing as a food-safety "mistake." And some have gone so far as to imply the possibility of combating public violations with lawsuits.

For a study published in the November–December 2016 issue of *Food Protection Trends,* researchers at the USDA and UC Davis scrutinized four popular TV food shows and their hosts, by name. The researchers logged the purported violations committed on camera, which included not washing hands, not washing cutting boards, licking fingers, and washing—or even mentioning the washing of—meat or poultry. Noting first that food companies are increasingly likely to be held liable for causing illness and deaths, the study concludes: "In the future, will cooking programs also be held responsible if they fail to model safe-handling practices?" There's a food trend to follow!

That ominous escalation got me to wondering about a couple of things. First, what evidence is there that washing chickens is a significant threat to public health? And then, to turn the study's concluding sentence around, should food-safety programs be held responsible if they fail to generate confidence and respect for their guidelines?

The evidence against chicken washing—what Science really has to say about it—turns out to be practically nonexistent. I scoured the food-safety literature for any studies of meat-washing splatter and its contribution to the risk of foodborne illness. I found not a single peer-reviewed study—just one 2003 report from Campden BRI, an independent British food-research consortium, with the title "Microbiological risk factors associated with the domestic handling of meat." To analyze the risk posed by washing, the authors covered the work surfaces around a sink with paper, coated a chicken with red food dye, washed the chicken for ten seconds, and noted that red spots appeared on the paper as far as 70 centimeters, more than 2 feet, from the sink.

That's it! The report includes no actual microbiology to see whether splashing water picks up bacteria and carries them in significant numbers—a real question, since half of the argument against washing is that it *doesn't* remove significant numbers of bacteria from foods. Nor does it estimate the risk splashing might pose compared to less ambiguous hazards, like handling a leaky supermarket package of raw meat, or not washing hands diligently during cooking, or using the same towel to dry clean hands and not-so-clean countertops.

To make sure that I wasn't missing something, I checked with half a dozen food-safety professionals. They generously responded with links, reports, and USDA information sheets—all of which assert the risk of washing meats but don't cite an actual study of the risk. Dr. Donald Schaffner, a professor at Rutgers, agreed that "definitive peer-reviewed data do not seem to exist."

And I wasn't entirely convinced by that Campden BRI report. As a longtime chicken-washer, I found it hard to believe that the water flies 2 feet from the sink. So I replicated that simulation in my own kitchen. I calibrated the flow rate from my faucet to match the report's moderate 35 milliliters (about 2 tablespoons) per second, and put the chicken under the stream.

I did see some splashing outside the sink, but only when I held the chicken high up, almost level with the countertop, and put the faucet on spray mode so that its flow was accelerated through a couple dozen small holes. I also felt that splashing. I was standing less than a foot away from the bird, so of course my paper-coated shirt got wet with chicken rinse. Disgusting! When I did what I usually do, put the chicken on a plate at the bottom of the sink and let the water flow normally, there was no discernible splatter on the countertops or me.

My unsurprising conclusion: it's possible to wash chicken carelessly, in a way that might spread contamination onto countertops and draining boards and the cook. It's also possible to wash chicken carefully, in a way that confines its microbes largely to the sink, where other unclean things also get cleaned.

And the same is true for those other unclean things. Everything that goes into the sink, and the sink itself, can be washed carelessly or carefully. That includes hands, cutting boards, utensils, and scrubbing pads. It includes the vegetables and fruits that the food-safety pros say we *should* wash, and that are reported to be responsible for about as many annual cases of foodborne illness as meat and poultry.

It seems to me that instead of discouraging the laudable general impulse to start cooking with clean ingredients and creating dubious categories of the should-be-washed and the unwashable, it makes much more sense to define and encourage careful washing and sink-faucet-towel work in general. And to do the definitive experiments to clarify what the real risks are and what the best practices would be. As Dr. Schaffner at Rutgers wrote to me when he couldn't find any studies of washing, "This is a research opportunity." A big one!

The Don't Wash Your Chicken! storm offers another kind of opportunity, an obvious occasion for the food-safety community to reevaluate the way it approaches its mission. The PR campaign garnered a lot of media play and views for its videos. But it also got spectacular blowback from respected figures with millions of followers in the cooking world. Inviting that kind of mockery and then backpedaling on the message only deepens confusion and doubt about food safety and diminishes the credibility of its authorities. Nor is their image likely to be improved by sitting in judgment of popular food personalities and hinting at legal action.

We absolutely do need credible sources of information—and good practical advice. Foodborne illness kills thousands of people every year, and neither the food industry nor the USDA is doing all it could and should to make the food supply cleaner. If you're not especially concerned about this, take a look at Lynne Terry's award-winning 2015 report "A Game of Chicken" in the *Oregonian*. During her investigation of several salmonella outbreaks over several years, all cases traced back to Foster Farms. In a follow-up to the story, she asked an Oregon epidemiologist for his advice on cooking chicken, and his answer was, "Treat it like hazardous waste."

Sure, it's a challenge to convince home cooks to keep invisible hazards in mind, or change daily habits, or correct misconceptions. That makes strategy especially important. Here are a few moves that have proved to be counterproductive: Misrepresent very preliminary science as settled scary fact. Discourage behavior that's rooted in an instinct for cleanliness. Caricature what cooks actually do. Make strong statements and then mostly retract them. Provoke ridicule from leaders in the community you're trying to influence.

What might be a more productive path? It seems pretty obvious: engage with people who actually cook.

The safety pros should take a break from the echo chamber of technical conferences and journals to spend time with cooking pros, chefs, and Ruhlmans and Browns. They should visit the country's best kitchens not to log violations but to listen and learn, to understand why cooks handle food the way they do, how they think and feel about making tasty and attractive and wholesome things with their hands. They should invite collaboration on coherent, workable guidelines that the culinary pros can actually recommend to their communities.

One expert I particularly admire for his critical approach to safety guidelines wrote to me apropos of unnecessary and risky handling, saying that "the home cook sees the leftover innards of the chicken and thinks that they have to be removed . . . There really is no reason to remove the intestinal organs as a part of preparing the chicken/poultry for cooking." This may be true from a strictly hygienic and nutritional point of view. But from that point of view, there's no reason for most of the things that cooks do!

Cooks may remove the innards from a chicken because they're in an inedible bag, or because they hate innards, or because they love them and want to cook them perfectly. They go to the trouble of washing chickens, brining and massaging and stuffing them and tying them up, because they seek not just to detoxify foods but to make them as delicious as they can be. Cooks have their own good reasons, and most eaters are glad they do.

Born in the USA: The Rise and Triumph of Asian-American Cuisine

FROM *T Magazine*

ON THE PLATE, the egg looks like an eye plucked from a baby dragon. The yolk is the green-black of smoked glass, with a gray, nearly calcified halo, trapped in an oval of wobbling amber and emitting the faintest whiff of brimstone.

So begins the $285, nineteen-course tasting menu at Benu in San Francisco. The egg is a traditional Chinese snack, often called (poetically, if inaccurately) a thousand-year-old egg, preserved for a few weeks or months in lye or slaked lime, salt, and tea. It's sold by street vendors, tossed into stir-fries, and scattered over congee throughout China, parts of Southeast Asia, and the world's China-towns. To more than a billion people, it is an utterly commonplace food.

But to present it as an amuse-bouche at one of the most ac-claimed fine-dining restaurants in the United States, to a predom-inantly non-Asian clientele, is radical. For despite America's long, complicated love affair with Asian cooking, it is hard to imagine such a food, so alien to Western culinary ideals in appearance, aroma, flavor, and texture, being served in this kind of setting, let alone embraced, a decade ago.

This, though, is the new American palate. As a nation we were once beholden to the Old World traditions of early settlers; we now crave ingredients from farther shores. The briny rush of soy; gin-ger's low burn; pickled cabbage with that heady funk so close to rot. Vinegar applied to everything. Fish sauce like the underbelly of the sea. Palm sugar, velvet to cane sugar's silk. Coconut milk slowing the tongue. Smoky black cardamom with its menthol aftermath. Sichuan peppercorns that paralyze the lips and turn speech to a burr, and Thai bird chilies that immolate everything they touch. Fat rice grains that cling, that you can scoop up with your hands. (As a child raised in a Filipino-American household, I was bewildered by commercials for Uncle Ben's rice that promised grains that were "separate, not sticky," as if that were a good thing.)

These are American ingredients now, part of a movement in cooking that often gets filed under the melting-pot, free-for-all category of New American cuisine. But it's more specific than that: this is food born of a particular diaspora, made by chefs who are "third culture kids," heirs to both their parents' culture and the one they were raised in and thus forced to create their own.

Could we call it Asian-American cuisine? The term is problematic, subsuming countries across a vast region with no shared language or single unifying religion. It elides numerous divides: city and countryside, aristocrats and laborers, colonizers and colonized — "fancy Asian" and "jungle Asian," as the comedian Ali Wong puts it. (She's speaking specifically of East and Southeast Asians, who followed similar patterns of immigration to the U.S. and who are the primary focus of this piece.) As a yoke of two origins, it can also be read as an impugning of loyalties and as a code for "less than fully American." When I asked American chefs of Asian heritage whether their cooking could be considered Asian-American cuisine, there was always a pause, and sometimes a sigh.

But this is what happens in America: borders blur. When there aren't many of you—Americans of Asian descent are only 6 percent of the population, a legacy of decades of immigration quotas and denial of citizenship—you find common cause with your neighbors. The term *Asian-American* was not imposed on us, like *Yellow Peril* in the late nineteenth century, or *Oriental;* it was coined in the 1960s by Yuji Ichioka, a California-born historian and civil rights activist, to give us a political voice. If we call this kind of cooking *just* American, something is lost.

The rise of contemporary Asian-American cuisine began with Korean-American chef David Chang's Momofuku Noodle Bar, which opened in New York in 2004 and was followed four years later by fellow Korean-American chef Roy Choi's Kogi BBQ truck in Los Angeles. Their approach to cooking is typically, reductively framed as an East-meets-West marriage of big flavors and elevated (i.e., French) technique—as if every Asian cuisine were hell-bent on storming the palate (some, like Cantonese, are in fact renowned for their subtlety); as if culinary refinement were proprietary to the West.

But the history of Asian-American cuisine goes further back than that, to the first tearooms and banquet halls set up by Chinese immigrants who came to seek their fortune in Gold Rush California in the 1850s. By the end of the nineteenth century, despite Congress's passage of the Chinese Exclusion Act in 1882 and attempts to condemn San Francisco's Chinatown as a threat to the American way of life—"in their quarters all civilization of the white race ceases," declared a pamphlet published by the Workingmen's Party of California in 1880—Cantonese restaurants were all the rage in New York. The food was cheap and fast, swiftly stir-fried in woks, a technique that remained a mystery for decades to most in the West. (One journalist, touring a Chinatown kitchen in 1880, did wonder if "the funny little things we saw at the bottom of a deep earthen jar were rat's-tails skinned.")

When outsiders came flocking in the 1890s, Chinese chefs altered and invented dishes to please them. This was less concession than calculation, capitalizing on opportunity. The work of immigrants—in food as in the arts—has always been dogged by accusations of impurity and inauthenticity, suggesting that there is one standard, preserved in amber, for what a dish should be or what a writer or artist with roots in another country should have to say. It's a specious argument, as if being born into a culture were insufficient bona fides to speak of it. (Immigrants are always being asked to show their papers, in more ways than one.) The history of food, like the history of man, is a series of adaptations, to environment and circumstance. Recipes aren't static. Immigrant cooks, often living in poverty, have always made do with what's on hand, like the Japanese-Americans rounded up and shipped to internment camps during the Second World War, who improvised rice balls with rations of Spam, and the Korean- and Filipino-Americans who, having survived on canned goods in the aftermath of war, eked out household budgets by deploying hot dogs in kimbap and banana-ketchup spaghetti.

Sometimes the nostalgia for this kind of food can be difficult to convey to those who don't share the same history. At Bad Saint, a Filipino restaurant in Washington, DC, the chef Tom Cunanan makes adobo with pig tails, a cheap, snubbed part of the animal that was treasured by Depression-era Filipino immigrants working in California labor camps. Diep Tran, the Vietnamese-American chef of Good Girl Dinette in Los Angeles, told me that she wishes she could serve a breakfast of nothing but baguette accompanied by condensed milk diluted with hot water, for dipping. "It's refugee food," she said. "Proustian, kind of like Spam. But people get upset; they think they're being ripped off."

Almost every Asian-American chef I spoke to—most of whom are in their late twenties to early forties—came to the U.S. as children or were born to parents who were immigrants. (In 1952 the last racial barriers to naturalization were lifted, and in 1965 immigration quotas based on national origin—for Asia, 100 visas per country per year—were abolished.) Almost all had stories of neighbors alarmed by the smells from their families' kitchens or classmates recoiling from their lunchboxes. "I was that kid with farty-smelling food," said Jonathan Wu, the Chinese-American chef at Nom Wah Tu in New York. "I still feel that, if I'm taking the train with garlic chives in my bag."

So these chefs' cooking, born of shame, rebellion, and reconciliation, is not some wistful ode to an imperfectly remembered or never-known, idealized country. It's a mixture of nostalgia and resilience. It wasn't taught—certainly not in the way other cuisines have been traditionally taught. Graduates of the Culinary Institute of America in Hyde Park, NY, recalled that little time was devoted to Asian cooking; at Le Cordon Bleu in London and in Paris, none. One instructor took offense when Preeti Mistry, whose Indian-inflected restaurants include Juhu Beach Club in Oakland, CA, likened a French stew to curry. Another told David Chang that pork stock, essential to tonkotsu ramen, was "disgusting."

Neither does their cooking have much kinship with the "fusion" cuisine of the early 1990s, when non-Asian chefs like Jean-Georges Vongerichten and Gray Kunz began folding Eastern ingredients into otherwise Western dishes. (*Fusion* is another term that sits uneasily with Asian-American chefs. "I wouldn't call myself fusion," said Maiko Kyogoku, the owner of the idiosyncratic Bessou in New York. "To describe food that way? It's an extension of myself.") In spirit, Asian-American cooking is closer to other American-born cuisines with tangled roots: the Lowcountry cooking of coastal South Carolina, which owes a debt to slaves from West Africa who brought over one-pot stews and ingredients like okra, peanuts, and black-eyed peas; and Tex-Mex, which is not a bastardization of Mexican food but a regional variant of it, cultivated by Tejanos, descendants of Hispanics who lived in Texas when it was part of Mexico and, before that, New Spain.

There's also no one cultural touchstone or trauma that binds Asian immigrants: no event on a national scale that has brought us together. But part of what distinguishes our experience from that of other immigrants and people of color is the fraught, intimate relationship between our countries of origin and the U.S., which has been foe and protector, oppressor and liberator, feared and adored. In 1899 the British writer Rudyard Kipling urged the U.S. to "take up the White Man's burden" in the Philippines after the Spanish-American War:

> Go send your sons to exile
> To serve your captives' need
> . . . Your new-caught, sullen peoples,
> Half devil and half child.

This begot more than a century of American military intervention in East and Southeast Asia and a history of conflicting images: Pearl Harbor and Hiroshima; the Vietcong in black pajamas and the American atrocities at My Lai; teeming refugee camps and smiling American GIs handing out candy, decade after decade, to throngs of dark-haired, starving children.

Any immigrant is an outsider at first. But for Asians in America, there is a starker sense of otherness. We don't fit into the American binary of white and black. We have been the enemy, the subjugated, the "lesser" peoples whose scramble for a foothold in society was historically seen as a menace to the American order. And yet we've also been the "good" immigrants, proving ourselves worthy of American beneficence—polite, humble, grateful, willing to work twenty-hour days running a grocery store or a laundry or a restaurant that will never be "authentic" enough, to spend every dime on our children's test prep so that they get into the best schools, because we believe in the promise of America, that if you work hard, you can become anyone. If you try hard enough, you might even be mistaken for white.

Among the children of immigrants, Asians in America seem

most caught in a state of limbo: no longer beholden to their parents' countries of origin but still grasping for a role in the American narrative. There is a unique foreignness that persists, despite the presence of Asians on American soil for more than two centuries; none of us, no matter how bald our American accent, has gone through life without being asked, "Where are you from? I mean, originally?" But while this can lead to alienation, it can also have a liberating effect. When you are raised in two cultures at once —when people see in you two heritages at odds, unresolved, in abeyance—you learn to shift at will between them. You may never feel like you quite belong in either, but neither are you fully constrained. The acute awareness of borders (culinary as well as cultural) that both enclose and exclude, allows, paradoxically, a claim to borderlessness, taking freely from both sides to forge something new. For Asian-American chefs, this seesaw between the obligations of inheritance and the thrill of go-it-aloneness, between respecting your ancestors and lighting out for the hills, manifests in dishes that arguably could come only from minds fluent in two ways of life.

Thus the *kaiseki* at Niki Nakayama's n/naka, in Los Angeles, always includes a pasta course. Her slyly voluptuous "carbonara" of abalone livers and egg yolks is a homage to Tokyo-style wafu spaghetti with briny pickled cod roe—only here it's capped with shaved truffles. At Tao Yuan, in Brunswick, ME, Cara Stadler takes tiles of goat cheese made by a local creamery and sears them, as is done in Yunnan, to approximate *rubing*, a sturdy farmer's cheese. But instead of merely sprinkling the cheese with sugar or salt, she counters its meatiness with a bright grace note of mint and watermelon from summer's height. A Caesar salad might be supplanted by a canoe of romaine, grilled for a hint of smoke, and loaded with dainty *jako* (dried baby sardines) and quail eggs as anchors, as at Bessou in New York. Or, as reenvisioned by Chris Kajioka at Senia, in Honolulu, it might be a mossy cliff of charred cabbage —a wink at an iceberg wedge—dusted with *shio kombu* (shredded kelp boiled in soy and mirin), soaked through with dashi and ginger, and surrounded by daubs of heady green goddess dressing and buttermilk turned to gel. It's not so much a salad as a cheeky biography of it by the barbarian at the gates, achieving the quintessence of an American classic through Asian ingredients.

And while Asian-American cooking may not be expressed in or

identified by a single set of flavors, one thing that does unite such disparate traditions is an emphasis on textures. Indeed, if the cuisine can be said to have revolutionized American food, it's by introducing unfamiliar mouthfeels—crackle where one doesn't expect it, slime in a country that's always shied away from that sensation —into our culinary vocabulary. Justin Yu, who recently opened Theodore Rex in Houston, rhapsodizes about "the crunch that you can hear in the back of your head"; unrendered, gelatinous animal skin, "a fun burst of fat and softness"; broths barely skimmed, or with a spoonful of fat added "to coat the lips." The maverick Katsuya Fukushima, of Daikaya in Washington, DC, once turned *natto* —a gooey, slippery skein of fermented soybeans, with the perfume of castoff socks—into an earthy caramel over soft-serve. Like Latin American food, which made Americans crave heat, Asian-American cuisine has made "difficult" textures not only desirable but as integral to food as flavor itself. That certain ingredients still make some Western diners squeamish is part of its provocative fun.

But the question remains: does calling this kind of cooking Asian-American cuisine deepen and contextualize our understanding of it, or is it just a label, like speaking of Asian-American art or fiction—a way of simplifying a complex story and making it a marketable cliché? The danger is fetishizing Asian features, a tendency that diminishes: if you are an exotic object or phenomenon, you may never become recognized or acknowledged as more. "White chefs are using these ingredients and saying, 'Oh, it's so strange,'" Tin Vuong, of Little Sister in Los Angeles, said. "It isn't." Instead of a historical matrix of Asian culinary traditions, "young cooks just see a big pantry," Fukushima said. "Take a little bit of this, a little bit of that—there's no soul to it."

Chang believes that food "has the potential to sort of show that we're all the same." But even he isn't entirely comfortable with the ubiquity of kimchi. "Let's say you spent no time in Asia, you just found a recipe on YouTube," he said. "That's appropriation. It's not about skin color. You have to have a story, pay respect to what it was and what it means." At the same time, it seems reductive to expect Asian-American chefs to make food that somehow reflects their personal "story." On season three of *Top Chef*, Hung Huynh, a Vietnamese-American contestant, was faulted for cooking that was technically dazzling but lacked explicit reference to his roots. "You were born in Vietnam," Tom Colicchio, the head judge, said.

"I don't see any of that in your food." (It's hard not to hear an echo of the trope of the inscrutable Oriental, whose motives can't be deciphered, and the common criticism of Asian-Americans at school and at work as being overly cerebral and lacking feeling.) The strictures of reality TV do demand a baring of the soul, but not all Asian-American chefs want to work with Asian flavors—and when they do, it's not always in expected ways.

Must every Italian chef make lasagna, every French chef coq au vin? Anita Lo, who closed her fine-dining restaurant Annisa in New York earlier this year, cooked there for seventeen years without fealty to one region or cultural tradition. This puzzled some diners. "I had someone come in and say, 'Where's the big Buddha head?'" she said. When publications request recipes and she submits one without Asian ingredients, the response is often, "We were really hoping for something Asian"—or Asian-ish: anything with soy, apparently, will do. "I send in Japanese, which isn't even my background, but that works," she said.

Corey Lee's *Benu* cookbook is filled with stories: of his grandmother foraging for acorns; of his mother forcing him to drink a tonic of brewed deer's antlers; of his father bringing home live lobster for his son's birthday; and of the joys of eating tomalley (the wet gray-green paste that acts as a lobster's liver and pancreas) on buttered bread. All suggest that Lee's dishes, however rarefied, are also deeply autobiographical. But Lee demurs, the way a novelist might, fending off a critic's attempt to find in his books correlations to actual events, wanting them to stand alone as fully imagined works of art. "There's great pressure for chefs to have a story," he said. "Maybe there's no story beyond 'I want to serve this food and it tastes good.'"

It's the eternal plea of the minority, to ask to be judged not by one's appearance or the rituals of one's forebears but for the quality of one's mind and powers of invention. Certainly our country was predicated on the right to shed one's past and be reborn, to come from nothing and work your way up; in this, Asians may be among the most American of Americans. But why is the choice always between exotic caricature and rootlessness? The philosopher Slavoj Žižek argues that the embrace of "ethnic" restaurants is merely "tolerance" of a "folklorist Other deprived of its substance": "The 'real Other' is by definition 'patriarchal,' 'violent,' never the Other of ethereal wisdom and charming customs." Too often

Asian-American chefs are presumed to double as educators or ambassadors, representing an entire race, culture, or cuisine.

In the end, doesn't it matter—not to others, but to ourselves—where we are from? And no, I don't mean "originally." I mean the forces that made us: the immigrants who raised us, with all their burdens and expectations, their exhortations to fit in but never forget who we are; and the country we grew up in, which is our only home, which taught us we are "other" but also seems, in some confused, tentative way, to want to learn something from us.

For Asian-American chefs, this is the conundrum, and the opportunity. The foods of their childhoods were once mocked and rejected by their non-Asian peers (and by their ashamed or rebellious younger selves), then accepted in dilute, placating form, and now are able to command audiences who clamor for their sensations and aggressive flavors and who might be unnerved if they knew exactly what they were putting in their mouths. What may be most radical about Asian-American cuisine is the attitude that informs and powers it, reflecting a new cockiness in a population that has historically kept quiet and been encouraged to lay low. It's food that celebrates crunchy cartilage and gelatinous ooze, that openly stinks, that declares, *This is what I like to eat. What about you? Do you dare?*

Who Owns Uncle Ben?

FROM *The Bitter Southerner*

Take a pint of rice well picked and clean'd. Set on a sauce-pann [*sic*] with one gallon of water and a handful of salt, when the water boils put in the rice, about a quarter of an hour will boil it enough according to the quickness of the fire or by tasting it; but be sure to avoid stiring [*sic*] the rice after 'tis in the saucepan for one turn with a spoon will spoil all.
—Rect. Book No: 2, Eliza Pinckney, 1756

"DON'T STIR THE pot," said Nana.

Crowded together at the stovetop in her Queens Village apartment, my grandmother grabbed my hand away from the rice spoon. Her narrow kitchen contained an enamel sink, gas oven, and a Coldspot refrigerator stuffed with the mystery scraps that elderly women can't bear to throw out, a sign of lifelong frugality or early-stage dementia, both possibilities that wouldn't occur to me as a rude teenager who showed up occasionally to abuse her generosity—a quiet bedroom to myself, hot meals, season tickets to the opera—and in return would clean out the frost-crusted liver pudding, half-eaten bowls of grits, mold-crusted jars of improperly sealed pepper jelly. But I also never stayed long, because, this being the late 1970s, our conversations were haunted by uncomfortable truths about our family history.

"Please don't bring your friends around."
I stared at her, confused. She sounded afraid.

"I mean those people who work with you."
Counselors at a summer camp for disadvantaged inner-city youth.

Her beliefs held steadfast through the civil rights era: My grand-mother was raised on one of the sea islands near Charleston by parents who lived through the Civil War and passed their complicated attitudes to the next generation. After witnessing battles over racism, over religion, over politics, all over the turkey and greasy gravy at Thanksgiving gatherings in her apartment with my slightly more progressive parents, who passed their attitudes onward as well, I had learned to simply let Nana show me how to cook rice properly.

She preferred Uncle Ben's Converted.

Yeah, I know.

Like White on Rice

Q: What do Charlestonians and the Chinese have in common?
A: They eat rice every day and worship their ancestors.

My people are rice eaters. Marry into my family a potato or pasta eater and we will convert you. To brown rice, red rice, basmati and jasmine, Forbidden rice, Arborio, and yes, even commercial brands of white rice like Uncle Ben's.

But here's the issue. The roots of rice in the South have always troubled me. The story begins on fertile coastlands that belonged to ancestors who first settled there over three hundred years ago. My grandmother, Lydia Alta Anderson Mitchell, was born in 1893, one of seven daughters whose father was a storekeeper and circuit court judge. He managed to send them all to college in an era when many southern women didn't have that opportunity. They were beautiful, funny, elitist, stubborn, both vengeful and loyal. Their collective nickname: the Queens of Edisto.

My grandfather was Nana's childhood sweetheart, a neighboring farmer's son with artistic aspirations, by all accounts a charming rascal who hauled her north during the 1920s. When he died of an aneurysm in the middle of the Depression, Nana was left to raise their three sons alone on a teacher's salary, and despite the urging of her family, never remarried or moved back home; but she always put food from home on the table, boiling hog heads in that little kitchen, diligently pouring bourbon on fruitcakes kept in a hallway closet, preserving pumpkins, Jerusalem artichokes, watermelon rinds, serving age-old dishes based on rice raised with blood, sweat, and tears. Without her cooking I would not have such a strong connection to my culinary legacy or the desire to rectify it. Over the past year, on multiple trips to Charleston and beyond, I talked to others wrestling with the same issue, around the time when a white supremacist was on trial for murdering nine AME parishioners and a Black Lives Matter activist was arrested for tackling a Secessionist Party protester waving the Confederate battle flag.

First, a history lesson.

Rice is fundamental to the Carolina Lowcountry kitchen, where the pot contains ingredients introduced from West African, French Huguenot, and Caribbean Creole cultures, where Senegambian *jollof* turned into red rice and Parisian *beignets de riz* became calas and johnnycake. While imported grain established rice as a cash crop on the southern Atlantic coast as early as the late 1600s, a farmer named Hezekiah Mayham in 1786 planted the first documented field of the subtropical japonica that would eventually be called Carolina Gold.

No one is exactly sure where it came from — the origin story of this "gold seed" is one of those quandaries that still give food historians and geneticists heartburn. (Scientists may be getting closer to cracking the genomic mystery, curiously enough, by tracing funeral practices involving rice that traveled from the Tana Taraja region in South Sulawesi to Madagascar.) The name not only derives from the hue of the grain as it ripens but also references the fortunes created as the demand grew for the starchy new variety. Cookbooks, plantation diaries, and oral histories document the profound influence of this crop on the Lowcountry. The wealthiest planters slept in Chippendale-style mahogany or cherry four-poster beds carved with panicles of rice. A long-handled silver spoon originally used in England for serving stuffing became a treasured heirloom on Charleston sideboards when placed next to bowls of rice instead. The spoons are still in demand. A cousin gave me one as a wedding gift.

Sarah Rutledge's *The Carolina Housewife* (1847), published at the height of antebellum rice culture, contains recipes for every meal, including rice crumpets, rice sponge cake, rice waffles, rice flummery, rice blancmange. Her golden-crusted rice casseroles echo the masterpieces of Carême, in particular his Casserole au Riz à la

Moderne; her pilau traces the journey of that most fragrant dish from the Persian Empire after the Arab conquest scattered the recipe to the four winds in the seventh century, and evolved into both paella and pullao, as well as arroz con pollo, jambalaya, and Hopping John. Even birds that feasted on Lowcountry rice became a prized dish — the New World epicurean equivalent of the ortolan, *Dolichonyx oryzivorus,* or bobolink, derives its Latin name from a voracious appetite for the grain — it's still known regionally as the rice bird.

But Rutledge did not cook for herself. She had slaves to do that.

As more planters shifted to growing Carolina Gold, they paid a higher premium for slaves from the ancient rice regions of Sierra Leone and the Upper Guinea Coast; traders were quick to advertise these skills in auction posters at the Old Market in Charleston. Fields were dug by hand in the lowland meadows and cypress swamps surrounding the region's great tidal river deltas. Grain was sown by pressing it into the muddy ground with the bare heel, a technique first practiced in the freshwater floodplains of the Sahel of Africa. Harvest in the Lowcountry took place at the height of hurricane season. Panicles were cut and baled. Women pounded the hulls with a wooden mortar and pestle and then winnowed while tossing handfuls from coiled grass fanner baskets, husks blowing away in the wind. The grain was absurdly delicate and fractured easily during milling, producing "middlings" or "brokens" that became a delicacy of sorts as well. The entire process, from planting to polishing, was punishing work under a subtropical sun, with risk of exposure to malaria, cholera, and yellow fever. Malnutrition and mortality rates were high.

Until recently, I didn't know slaves grew their own rice.

Other species — particularly upland bearded rice introduced from Guinea — were planted in provision gardens, plots granted by overseers to supplement meager rations of cornmeal and pork. The husk of this African rice was reddish brown to purple in hue, and unlike the golden Asian cultivar served at tables in the "big house" thrived in dry soil conditions rather than flooded fields. Its origin story is also murky, and involves Thomas Jefferson trying to grow some in a flowerpot, but crops up wherever slave cultures existed in the New World, including Trinidad, El Salvador, and French Guiana. Upland bearded rice is still grown by the Maroons of Suriname and plays a central role in their ancestor meals. The ceremony called *ala mofo nyan,* or food for all mouths, often includes offerings of African-origin foods like pigeon peas and rice. (Hold that thought, okay?)

When Emancipation liberated the enslaved labor force in the Lowcountry, commercial production of Carolina Gold gradually ceased. Berms, sluices, trunks, and dikes rotted and returned to swampland; the grain barges and settlement houses, abandoned, crumbled in decay, strangled by creeper vines. A series of devastating hurricanes between 1881 and 1911 wiped out the last vestiges of viable rice agriculture in the Lowcountry—the cost of repairing fields outweighed the potential profits. Carolina Gold barely escaped extinction as large-scale farming of inferior grain in Louisiana and Texas supplanted it. Upland bearded rice also disappeared as the rural population that raised it began to shift to northern industrial cities during the Great Migration. Certain stubborn seedsmen planted them as a hobby, or to attract ducks during hunting season. Carolina Gold eventually had a comeback, but only as a specialty crop, not the goldmine of the antebellum period.

Why would anyone preserve a crop, no matter how flavorful and aromatic, with such a disturbing heritage?

Broken Rice

> Us being geechees, we had rice every day. When you said what you were eating for dinner, you always assumed that rice was there. A source of pride to me was that I cooked rice like a grown person. I could cook it till every grain stood by itself.
> —Vertamae Smart-Grosvenor, *Vibration Cooking, or, The Travel Notes of a Geechee Girl,* 1970

Sean Brock's "Charleston ice cream" is an intellectual construct. A quenelle of creamy white rice snuggled next to a morsel of crab topped by artfully arranged petals in a hand-blown glass bowl, it is featured on a tasting menu at one of his fine-dining restaurants, McCrady's, on East Bay Street.

Surrounded by vibrant paintings of the salt marsh, he sat there and obsessed about this stubbly grain.

"It's the star," he said. "I don't want to mess with it."

Brock rubbed his eyes and removed a baseball cap embroidered with MCC.

"From my perspective as a chef, I treat it like a white truffle from Alba. Pondering the aroma and flavor leads you to another realm of respect."

"It tastes wrong to me," I said. "Especially smothered in my grandmother's gravy. Cooks up gummy or burns to the bottom of the pot. I've had to completely reconsider what she taught me about the food from here."

Brock has a great belly laugh.

He opened a plastic container of Carolina Gold fetched by one of his kitchen staff. I grabbed up a handful of the uncooked grain, polished like pearls, almost as precious at $10 a pound, and let it trickle through my fingers as he continued.

"When those dishes were born, it was a much more subtle cuisine."

Brock told me he bought a copy of *The Carolina Housewife* when he was nineteen. "I became fascinated with this culture and cuisine," he said. "It was so drastically different from the hillbilly cooking I grew up eating."

So I asked where he did research in Charleston.

"I ate at Nana's Seafood and Soul yesterday, and Hannibal's Kitchen the day before. Rice with fried cabbage and stewed limas. Shrimp and crab perloo. Pig tails and rice. Crab rice for breakfast."

At Hannibal's Kitchen, Safiya Grant's rice was righteous.

Hannibal's has a narrow dining room with padded vinyl banquettes, a takeout counter, and a pass-through window offering a tantalizing view into a steamy kitchen. On a side street bounded by housing projects and industrial port facilities, in a squat cinder-block building painted haint blue, this soul-food restaurant has resisted the gentrification swallowing gritty East Charleston block by block. It is slightly north of Emanuel African Methodist Episcopal Church, better known as Mother Emanuel to its parishioners, where Dylann Roof was welcomed to pray during Bible study on the evening of June 17, 2015. Like the church, Hannibal's Kitchen is a community pillar. A pillar built of collards, lima beans, turkey wings, and smoked neck bones, one of the few black-owned restaurants south of the Neck. (Hannibal was the nickname of family patriarch Robert Lawrence Huger.) At the front door, a crowd waited for their orders. Waitresses dodged around with pitchers of sweet tea and platters of crab rice.

The crab rice here is an entirely different construct from that served by Brock, not subtle at all, closer to its Gullah roots and a distant relative of Senegalese *thiébou diène*, a fish and rice stew. Drenched in butter and topped with shredded crabmeat and shrimp sautéed with bell pepper, celery, onion, and bacon, it references the mangrove swamps of West Africa as well as a Provençal pilau. (Karen Hess devoted a whole chapter to diaspora pilaus of this kind in *The Carolina Rice Kitchen: The African Connection*.)

Blue crabs dwell in the creeks and salt marsh of the Lowcountry estuarine system. While only a few recipes are mentioned—deviled or stewed—in the earliest regional cookbooks, crab is foolishly easy to catch. An apocryphal tale has circulated in my family involving one of my great-uncles, a rope, and a dead dog, but usually a rank chicken neck will get their greedy attention. For several summers my grandmother brought me down South on visits to her sisters who still lived in the Lowcountry, and one of my happiest childhood memories was the time spent barefoot and sunburned on the end of a ramshackle dock jutting into the Folly River, net poised as crab after crab rose in the muddy brown water to my bait. Nana and my great-aunts got so fed up picking crab day after day that they would sneak the full bucket out of the kitchen and dump them back into the spartina grass to crawl away again. Nana never mixed crab with rice. Shrimp, yes. Crab, no. Not sure why, but it may have something to do with that dog. So I was grateful for this version at Hannibal's Kitchen.

Safiya Grant had a long, thin face framed by gold earrings. She slid into a booth opposite me, and her daughter, dressed for a dance class, climbed into her lap.

"You want a little something-something with that? Get the red rice and collards too."

Another platter arrived. Her red rice was the real deal, the consequence of tomatoes and chili peppers introduced to Africa and brought back again on the Middle Passage.

Grant tilted her head in concentration when I asked how she cooked it.

"First you fry the meat," she said. "And you can use any flavor meat, that's the flavor your red rice is going to be. Italian sausage, beef sausage. Then you add some veggies, onions, and bell peppers and put the sauce in, whatever seasoning, and water, stir it up to make it smooth, some salt and pepper, and whatever rice you want. It's an equal share, one to one, cook it until halfway, and for your eye, if you want it a little redder, add some more sauce."

"What kind of rice?" I asked.

"Any kind. It doesn't matter." She shrugged.

Before Grant's family bought the business, two other owners operated soul-food restaurants at the same address. The Hugers eventually changed the menu—she is the third generation to cook there.

"In the sixties they used to have bologna sandwiches, cornbread, that kind of thing," said Grant. "People who went to school around here, they used to jump the fence—hope you don't get caught—it was like a snack place for them. Teachers would send across to get lunch and stuff too."

Grant's daughter squirmed out of her lap and danced away. I scraped the rest of my lunch into a plastic clamshell. Before she disappeared back into the clatter of the kitchen, I asked Grant a parting question.

"Where do you get your rice?"

She smiled.

"Bulk, from Costco."

Grains of Wisdom

> Promisin' talk don' cook rice.
> —Gullah version of a Hausa proverb

Not long after rice production failed in the Lowcountry, German scientist Erich Gustav Huzenlaub and British chemist Francis Heron Rogers invented a method of parboiling commercially produced rice to retain greater nutritional value. The Huzenlaub Process yielded a less starchy grain resistant to weevils. It was also the color of a manila folder. The original patent number 368,092 application filed in Great Britain on November 30, 1939, claims:

The method of this invention produces the highest degree of gelatinization possible in a rice grain, leaving it totally free from any white, chalky, light refracting spots or sections on the grain surface or grain interior, it produces a rice grain without any hint of colouration [*sic*] beyond the slightly creamy tint which is usually regarded as a characteristic of the very highest grades of rice, and it produces further a rice grain which is free from any objectionable odor during subsequent cooking.

Objectionable odor?

American businessman and candy heir Forrest E. Mars Sr. acquired a stake in the patent for this easy-to-cook "converted" rice in 1942. The first Converted Rice Inc. plant set up in Houston subjected Gulf Coast grain to Huzenlaub's parboiling; the company swiftly obtained a wartime government contract to supply rice to U.S. Army mess kitchens on fighting fronts from Europe to Africa. By 1947, when it arrived in American grocery stores, the new brand acquired a name and a face on the packaging: a genial elder servant wearing a waiter's jacket and bow tie, with an honorific historically reserved by southerners who avoided calling black men "Mister."

Uncle Ben may never have existed, although Mars Food corporate lore references a black rice farmer, last name unknown, in Beaumont, Texas, as his inspiration. A waiter named Frank Brown, however, who worked at the Tavern Club in Chicago, did consent to have his portrait painted for $500. The restaurant was a favorite haunt for the agency reps who created the first advertising campaign featuring his image, which appeared in *Life* magazine on October 27, 1947. Tag line? "The sunny-colored rice that cooks white." In six years the brand became the top-selling packaged long-grain rice in the country.

A curious thing happened in 1971. Uncle Ben disappeared from the packaging. This was the tumultuous year when President Richard M. Nixon made disparaging remarks about women, blacks, Mexicans, and Italians on secret White House tapes. The U.S. Supreme Court overturned the draft-evasion conviction of Muhammad Ali and, in *Swann v. Charlotte-Mecklenburg Board of Education,* also upheld the use of busing to achieve racial desegregation in schools. Three drunken white males in Drew, Mississippi, killed Jo Etha Collier, an eighteen-year-old black woman. James Earl Ray, Martin Luther King Jr.'s assassin, was caught in a jailbreak attempt in Tennessee. The Black Panthers were accused of an attack at the

Ingleside police station in San Francisco that left one officer dead. Don Cornelius debuted as the host of the new musical variety show *Soul Train.*

Uncle Ben returned to the box in 1983.

Nana died the next year.

"Help yourself."

Not only was this her invocation at the table, the invitation to an open refrigerator, and even the welcome to a stash of bourbon in her liquor cabinet, but also a battle cry for an independent woman who lived ninety-two years, never said a peep about money missing from her purse or unwritten thank-you notes, and cried down the phone line when her uppity granddaughter got a scholarship to Vassar. Until the end, she also never burned a pot of rice on that modest apartment stove so far from the salt marsh.

Two decades later Mars Food hired another agency to promote Uncle Ben to chairman of the board. He was reimagined in a lavish corner office, in a bright blue suit, still wearing the same bow tie and dispensing "grains of wisdom." Socially minded critics were ambivalent about the campaign's intent.

The series titled *Unenslaved: Rice Culture Paintings* by artist Jonathan Green is kaleidoscope-bright and full of movement. Men pole barges loaded impossibly high with grain. A woman in a polka-dot dress and headscarf tosses rice with a sweetgrass basket. Others tote sheaves in fields stretching to a low marshy horizon. For its debut at the Gibbes Museum of Art in Charleston, the series was paired with the earlier work of watercolorist Alice Ravenel Huger Smith, who depicted life on an antebellum rice plantation in softer hues but with more racially fraught themes.

"I wanted to capture it from the perspective of Africans in touch with their own humanity and dignity," said Green, who showed me a painting from the series when we first met in his Charleston studio. "I wanted to think of the history of the Lowcountry and rice as I know it from *my* ancestors."

The soft-spoken artist was born in Gardens Corner, not far from the sea island where Nana grew up.

"I love the fact that you can have two impressions of the same culture," Green said. "How we do not know each other, even though we've been living side by side for hundreds of years. How is it that we have allowed ourselves to treat each other like this for so long?

Painting this series as if Africans came here like everyone else, that helped me overcome this fog of slavery."

"What rice did you eat growing up?" I asked.

"My grandmother cooked Carolina Gold. She grew it. But my mother didn't go out into the rice field," he continued. "She used Uncle Ben's or Mahatma. I cook the way my grandmother did. She put some oil in the pan and then the rice. Threw vegetables in there with the rice, peas or whatever, and when the vegetables were cooked and the rice brown enough, she added the liquid."

The Requiem for Rice is Green's next project. According to the website, the multimedia collaboration with filmmaker Julie Dash and composer Trevor Weston is "a lamentation for repose of the souls of the dead who were enslaved, exploited, and brutalized on Low-country South Carolina and Georgia's rice plantations and who remain unburied, unmourned, and unmarked." A preview debuted in 2017 at Charleston's Emanuel AME Church, the same place of worship where Dylann Roof shot nine parishioners in cold blood two years earlier. The fully realized requiem will have its world premiere at a later date. Green commissioned scholar Edda Fields-Black, who teaches the transnational history of Gullah-Geechie culture at Carnegie Mellon University in Pittsburgh, PA, to write the libretto. She is an expert on rice agriculture in West Africa.

Dr. Fields-Black told me, "Never met a rice field that I didn't love, and literally would have to pull on my boots and want to get into."

She also spent childhoods visiting her Lowcountry family; her father's ancestors are buried on several plantations that once belonged to Nathaniel Heyward, whose vast estate included 1,648 slaves at the time of his death. For her libretto she draws on diaries of plantation mistress Fanny Kemble and oral histories from the Depression-era Works Progress Administration Slave Narrative project.

"I want to bring these experiences to light and create something beautiful about a labor system that was pretty horrible," Fields-Black said. "We're using the metaphor of a mass said for the dead, but it's very much our own creation, an African-American requiem."

When I talked to her on the phone in Pittsburgh, she admitted never eating rice as a child. "White bread, white potatoes, white rice. My father associated these with poverty and obesity. Now if I don't eat rice—brown rice—every day, I get cranky."

Ghost Rice

> If a breath of life was left in her, she would sit up and eat, but
> if she smelled the hopping-john and did not stir, then they
> could just nail down the coffin and be certain she was truly
> dead.
>   —Carson McCullers, *The Member of the Wedding*

Lucie Kulze climbed on the vintage Allis-Chalmers combine when
it stalled. She peered into the unloader as her uncle and father
fixed the belt drive. The autumn sky was streaked with cloud, insects hummed in the heat, and a breeze rattled the palmettos.
Grain hung heavy, all green and golden. Everyone wore snake boots
and kept an eye on the riverbank when a bull alligator coughed.
White egrets startled as the combine lurched back into motion,
rattling away and burping out chaff, chomping through a rice field
bounded by centuries-old canals. Despite the calm day, however,
Hurricane Matthew barreled toward the Carolina coast. Lowcountry farmers scrambled.

Kulze is a cousin, our blood tied by multiple generations and en-
twined family trees. Nana and her great-grandmother were sisters.
The twenty-two-year-old brunette has ramrod posture, prefers sec-
ondhand work clothes from the Salvation Army store, and instead
of pursuing mainstream higher education chose apprenticeships
ranging from permaculture to animal husbandry. Kulze attended
the Young Farmers Conference at New York's Stone Barns Center for Food & Agriculture and forages mushrooms for Charleston restaurants like Fig and Husk. One of her mentors is Dr. Brian
Ward, of Clemson Coastal Research and Education Center, an heirloom seedsman and founding member of the Carolina Gold Rice
Foundation, which provides seed free of charge to planters interested in experimental and heirloom revival crops. (Full disclosure:
I nudged her a tiny bit by introducing him.) When the family got
a grant to restore the ruined dikes and trunks on their Combahee
River property, they started growing Charleston Gold.

This was rice I could respect.

In 1998 two rice scientists collaborated on a new cultivar by
cross-breeding Carolina Gold with sturdier japonica varieties. After
ten years of testing and selection, Gurdev Khush and Merle Shepard brought the grain to Anna McClung, a geneticist at the USDA

Agricultural Research Service in Beaumont, Texas. (Remember Beaumont, Texas? Where a black rice farmer named Ben reportedly toiled?)

Dr. Shepard told me, "One of the parents of Charleston Gold is a modern, high-yielding 'green revolution' rice, but I asked Dr. Khush to keep the gold color on the hull and add an aromatic gene from a basmati. Dr. McClung did the final 'cleaning up' of the variety and grew it in regional trials." Of the eleven historical "rice rivers" in the Lowcountry, the Combahee is the tenth in succession from north to south, where Alice Smith painted her plantation scenes and several present-day landowners, including my cousins, are growing these new cultivars.

The Allis-Chalmers made several more passes through patches of rice ready to harvest, filling two large totes with 700 pounds of grain, which Kulze hauled by tractor back to her parents' house. She transferred the raw rice to smaller plastic bins and bags, setting up electric fans in the kitchen to aid the drying process. The room smelled of grass. A pot of rice simmered on the stove for dinner.

"What is ghost rice?" I asked.

"That's when the plant makes a panicle and the hull is there, but with no grain inside," Kulze said. "Like it didn't fill. Dr. Ward says it happens when the soil is high in organic matter."

Before driving down from Charleston for the harvest, I stopped at the weekend farm market in Marion Square and bought bags of freshly picked field peas.

If I had an ancestor meal, food for all mouths, it would be Hopping John. Nana said my grandfather ate his cowpeas and rice topped with a big glob of mayonnaise. My father preferred it that way as well. Yes, it's gross, but as tribute to them, so do I. Always cowpeas, never black-eyed peas. Everyone in the Lowcountry has opinions about the potlikker and whether the flavor meat should be bacon or a smoked ham hock.

No one can agree about the name. Some argue Hopping John (or Hoppin' for the colloquially precious) is a bastardization of *pois de pigeon*. Others swear a lame pea vendor named John once limped through the streets of Charleston. The earliest reference in an American cookbook is credited to Sarah Rutledge, who recommended garnishing the dish with a sprig of mint. (So don't give me grief about mayonnaise.) In *The Savannah Cookbook* (1933), Harriet Ross Colquitt wrote: "As children, it was our custom, when the word went around that we were to have Hopping John for dinner, to gather in the dining-room, and as the dish was brought on to hop around the table before sitting down to the feast." Her society-lady recipe collection was illustrated with cartoonish images of possum hunts and vegetable sellers, and headnotes peppered with disparaging remarks about "coloreds" and "dark horses," ugly names close to those Nana used as well.

Dinner with Lucie Kulze was plain and simple. Rice with peas, the last bolted greens from the vegetable garden, some leftover succotash, and venison shot in the piney woods that back up against the golden fields where, in two days' time, the remaining crop would be obliterated by hurricane-force winds and rain. The Charleston Gold was aromatic and fluffy, not split or starchy—complaints I often have against rice that hasn't been converted.

"What do you think about the history of rice here?" I asked.

"Truth is truth," she replied. "When I'm out there working, I can't understand how it used to be done by hand, turning those swamps into fields. It's almost like Machu Picchu, but in a more buggy, snakey, alligatory environment. Tough as hell."

Kulze spared me two pounds of Charleston Gold to take home. I hugged this young girl who wears scruffy overalls and eats table scraps cold out of the fridge because she can't stand to see them go to waste.

At first light she dragged the salvaged rice out into the last sun prior to the storm, in hopes of dehydrating the grain more before shipping it to a mill in Orangeburg. As I left her to it, she said, "Every single step has been a mountain and this year has more mountains than last."

Pot, stirred.

Georgetown One Stop

FROM *Oxford American*

I'D BEEN FISHING alone in the rain, catching squat, some runt largemouth was all, when on the third day I drove to Searcy, Arkansas, where the spell was broken. It wasn't redemption I was after so much as I wanted to test a theory that I could fish just as poorly among friends. My pal Dacus and I spent an evening hauling corpulent bluegill from a roadside pond with his father, Bobby T, who hollered "Whooo-weee!" whenever one of us got a strike. It felt good to prove my theory wrong.

Bobby T called them *bream* (pronounced "brim"), not bluegill, as we did in Michigan, and said what he'd really like is some catfish. So we headed over to the Georgetown One Stop for supper, about the only place left, he said, where you could still get genuine White River–caught catfish, short of catching one yourself. We had catfish in Michigan, but it had never occurred to me to fish for them, let alone eat one. Not out of any bottom-feeder snobbery; I inhabited a salmon-patty milieu was all. But Bobby T was from Newport, Arkansas, the heart of White River catfish country, and I was given to understand that as a fisherman I was obliged to educate myself about catfish. It followed that if I wanted to have a lucid conversation about catfish, I needed to eat at the One Stop.

This was maybe five years ago, so some of it's a blur: a dozen unbending miles down AR-36 to Georgetown, through rust-colored fields and forests in spring twilight, the Little Red River, a branch of the White, sailing along beside us. Swaybacked porches. A sky stretched out darkly like a country lake. In that short distance I noticed a shift from the eastern edge of the Ozarks to Delta bottomland, where there were fewer trees and cars and more fishing shacks. I'd just read that Hernando de Soto, while fording the White River not far from here in 1541, saw "no end of fish." It comes back to me that in Kensett we passed a yard where a zorse, or it might've been a zedonk, was tied to a stake. Dacus, without elaboration, said its name was Trouble.

The highway dead-ends at Georgetown, which was once a proper mill town with a hotel, drugstore, mattress factory, the mill that made hammer and ax handles, two churches for upward of five hundred souls, even a movie house. No longer. Just the One Stop, the name meant literally. When the river is up, AR-36 can flood out, ditto the other road in and out of town, cutting Georgetown off completely.

The One Stop, set off Main Street, looked like a deserted barracks or a survivalist's cabin: porch roof of corrugated tin, slack American flags. Inside were newly minted Sam's Club folding tables and chairs and hundreds of photographs of people holding strung-up catfish and trout or kneeling over dead whitetail deer that looked oddly animate, like they might get up and run off. We arrived when most folks would be quitting work, but it was packed. I think the plate was $9, all-you-can-eat, and I might've stopped after two. The owner, Joann Taylor, brought them out three or four at a time, white enamel ovals pyramided with catfish fillets, hush puppies, sliced white onion, cupped coleslaw, pickle, and lemon wedge. Dacus, a de Kooning of the condiment school, whipped together tartar sauce, ketchup, mustard, and Tabasco into a purplish glop. As we ate I could see steam rising out of the kitchen, hear the clang of cast iron.

This was none of your salmon-patty mealiness, no gummed-up Progresso crumbs feebly masked by Mom's dill sauce. It struck me that I hated salmon patties. By contrast, the catfish was tawny and sweet, faintly smoky, and it cracked apart on the tongue, tumbling weightlessly down the hatch. We overdid it, the three of us, grunting and lip-smacking, sweat blooming under our caps, balled-up paper napkins everywhere, catfish remnants smeared across our faces. I won't lie. The gastric repercussions were thunderous, but at our table a mutual amnesty presided. That night a morsel popped from my rolled shirtsleeve. It still tasted good.

Joann landed in Georgetown in '97, pitching in with her sister, Jeanie, to run a minimart and wildlife-check station that had some gas pumps. She served catfish lunches on the side—but no frozen, farm-raised stuff. Joann, a purist, bought cats directly from White River fishermen. By then just about everyone else had gone over to farmed cats—Dondie's in Des Arc, Murry's over in Hazen, the Riverfront Fish Market on the Cache River near Fredonia. Her recipe, Bobby T said, was beside the point. The salient detail was *White River catfish.* Joann's lunches became so popular that she tore out the gas pumps and tossed the Skoal racks and went full-on catfish, becoming, in a few months, a kind of desert prophetess working to preserve (albeit inadvertently) an obscure regional tradition before it was lost forever. By conventional measure, Georgetown had gone to seed. By another, it was flourishing.

Although some Food Network stooge would surely find the One Stop eventually, for the moment it lacked any officious culinary sanction, which seemed important. Joann was cooking for her neighbors, sawdust clinging to some of them, others redolent of fish slime and beer and gasoline, excepting the ladies of course, painted up ferociously in brilliant crimsons and blues. Everybody momentarily at peace. The hottest part of the day gone. Not an ironic mustache in sight. Fried catfish like you couldn't get anywhere else.

The biggest catfish on record, an adult female Mekong giant caught in Thailand in 2005, measured 9 feet long and weighed 646 pounds. By comparison, North American catfish are plausibly sized (a 60-pound channel cat is Guinness territory and blues rarely top 100), though it's true they'll eat almost anything. In the South, catfish have been found with the remains of raccoons, rattlesnakes, baby turtles, menthol cigarettes, and a mini-basketball in their stomachs. Anglers sometimes target them with "stink bait" —typically a slaw of raw chicken liver, fish blood, and Limburger cheese that has sat around in the sun for a few days. Of our fifty or so native species, three in particular are worth knowing about: blues, channels, and flatheads. They live basically everywhere east of the Rockies, from Manitoba down through the Mississippi and Ohio river basins, the Great Lakes, the Dakotas, and south to Louisiana, Arkansas, Georgia, and the Mobile Bay drainage, all the way into Mexico. Our polymorphous regionalisms give a sense of their dispersal: chucklehead, shovelhead, mud cat, granny cat, tabby cat, johnnie cat, Op cat, Appaloosa cat, Russian cat, bashaw, humpback, forktail, fiddler, eel cat, willow cat, Morgan cat, Mississippi cat, to name a few. Blues are the biggest. Channels the most common. Flatheads the best eating.

An inescapable attribute of catfish is their remarkable hardiness. They've evolved over millions of years to tolerate murderously sluggish, oxygen-poor, alkaline-rich water. Catfish can even survive without water for several hours, and should the need arise, some can crawl a fair stretch from one body of water to another, and even scale cave walls and rapids. The Eurasian wels catfish will hurl itself ashore to seize a pigeon, casually swallowing it whole.

Another inescapable attribute of catfish is how unsightly they are. Downright revolting. Comically so. Barney from *The Simpsons* shares a likeness. Admiral Ackbar. The bug-eyed Marty Feldman as Igor in *Young Frankenstein*. For some people, for instance my wife, this presents a culinary impasse—just to harmlessly float the idea of eating catfish on an otherwise lovely night out, let alone to suggest frying one at home, is to cast a dark shadow indeed. We northerners are fairly clueless about catfish. As much as anything else at the seafood counter, they can educe for us a heady, collective shudder, like a nightmare drug up from some primordial chamber of horrors. It must be admitted that their cadaverous, thick-lipped, thin-whiskered mugs have something of the pederast about them. But to catfish chauvinists I say, take a good look at a flounder. It doesn't help that fried catfish are often thought of as a poor person's food—cheap, artery-clogging, abundant. Not to mention they're a pain in the ass to clean. Our bias against catfish is also rooted in the widespread notion that bottom-feeders have more pollutants than other fish. This isn't always the case; imported catfish can be a dicey proposition, but domestic cats do not contain mercury or other neurotoxins.

Most sensible people would agree that, beheaded and fried in lard, catfish are delicious, and a few hush puppies don't hurt either. This is notably true in the South. In his excellent *American Cooking: Southern Style*, Eugene Walter writes that "to a Deep Southerner, black or white, the very word catfish sets up a chain reaction of associations, all pleasurable." Walter, who grew up in Mobile and helped start the *Paris Review*, preferred channels to flatheads, judging their sweet, pale flesh superior, and found that a platter of fillets dusted in water-ground cornmeal required a "drooling-bib" and "stretcher service afterwards." He was writing in the 1970s, under contract to add a southern cookbook to Time-Life's Foods of the World catalogue, though to call *American Cooking: Southern Style* a cookbook isn't quite right: a culinary lexicon is more apt; a lyric treatise on the salutary rewards of cooking with pig fat; a discursive, reverential road trip through the South's hallmark cuisines. It's fitting that by the time Walter gets around to catfish, he's in Arkansas —Stuttgart, to be exact, a Delta town practically within casting distance of the White River.

Shaped like a fishhook, the White skulks across a 28,000-square-mile watershed from the Ozarks in northwest Arkansas on up through Missouri, where it runs past Branson, then turns south again, flattening diagonally across the top right quadrant of Arkansas, sprouting nine tributaries in a 700-mile dash to the Mississippi. Its hypothermically cold water and abundant baitfish like shad and herring produce a year-round Nathan's Hot Dog Eating Contest for predatory fish. Among anglers of outsized ambition, the Upper White is a famous trout fishery—browns in the 2-foot range aren't unheard of—while the Lower White, starting below Newport, is hallowed catfishing grounds.

It used to be that if you were talking about Arkansas catfish, you were talking about White River catfish. From the 1940s to the early '70s, catfish houses all over the state made a point of advertising it. On menus, and on signs out front: WE SELL WHITE RIVER CATFISH. The implication being that anything less was cut-rate, bottom-shelf. Outpost towns on the Lower White—Des Arc, DeValls Bluff, Augusta, Clarendon, St. Charles—drew weekend nomads from far-off rangeland and Little Rock and Memphis, spilling outside on buffet lines, fanning themselves under Delta skies, seeking something wild, pure, cold-river caught. One felt lucky to partake.

All that changed. It wasn't overnight, and I'm simplifying here, but to start, a guy named Edgar "Chip" Farmer out of Dumas more or less birthed the U.S. commercial catfish industry in the '60s. From a dozen fingerlings in ponds chopped out of his rice fields, Farmer expanded into one of the largest aquaculture outfits in the country. The Delta's thick alluvial clay made excellent catfish ponds. A few silty, marginal acres can support upward of 100,000 fry. Eventually Alabama, Louisiana, and Mississippi caught on. When the domestic cotton market tanked in the '70s, catfish saved many southern farmers from foreclosure. At one point Arkansas had 35,000 acres in production, yielding hundreds of thousands of pounds of cats a year, so much that most of them got exported. You can hardly blame restaurant owners for shifting toward abundance and a reliable delivery schedule (the old "river rat" anglers tended to fish when it suited them) and a price point more within the local purse.

Then people started worrying about the rivers. Right about when Chip Farmer was getting started, catfish in the state's big three arteries—the Mississippi, Arkansas, and White—were found to have traces of endrin, an insecticide linked to neurological abnormalities in humans (so too were commercial catfish, but that news didn't travel). So farm-raised cats became the thing. Even Eugene Walter, drooling over his golden fillets a mere dozen miles from the White River, was eating commercial catfish.

Like much of what we eat today, Arkansas's cats have been thoroughly and profitably denuded, standardized, made invariable. They originate in rectangular, 5- to 15-acre, 4- to 6-foot-deep levee ponds with a capacity of about 7,000 fish per acre, most of them in southeast Desha and Chicot Counties. Because of algae and aquatic bacteria, ponds can cast a glow. This, combined with toxic effluent from pesticides and antibiotics from modern farming, is why a good chunk of Arkansas bottomland today resembles Sherwin-Williams color samples: Quench Blue, Sea Salt, Jacaranda, Oh Pistachio. To deal with parasites, commercial farms maintain robust biosecurity programs, including kill permits for predatory cormorants and propane cannons to scare off pelicans that defecate in the water.

Not to shit all over farm-raised catfish, which tastes just fine to me; put some fries or hush puppies on that plate, a splat of tartar, coleslaw, pickles, then, yes, stretcher service would be appreciated. But there are those who feel that something has been lost, something momentous, something like the very essence of catfish, which from our earliest association has been bound up in the hidden enticements of a river or lake. We've become depressingly conversant with the industrial variants of our food. The original versions often fail to retain any meaning. No doubt many people prefer it that way: an efficient, predictable hell of sameness.

Except that, not *everybody*. For some, catfish has a default setting. Consider this, from the angling classic *Fishing for Catfish,* a rare literate gem of the how-to genre written by Arkansas native Keith "Catfish" Sutton, our most eloquent evangelist for a species once universally dismissed as a "trash fish" by anglers and diners alike (I'm quoting from the editor's introduction): "Catfish and the places they reside make us smile, and we are drawn to the fish and to those places with a longing that is life changing, and eventually, life defining."

A sad corollary to all of this is that the U.S. commercial catfish market tanked too. By 2007 a cheap catfish import from Southeast Asia called "swai" had begun to undercut domestic sales and put farmers across the catfish belt of Arkansas, Alabama, Louisiana, and Mississippi out of business (swai, an endangered species of the Mekong Delta, was packaged simply as "Delta catfish" and as "grouper"). Rising feed and fuel costs, then a viral infection that rent farm-raised cats with a ghastly, measleslike rash, nearly sank the entire industry. Arkansas's 35,000 acres shrank to 5,000.

I can't help but think of two characters in Larry Brown's last novel, *A Miracle of Catfish:* Ursula, the lugubrious 40-pound channel cat plucked from a riverbed to become brood stock for a catfish operation, who flails against her aquarium life of fishmeal and glass walls, and her human counterpart, Tommy Bright of Arkansas, a flawed but honorable guy in the Brownian mode, overextended financially and romantically and probably morally, though resonating inner-core warmth. Briefly successful in the fish-stocking business, Tommy loses everything in one bad roll at the "Indian casino." It's the last straw for his old lady. And the bank. And Tommy himself, who's too old to start over. The last we see of him, he's careening into the tremoring dusk, taillights flashing. Before leaving town, his penultimate act is to do right by Ursula, to whom he feels indebted—his prosperity, his one hot streak in life, was her work. In a roundabout way, he loves her. So he sets her loose, plops her in a Mississippi catfish pond to resume a version of her former existence.

Fish. Why did he think they were the answer? For a long time they had been . . . He wished he could go back to that time and live there again. But that world was gone.

I too had always wanted to return. Not just to the One Stop, but to Searcy, to Georgetown. In Michigan, snow on the ground, the sky achieving the consistency of gruel, Arkansas was light-years away. I got an occasional email from Dacus, a voice message from Bobby T: "When we going back?"

In 2011 the White River flooded its banks, nearly carrying off the One Stop's fridge. Georgetown rallied. Folks chipped in to help Joann rebuild. Still we dithered, Dacus and Bobby T and I, figuring there'd be time. A couple of years later things were conceptually coming together—a One Stop pilgrimage and fishing trip up and down the White and Little Red: a johnboat, Old Milwaukee, six or eight rods out, drift fishing in the current, or just finding a hole and sitting on it—when word arrived that we were too late. Joann had retired. The One Stop was finished. The dream was dead.

In May 2015 a Yelp post announced the One Stop's return. New owners, same fish, it said. I'd been in the habit of checking the site for updates, my feeling being that insofar as I could distill hope to a manageable size, the One Stop's resurrection would definitely, providentially arrive. And out of the blue, an all-caps missive from Wally J. of Searcy: "It's back . . . original recipe . . . OH THE FISH. EXCELLENT!! Absolutely THE BEST CATFISH I ever put in my mouth."

Plans were hatched. Bobby T would do reconnaissance, see how the cooking measured up to Joann's. Dacus, coming from New Orleans, would meet us in Searcy. I started looking for flights, went and bought a gang of 30-pound test line. Then a bunch of stuff happened. My daughter was born, for starters. Logistical paroxysms. The short of it was, plans were squelched.

From Yelp came more One Stop news. Justin S. wrote: "We drove by it 3 times before we realized it. That would be my only complaint —poor signage. The food was great." Morris R.: "The new owners are family . . . Three generations of ladies . . . I asked our server who made the pies and she said: 'Grandma makes all the deserts [sic].'" I finally picked up the phone.

Grandma turned out to be Jason Goodwin, thirty-six. He and his wife, Brandy, had bought the One Stop from Joann more or less on a whim. Although he'd never set foot in a commercial kitchen, Jason did all the cooking himself. He'd been working at a packaging plant nearby and wanted a change, felt a harmonic tug from Georgetown. "It's probably one of the peacefulest places you'll ever be," he told me, sounding enamored, like a man who had suddenly changed the picture he had of himself.

Joann had included her recipes with the sale. Jason tweaked the hush puppies and coleslaw, added fried shrimp, cheeseburgers, and cobblers to the menu. But the catfish—350 to 400 pounds of

White River flatheads and channels bought weekly from a DeWitt river rat—was unchanged. The plate cost $11.50.

"The recipe is so simple, you'd flip if I told you," Jason said. "Heck, I'll tell you. It's Tony Chachere's Creole Seasoning and white cornmeal."

I started to ask him about White River catfish versus the inferior farm-raised kind, anticipating corroboration of my favored narrative. Of course, as with Tommy Bright, the stories we tell ourselves are often revealed upon closer inspection to be fragmentary, half-baked. It's the you-can't-go-home-again quandary. While it's tempting to load our desires with wistful hang-ups about the past so they feel freighted with meaning, the truth is more complicated.

"You can't tell no difference in taste between river fish and pond-raised," Jason insisted. We had a good connection. It was early spring. I could hear birds chirping in Georgetown. I asked him to clarify. "The only reason I use White River catfish is because it's way cheaper," he insisted. "The trick is cutting it. You have to cut out the mud vein. If you go to a supermarket and buy a box of catfish fillets and look at the backside, it's got this gray, veiny stuff on it. That's the mud vein. It's what makes catfish taste bad. You cut that off, it'd taste no different from the river fish we're serving right now."

I think he could tell he was upsetting me, because he backpedaled some, allowing that White River catfish was "a cleaner fish . . . it's in flowing water all the time . . . it's not pink like pond fish. It's white like chicken." But, and he said this emphatically, so I understood, so that it would close the subject, which was one he knew intimately, "It's real simple. If everybody knew how to cut mud veins, we'd be out of business. As far as taste is concerned, that's all there is to it."

Anyway, I'm not sure it mattered. The One Stop was back. AR-36 buzzed with weekend carloads of Georgetown pilgrims. We were headed there ourselves. Bobby T, who'd taken to calling me "Catfish John," had it on his calendar. Until a Facebook post from Jason appeared. I should've seen it coming.

He'd had a good run, Jason said, had kept it going for more than a year, but he couldn't make it work. The One Stop was kaput. Again. I tried calling him, emailing. Nothing. Bobby T drove over to Georgetown. The place was shut tight. It seemed as if Jason had gone into hiding. Even his Facebook page disappeared. I got it.

Things like this, it's like that mud-vein business: you want to core it out and toss it aside, move on.

I like to think you can't kill the One Stop, that it'll come back around eventually, in some form or another. It might take a while, but it wouldn't surprise me. In my head, I'm counting on it. I've got some stuff to take care of first. Up in Michigan, I'm digging myself out. Stocking my tackle box. Rereading *Fishing for Catfish*. Dacus thinks his car might even make it to Georgetown. We're awaiting a signal from Bobby T — "Let's go fishing," it'll say. It's been too long.

The Country Sausage
That's Going to Town

FROM *Oxford American*

IT HAS COME to my attention that within the dog-eat-dog un-
derworld of the culinary industry, there is a clandestine movement
afoot to discredit my food writing. The chief criticisms are that I
don't actually cook and my essays aren't about food. This has gotten on my last nerve! I put forth that any creature in possession
of an alimentary canal knows plenty about food. The basics are
simple: if you don't eat, you will die, and bacon tastes better than
rice cakes. Nutrition is for the food writer as ornithology is for the
birds!

To reassure the skeptics, my bona fides are as follows. For more
than a decade I worked in seventeen different restaurants, cafés,
and bars. My career began in Morehead, Kentucky, at a Burger
Queen and ended at Doyle's Cafe in Boston, Massachusetts. I
worked as a dishwasher, busboy, prep cook, steward, breakfast cook,
soda pop pourer, sandwich maker, barista, and waiter. I got fired
often, although never for reasons related to job performance. The
most common reason was a mysterious word — *insubordination* —
essentially a pretext used by power-mad bosses to shed themselves
of people they didn't like. Or in my case, a person who resisted
the lure of kissing the boss's b-hole. Of all the professional sadness
in the world, the most poignant is that of assistant managers at
a restaurant. Their priority is scheduling shifts for a waitstaff that
makes more money than managers. Their only recourse is firing
people.

A deeply personal matter led to my decade in the restaurant

business and subsequent "career" as a food writer. At age fifteen I met a girl. Nothing is as powerful as the extraordinary jolt of a teenager's first love. It's like seeing the world after a double cataract surgery. Life is suddenly exquisite. Each leaf becomes the bearer of unbearable beauty. Romeo and Juliet were so deliriously happy that they embraced murder and suicide as an ideal solution. I didn't go that far, but I fell deeply and totally in love with Kim. She was smart, pretty, and laughed at my jokes. I spent all my waking hours trying to talk to her, eventually moving up to walking around holding hands. Our six-week romance was the best of my life—virtuous, finite, and gloriously unprecedented. I never again knew such an all-encompassing joy.

We met doing summer-stock theater as part of a college recruitment program for promising high school students. This occurred before the advent of portable music devices, which meant we listened to the radio. Every lyric seemed to be about us, directed exclusively at the impermeable dome in which we lived. Our favorite song was "The Joker" by the Steve Miller Band, in which he spoke of the pompitous of love. Neither Kim nor I knew exactly what the phrase meant, but we felt it described what we had, a kind of purity and truth. We were pompitous. Our love embodied pompitousness. We sought pompity.

In mid-August Kim returned home to western Kentucky, two hours away. We wrote each other daily, a pace that dwindled to weekly, then monthly. We called each other a few times, long spells with both of us clutching the receiver silently, content to know the other person was on the line. She visited me once, driving with a couple of her friends who clearly evaluated me as deficient: too short, too poor, nonathletic. Plus I was from the hills and looked it. I didn't even own a car to reciprocate her visit. We stopped writing. I never saw Kim again, but I never forgot her.

Her grandfather was Fred Purnell, a former railroad man who founded Purnell's "Old Folks" Sausage company in Simpsonville, Kentucky. According to family lore, Fred loved listening to the elderly talk, a trait that earned him the phenomenal nickname of Old Folks. I deeply envy his sobriquet. As a child I also enjoyed hearing tales of the old days. This has evolved into a secret desire that young people would be interested in hearing me talk. As it is, I can't even get my wife to listen to a word I say. My nickname could readily be Husby Ignored or He Who Talks to Himself.

Purnell Sausage began as a family company and still maintains that status, which is quite unusual in the corporate era of Big Pork. For example, Smithfield Foods began as a family operation in North Carolina and was America's biggest pork company until it was bought by a Chinese corporation for $7 billion. (Yes, that's 7,000,000,000 bucks!) Industrialized pork created a lucrative side business, the never-ending disposal of hog feces. If you can withstand the dreadful smell, it's a wide-open field for a "manure entrepreneur."

The packaging of Purnell's sausage features a drawing of a cheerfully grinning pig's face. It's a great design: simple, bold, and memorable. At least as long as you ignore the obvious—what the hell does that pig have to be happy about? His entire family is encased in frozen wrappers for sale! Setting aside the complex emotional life of a hog, what enthralled me most was the slogan: "The Country Sausage That's Going to Town!"

When I was a child living on a dirt road in the country, there was nothing better than going to the nearest town. Morehead had paved streets, multiple two-story buildings, and sidewalks. One structure was rumored to contain an elevator. A ten-cent store sold model cars and Hot Wheels. The corner drugstore had comic books and nickel Cokes. The prospect of going to town on Saturday sustained me throughout the tedious week of attending school. My mother's greatest punishment was forbidding her kids from accompanying her to town. Merely the threat impelled me to prompt obedience. (The worst period of my life was being banned from Morehead for a month. After reading that Daniel Boone had stained his skin with walnut juice to pass as a Shawnee, I smeared the brown inner oil all over my body. It didn't wash out.)

The phrase *going to town* has another, more generalized and colloquial definition. It means to carry out something with great enthusiasm, fully committed and doing the best you can—such as eating. *That boy is going to town on that sausage!* As a food slogan, it connotes the ambition of a country staple that's heading out, putting the farm behind, eager for the bright lights. Maybe that's why the pig was so happy. Its zeal for departure was a form of ignorance at the true destination—the bloody fate of a slaughterhouse. Like me in later years, that pig would often wish it had stayed home, safe in the hills.

I recently learned that the Purnell motto was discontinued

sometime in the mid-1970s. The new slogan, currently in use on all their products, is bland and innocuous: "It's Gooo-od." The phrase is better used in a verbal fashion, drawing out the syllable for emphasis. Written, it's harder to comprehend, leading one to mentally pronounce it as "gew-odd." Still, it sounds less old-fashioned and is faster to say on TV and radio. (I guess they had to go with an elongated form of *good* because Tony the Tiger had already appropriated "They're Gr-r-reat!" to endorse Frosted Flakes.) Most important, it's true. Purnell's sausage is the best sausage in the world.

I began wondering if the new motto was a business decision or a family mandate due to Kim's interest in me around the same time. Maybe the Purnells didn't want my country sausage coming to Louisville. *It's gooo-od that we got rid of that bumpkin early!* Feeling rejected, I realized I could simply call Kim and ask her what motivated the new motto. I immediately became terrified that she wouldn't remember me, or that she'd consider me a stalker with a forty-year delay. The best-case scenario would be if we talked for hours, met in person, fell in love, and I left my wife to move to Louisville and eat sausage forever. That would also be the worst-case scenario.

It took two days to generate the courage necessary to make the call, and I immediately ran into a problem—there were dozens of people with her name living in the USA. I got in touch with a local private detective named Larry, who advised me of a cheap online search engine that he used to track down deadbeats and bail jumpers. My Internet sleuthing resulted in calling her father, who said Kim was on vacation in the Bahamas, had two kids, and was celebrating her fortieth wedding anniversary. He said I could call back later and get Kim's cell number from his wife. I thanked him and hung up.

While waiting impatiently, I received a telemarketer's call, which irritated me with its rude intrusion. I then felt bad for bothering an old man at home. I decided to return to the Internet, that great fount of public knowledge. Kim had little online information aside from one designation as "homemaker." Incidentally, my birth certificate lists the same occupation for my mother. Maybe it is nomenclature particular to Kentucky. I quickly ran a search on the term and learned that the actress Jennifer Garner might be "the perfect homemaker" because she organizes the schedules for her three kids and husband. On the same "news" site I learned that Nicole Kidman still doesn't know why it took her husband, Keith Urban, four months to ask her on a first date. (OMG!) And that there are at least eight "Royals" I should follow on Twitter.

Elsewhere I found out that Kim's husband was a successful businessman who owned a tractor dealership. Like a modern-day *Game of Thrones* episode, two prominent business families had merged —vehicles and sausage—and I wondered why they didn't combine them into a car that ran on hog manure instead of gasoline. (Toyota is already on this with its recent production of the Mirai, an automobile that runs on hydrogen produced by cow dung.) From the looks of things, Kim had a nice life, a good husband who golfed, and grown kids with no criminal record.

For some unknown reason the whole thing made me feel sad. The search had been more enticing than achieving the goal, similar to the excitement of going to town. Once I got there, it was full of stores I couldn't afford and people who knew I was from the bad part of the county, home to bootleggers, arson, and gunplay. In my melancholic state, I imagined that Kim was sad too. Her life as a homemaker surrounded by golf equipment and tractors was unfulfilling. I understood that I was projecting my own sadness onto her, and I began feeling profound despair. It made no sense. Perhaps I was envious. Maybe I yearned less for her than the life I believed her family led—privileged, entitled, part of the social elite of western Kentucky.

I wanted box seats at the Kentucky Derby, a vacation home on the beach, and a fleet of luxury automobiles. I wanted a low golf handicap and an air-conditioned tractor cab. I wanted to be a happy pig smiling on the package, exuberant about going to town. What I really wanted was to be fifteen years old and walking around in the summer holding hands with a girl as innocent as I was, an innocence that would end quickly and harshly for me. That's why I was sad. But one thing always makes me happy: eating Purnell's "Old Folks" Sausage.

Later it occurred to me that my despondency was not new but refreshed, like a relapse, or in my case, "a re-sad." It was the slippery sadness of knowing that at age fifteen I'd inadvertently brushed against a world into which I could never fit. The "right way" of living life in America. A marriage of forty years. Money and tractors, trips to the Bahamas, tailored suits. I wasn't cut out for that kind of life, but having grown up in the land of opportunity, I felt as if some part of it should be mine. Face-to-face with my own past and an imagined life that could have been, I underwent a terrible epiphany. I'd spent decades convinced that I didn't want something simply because it wasn't available to me. I'd persuaded myself that striving to live well in middle America was false and empty, not for me. But I hadn't discarded those values, I'd been denied them in the first place. The lack of access made me judge the people who'd accomplished their version of the American dream. Now, like most of us, I was trapped with the life I'd made: car payments, sore back in the morning, worries about money. Instead of seeing what I had, everything that lay before me reminded me of my own failures. I would never own a tractor.

Later my wife told me I was too sensitive for the Internet. But it wasn't the Internet, and it wasn't Kim or the life I'd imagined for her. It wasn't even sensitivity or sadness, but a kind of wistfulness, a yearning for something beyond reach. I've known many people who strove upward. They shed their accents and preferences, pressuring themselves to pass at what came easily for others. They lived under perpetual duress. They seemed brittle around the edges, tense through the neck and face, as if afraid of being found out —an imposter from the dirt living in the city. Too often they died young, the strain eventually getting the better of them. At least, I told myself, I'd get old!

Despite my romantic concept of love at fifteen, there had never been anything for me in Louisville, or any of the big *villes*. I was more likely to work in the slaughterhouse than in sales; wear coveralls, not a suit; judge pies at the county fair, not a Miss Kentucky contest. I was destined to remain perpetually on the outside of whatever side was in.

I decided not to call Kim. I couldn't bring myself to tamper with the memory preserved. I needed the illusion of past perfection. What we had was puppy love, the stuff of movies and books. Over time she came to represent genteel society, socializing with elegant people in a gated community with a swimming pool. I'd have hated it. They would regard me as a "character" and I'd probably die young! What I really wanted was enough of a view into that world that I could discard it myself. As it was, I'd always felt barred from the upper-class order of niceties and etiquette, linen suits and bow ties.

I wouldn't call Kim because the worst-case scenario had shifted. Now I had a new fear. She would tell me that she had never forgotten our summer and was willing to change her life for me like the sausage changed its slogan. I'd patiently explain that as much I wanted to be part of her world, it was too late now. I'd be slumming at the country club the same way she'd been slumming in the hills all those years before. She found her life and I found mine. Kim was the only woman I'd loved who I hadn't hurt. I couldn't risk doing so now.

I resolved to never call her. I will live on my muddy acreage and drive my pickup truck and plant trees every fall. I will swing a sickle, not a golf club. I will wear my Carhartt jacket and my feed-store cap. I will eat Purnell's "Old Folks" Sausage twice a week. And I will always deeply miss the past, when every pork label proclaimed its glory: "The Country Sausage That's Going to Town."

Recipe
TRUE LOVE

Be fifteen.
Meet someone your own age.
Like that person more than anyone ever.
Hold hands in public.
Kiss in private.
Never do anything more.
Never see that person again.

JULIA O'MALLEY

The Teenage Whaler's Tale

FROM *High Country News*

BEFORE HIS STORY made the Anchorage paper, before the first
death threat arrived from across the world, before his elders began
to worry and his mother cried over the things she read on Facebook, Chris Apassingok, age sixteen, caught a whale.

It happened at the end of April, which for generations has
been whaling season in the Siberian Yupik village of Gambell on
St. Lawrence Island on the northwest edge of Alaska. More than
thirty crews from the community of seven hundred were trawling
the sea for bowhead whales, cetaceans that can grow over 50 feet
long, weigh over 50 tons, and live more than 100 years. A few animals taken each year bring thousands of pounds of meat to the village, offsetting the impossibly high cost of imported store-bought
food.

A hundred years ago—even twenty years ago, when Gambell
was an isolated point on the map, protected part of the year by a
wall of sea ice—catching the whale would have been a dream ac-
complishment for a teenage hunter, a sign of Chris's passage into
adulthood and a story that people would tell until he was old. But
today, in a world shrunk by social media, where fragments of stories
travel like light and there is no protection from anonymous outrage, his achievement has been eclipsed by an endless wave of online harassment. Six weeks after his epic hunt, his mood was dark.
He'd quit going to school. His parents, his siblings, everybody worried about him.

*

In mid-June, as his family crowded into their small kitchen at dinnertime, Chris stood by the stove, eyes on the plate in his hands. Behind him, childhood photographs collaged the wall, basketball games and hunting-trip selfies, certificates from school. Lots of village boys are quiet, but Chris is one of the quietest. He usually speaks to elders and other hunters in Yupik. His English sentences come out short and deliberate. His siblings are used to speaking for him.

"I can't get anything out of him," his mother said.

His sister, Danielle, seventeen, heads to University of Alaska Fairbanks in the fall, where she hopes to play basketball. She pulled a square of meat from a pot and set it on a cutting board on the table, slicing it thin with a moon-shaped ulu. Chris dragged a piece through a pile of Lawry's Seasoned Salt and dunked it in soy sauce. *Mangtak.* Whale. Soul food of the Arctic.

Soon conversation turned, once again, to what happened. It's hard to escape the story in Chris's village, or in any village in the region that relies on whaling. People are disturbed by it. It stirs old pain and anxieties about the pressures on rural Alaska. Always the name Paul Watson is at the center of it.

"We struggle to buy gas, food, they risk their lives out there to feed us, while this Paul Watson will never have to suffer a day in his life," Susan Apassingok, Chris's mother, said, voice full of tears. "Why is he going after a child such as my son?"

On the day they took the whale, Chris and his father, Daniel Apassingok, were cleaning a bearded seal on the gravel beach when they heard a cousin shouting. A black back cut the waves a few miles offshore. The three of them scrambled to their skiff.

Every whale is different, Daniel had told his son many times. An experienced crew captain knows to watch how each one moves and to calculate where it will surface. If they get it right, the boat will be 5 to 10 feet from the animal when it comes up. Then everything rests on the acuity of the striker in the bow, who holds a darting gun loaded with an exploding harpoon.

Daniel works as the maintenance man at the village school, supporting Susan, Chris, Danielle, and Chase, thirteen. Daniel is a decent hunter, but Chris is something else. The boy was born with a sense for the direction of the wind, an eye for birds flashing out of the grass and animals bobbing in the surf, Daniel said. He could aim and shoot a rifle at the age of five. By eleven he'd trained himself to strike whales, standing steady in the front of the skiff with the gun, riding Bering Sea swells like a snowboarder.

"He started out very young," Daniel said. "Chris kind of advanced a little bit faster than most people, even for me. He's got a gift."

From the boat, Chris and Daniel's village appeared in miniature, rows of weather-bleached houses staked in the gravel, four-wheelers parked out front, meat racks full of walrus and seal cut in strips and hung to dry. Across the water the other direction, mountains on the Russian coast shaped the horizon. Chris removed his hat to pray and scanned the glittering chop, his compact frame taut, his expression slack, as always. Daniel nudged the tiller.

When Daniel was a child, the village hunted in skin sailboats, chasing the whale in silence. Then as now, a boy started young, mastering one job, then another, until, if he was talented, he could try to make a strike. Daniel started as a striker at nineteen. He'd taken two whales so far.

The weather seemed to have changed permanently since he was a boy. He believed it was climate change. The ice didn't stay as long and wasn't the same quality. Whales passed at a different time. There were fewer calm days and more ferocious storms. The village was still recovering from one in 2016 that damaged sixty structures on the island, including their house.

Along with whale, the village relies on bearded seal and walrus for food. In 2013 hunting conditions were so bad, the village required emergency food aid to get through the winter. Subsequent harvests have been below expectations.

"It's always hard," Daniel said. "But it's getting harder."

They were a few miles offshore when the dark oblong of the whale passed their boat. Adrenaline lit up Chris. Just a few feet off the bow, the bowhead's back split the sea. Chris raised the darting gun, a heavy combination of shotgun and spear. He aimed.

"Please let us get it," he asked God.

He squeezed the trigger. The harpoon sailed, trailing rope.

Alaska Natives have been hunting bowhead in the western Arctic for at least two thousand years. The animals were hunted commercially by Yankee whalers from the mid-nineteenth century until the beginning of the twentieth century, decimating the population. Since then whale numbers have recovered, and their population is growing. In 2015 the National Oceanic and Atmospheric Administration estimated there were 16,000 animals, three times the population in 1985.

Alaska Native communities in the region each take a few whales a year, following a quota system managed by the Alaska Eskimo Whaling Commission (AEWC). The total annual take is roughly fifty animals, yielding between 600 and 1,000 tons of food, according to the commission.

Subsistence hunting of marine mammals is essential for villages where cash economies are weak. The average household income in Gambell, for example, is $5,000 to $10,000 below the federal poverty level. Kids rely on free breakfast and lunch at school. Families sell walrus ivory carvings and suffer when there isn't enough walrus.

Store-bought food can be two to three times as expensive as it is in Anchorage, depending on weight. In the village grocery, where shelves are often empty, a bag of Doritos is $11, a large laundry detergent is more than $20, water is more expensive per ounce than soda. No one puts a price on whale, but without it, without walrus, without bearded seal, no one could afford to live here.

The harpoon struck, but the wounded whale swam on. A second boat took another shot. The great animal lost power. It heaved over, belly to sky.

Soon Chris had congratulations in his ears and fresh belly meat in his mouth, a sacrament shared by successful hunters on the water as they prayed in thanks to the whale for giving itself. He had been the first to strike the whale, so the hunters decided it belonged to his father's crew. They would take the head back to the village and let the great cradle of the jawbone cure in the wind outside their house.

They towed the whale in and hauled it ashore using a block and tackle. Women and elders came to the beach to get their share. Every crew got meat. Whale is densely caloric, full of protein, omega-3s, and vitamins. People eat it boiled, baked, raw, and frozen. Its flavor is mild, marine and herbal like seaweed.

People packed it away in their freezers for special occasions. They carried it with them when they flew out of the village, to Nome and Anchorage and places down south to share with relatives. Everyone told and retold the story of the teenage striker. Then the radio station in Nome picked it up: "Gambell Teenager Leads Successful

Whale Hunt, Brings Home 57-Foot Bowhead." The *Alaska Dispatch News,* the state's largest paper, republished that story.

It used to be that rural Alaska communicated mainly by VHF and by listening to messages passed over daily FM radio broadcasts, but now Facebook has become a central platform for communication, plugging many remote communities into the world of comment flame wars, cat memes, and reality-television celebrity pages.

That is how Paul Watson, an activist and founder of Sea Shepherd, an environmental organization based in Washington, encountered Chris's story. Watson, an early member of Greenpeace, is famous for taking a hard line against whaling. On the reality-television show *Whale Wars,* on Animal Planet, he confronted Japanese whalers at sea. His social media connections span the globe.

Watson posted the story about Chris on his personal Facebook page, accompanied by a long rant. Chris's mother may have been the first in the family to see it, she said.

"WTF, You 16-Year Old Murdering Little Bastard!" Watson's post read. ". . . some 16-year old kid is a frigging 'hero' for snuffing out the life of this unique self aware, intelligent, social, sentient being, but hey, it's okay because murdering whales is a part of his culture, part of his tradition . . . I don't give a damn for the bullshit politically correct attitude that certain groups of people have a 'right' to murder a whale."

Until then Facebook had been a place Chris went occasionally to post pictures of sneakers and chat with his aunties. He heard about the post at school. By evening messages arrived in his Facebook in-box.

"He said, 'Mom, come,' and he showed me his messages in his phone, calling him names like 'You little cunt,' and 'I hope you choke on blubber,' 'You deserve to die,' and 'You need to harpoon your mom,'" Susan said.

A deluge of venomous messages followed, many wishing him dead.

Cleaning up after dinner, Danielle said she tried to keep count. She got to four hundred and they kept coming, from across the country and from Europe. Chris has been out of Alaska only once, to a church conference in Indianapolis, she said.

"There was this one message saying that, I read on his phone, that they hope that our whole community dies," Danielle said.

"It was pretty cruel," said his brother, Chase.

Chris said he tried to ignore the messages, to laugh them off. When he heard his parents and siblings talking about them, his eyes grew wet and he clenched his jaw.

"It never stops," he said.

Across the Arctic, people responded to Watson's post with comments, petitions, and private messages in opposition. The Alaska Eskimo Whaling Commission reported it to Facebook. Eventually it was removed. Across the region, whaling captains reminded hunters not to put pictures on social media.

Watson wrote another post, refusing to apologize.

"This has been my position of 50 years and it will always be my position until the day I die," he wrote.

Watson and Sea Shepherd declined to be interviewed for this story but sent a statement. "Paul Watson did not encourage nor request anyone to threaten anyone. Paul Watson also received numerous death threats and hate messages," it read. "It is our position that the killing of any intelligent, self-aware, sentient cetacean is the equivalent of murder."

Villagers have been familiar with Watson's opinions for many years. They have seen him on cable, and many remember 2005, when Sea Shepherd sent out a press release blaming villagers for the deaths of two children in a boating accident during whaling season.

Many environmentalists who object to subsistence whaling have a worldview that sees hunting as optional and recreational, said Jessica Lefevre, an attorney for the whaling commission based in Washington, DC.

"The NGOs we deal with are ideologically driven; this is what they do, they save stuff. The collateral damage to communities doesn't factor into their thinking," she said. "To get them to understand there are people on this planet who remain embedded in the natural world, culturally and by physical and economic necessity, is extremely difficult."

The organizations are interested in conservation but fail to take into account that Alaska Natives have a large stake in the whale population being healthy and have never overharvested it, she said. Some NGOs also benefit financially from sensation and outrage, she said, especially in the age of social media.

*

In the summertime village teenagers live in a different time zone in
the forever light of the Arctic. At 1 a.m. in June, their four-wheelers
buzz down to a large wooden platform basketball court in the gravel
by the school, where Drake pulses out of cell-phone speakers. The
girls wear polar fleece jackets, sparkle jeans, and aviator frames. All
the boys have Jordan sneakers. A half-dozen fidget spinners blur.

On a recent night Chris stood on the sidelines of a pickup game.
There was a girl with him. They didn't talk, but they stood close.
Occasionally someone threw him a ball and he made a basket.

It is hard to be alone in a village. Even if the adults are inside,
someone is always keeping track. Between blood relations, adop-
tions, and marriages, Chris's family is huge, with relatives in many
houses. Many are paying extra attention to him now.

Chris's grandfather, Mike Apatiki, lives just down from the basketball court. He has a freezer full of meat his grandson brought.
He worries less about Chris leaving school—hunting seasons have
put him behind for years—than he does about him feeling shamed.

"These people do not understand and know our need for food
over here," he said. "Like the rest of Americans need to have a
chicken and a cow to eat out there from a farm, we need our whale
and seal and walrus. Makes us healthy and live long."

Neqeniighta, the Siberian Yupik word for "hunter," doesn't have a
perfect equivalent in English, said Merle Apassingok, Chris's uncle,
who lives across the road from his grandfather. It means something
broader even than the word *provider,* and is tied to a role men have
played for generations that ensures survival and adaptation. When
a boy is a good hunter, he is poised to be a leader, Merle said.

"Hunting is more than getting a permit and fulfilling that permit with a grizzly bear or a Dall sheep or whatever," he said. "There
is happiness when a boy gets his first seal, there is joy. There is sadness when we have a tragedy. How can we isolate the word?"

He wishes that Chris's story had never left the island. He worries
his nephew has not lived long enough to process all that's happened.

"As far as day-to-day dinner on the table, hunters are everything
in the village," he said.

After basketball, when most of the village is asleep, Chris sometimes packs his backpack with ammunition, slips on his dirty camouflage jacket, and pumps up the leaky four-wheeler tire. Hunting,
he told his mother once, is like a story: suspense, conflict, resolu-

tion. He always prays the ending will be the animals showing themselves so he can take them back home, she said. As twilight edges into sunrise, he heads out alone down the coast, his rifle slung on his back. After a long ride, he crawls into a seal blind tucked behind driftwood on the beach, where he can stay for hours with only the birds and the smell of grass and the racket of the sea.

The Mad Cheese Scientists Fighting to Save the Dairy Industry

FROM *Bloomberg Businessweek*

IN A USUAL year Taco Bell juggles about four thousand new menu ideas. A dozen, maybe, will ever see the light of day. Trimming all this fat is the job of the chief food innovation officer, Liz Matthews, and a forty-person team of chefs, food scientists, nutritionists, microbiologists, chemists, and even one entomologist (he does food safety). Observers have unironically called this crew fast-food "disruptors." In the past five years Matthews's team has trotted out such blockbuster menu items as the Doritos Locos Taco (in Nacho Cheese, Fiery, and Cool Ranch varieties), a breakfast taco with a waffle for a shell, and a *chalupa* with fried chicken in place of its usual flatbread. Until a year and a half ago, however, one simple idea had foiled them: a fried tortilla full of oozing, molten cheese.

"Having this fabulous taco with melty cheese in every single bite was something we started dreaming about ten years ago," Matthews says. After a decadelong journey of dairy and failure and resolve, that dream eventually became the Quesalupa, a taco served in a cheese-stuffed fried shell whose 2016 arrival was heralded by a Super Bowl ad featuring a cackling George Takei. Costing somewhere from $15 million to $20 million, it was Taco Bell's most expensive ad campaign ever. And it paid off: the company sold out its run of 75 million Quesalupas during the product's four-month limited release. Chief executive officer Brian Niccol called the launch, which featured its own Snapchat filter, "one for the record books." Perhaps inevitably, the company began testing a Doritos Quesalupa Crunch in March.

Such is the influence cheese wields over the American consumer. Americans eat 35 pounds of cheese per year on average—a record amount, more than double the quantity consumed in 1975. And yet that demand doesn't come close to meeting U.S. supply: the cheese glut is so massive (1.3 billion pounds in cold storage as of May 31) that on two separate occasions, in August and October of last year, the federal government announced it would bail out dairy farmers by purchasing $20 million worth of surplus for distribution to food pantries. Add to that a global drop in demand for dairy, plus technology that's making cows more prolific, and you have the lowest milk prices since the Great Recession ended in 2009. Farmers poured out almost 50 million gallons of unsold milk last year—actually poured it out, into holes in the ground—according to U.S. Department of Agriculture data. In an August 2016 letter, the National Milk Producers Federation begged the USDA for a $150 million bailout.

That Taco Bell is developing its cheesiest products ever in the midst of an historic dairy oversupply is no accident. There exists a little-known, government-sponsored marketing group called Dairy Management Inc. (DMI), whose job it is to squeeze as much milk, cheese, butter, and yogurt as it can into food sold both at home and abroad. Until recently the "Got Milk?" campaign was its highest-impact success story. But for the past eight years the group has been the hidden hand guiding most of fast food's dairy hits—a kind of Illuminati of cheese—including and especially the Quesalupa. In 2012 it embedded food scientist Lisa McClintock with the Taco Bell product development team. She worked with the senior manager for product development, Steve Gomez, to develop a cheese filling that would stretch like taffy when heated, figured out how to mass-produce it, and helped invent some proprietary machinery along the way.

The finished product is mega-cheesy: with an entire ounce in the shell, the Quesalupa has about five times the cheese load of a basic Crunchy Taco. To produce the shells alone, Taco Bell had to buy 4.7 million pounds of cheese.

"Here's a little secret," says DMI president Barbara O'Brien. "If you use more cheese, you sell more pizza." DMI proved this decades ago: In 1995 the then brand-new marketing group worked with Pizza Hut on its Stuffed Crust pizza, which had cheese sticks baked into the edges. The gimmick was introduced with an ad starring a pizza-loving real estate baron named Donald Trump, and by year's end it had increased Pizza Hut's sales by $300 million, a 7 percent improvement on the previous year's. DMI has since estimated that if every U.S. pizza maker added one extra ounce of cheese per pie, the industry would sell an additional 250 million pounds of cheese annually.

The National Dairy Promotion Board created DMI in the mid-1990s to act as an umbrella company for state and local programs promoting the dairy industry. DMI is classified as a commodity checkoff program, a type of booster group for agricultural products funded by their producers. In addition to dairy, there are checkoffs for avocados, beef, cotton, softwood lumber, and an additional twenty or so commodities. The USDA's Agricultural Marketing Service loosely oversees these programs; they're authorized by Congress but ultimately answerable to the producers they serve. U.S. dairy farmers pay a compulsory checkoff fee of 15 cents on every 100 pounds of dairy they sell. It adds up: over the years DMI has collected hundreds of millions of dollars to promote and conduct research for dairy products.

DMI's original business plan was almost entirely direct-to-consumer advertising. But when consumers started eating out more in the late 1990s, the group shifted to working with companies that took products to the marketplace—particularly restaurant chains such as Pizza Hut and, eventually, Taco Bell. The DMI arrangement is unusual in fast food's highly competitive, proprietary world. Taco Bell isn't the only company benefiting from its expertise. The checkoff also puts DMI's agents inside Burger King, Domino's, McDonald's, Pizza Hut, and Wendy's, where they're privy to each restaurant chain's most closely guarded trade secrets.

Stuffed Crust was on the minds of everyone at Taco Bell as they welcomed McClintock, who was immediately assigned to the languishing Quesalupa project. "What Taco Bell usually needs is one person who's entirely dedicated to a product," she says—and sometimes, it seems, just one component of one product. "So that's what I was for—there to handle cheese."

It's worth pausing to note how serious a paradigm change Taco Bell credits DMI with causing. The company's innovation team once regarded cheese and sour cream as mere garnishes. Now dairy is often the focal point. Cheese use at the chain has increased

22 percent since the beginning of the DMI partnership. "Beef and cheese are the most important ingredients to our consumers," Matthews says. "But really, cheese." For proof, consult a menu. Eight items currently have the word *cheese* or *cheesy* in their name, vs. three with *steak* or *beef*. Breakfast items get a fancy cheddar shred; tacos get a three-cheese blend. Most of the chain's seven thousand U.S. locations also carry nacho cheese sauce and a spicy *queso* dip —the first in the company's fifty-five-year history—introduced to great fanfare last November.

No other cheese at Taco Bell, however, had to perform like the Quesalupa cheese. It had to be what CEO Niccol terms "an experience," a full five-sense extravaganza of melt and stretch. Before McClintock arrived, Gomez and his team had tested a glorified quesadilla folded in half, but consumers rejected it. "It didn't live up to the promise of a truly cheese-stuffed shell," Gomez recalls. Once they tried sealing off the sides, though, "it was like 'Holy crap, we can sell this.'"

How to mass-produce the shells became McClintock's problem. She applied her doctorate in chemistry to the cheese filling, comparing various varieties' chemical compositions, specifically the interplay between molecules of a protein called casein found in the space around milk fat. Think of casein as dairy glue that, at the right temperature and pH, gives cheese its pull by binding water and fat in a smooth matrix.

"If you tried using something like cheddar, you'd get too much oiling off," McClintock says. "It's a fattier cheese—it's not going to hold up well in terms of cheese pull." She also quickly nixed mozzarella. "Great stretch, but you expect something bold from Taco Bell," she says. "Pepper jack gave us the extra kick from the jalapeños." Crucially, it's also a high-moisture cheese, which means fewer casein connections and therefore a more reliable melt. She toyed with the idea of inserting a cheese "puck" into the tortilla pocket to see if that melted more uniformly, but grated cheese proved the most even. McClintock and Gomez recall intense competitions in the lab where they'd fry up a bunch of Quesalupas and tear them apart to see who could get the longest cheese pull. Winners sometimes stretched theirs a full arm span.

The final products were preassembled in factories using the Press, a proprietary machine Bloomberg wasn't allowed to see. Its basic function is to pressure-crimp the edges of two tortillas without squishing the cheesy center. "When I say it out loud, it sounds so simple," Matthews says, "but I can tell you, it took a huge team of engineers." McClintock spent four months traveling among supply facilities for Tyson Foods Inc., Taco Bell's tortilla vendor, introducing workers to the machinery, which had to be operated manually and was difficult to wrangle. "These 250-pound workers basically had to jump up and down while pulling on it to get enough pressure," she remembers. After observing it, Niccol told *Fast Company*, "It looks like that Lucille Ball skit." Since Taco Bell needed 75 million of these things for the January rollout, Tyson had no choice but to bring in a special team whose job was to yank the Press by hand 75 million times.

DMI argues that its prowess has helped slow Americans' declining desire for dairy, even as milk and cheese consumption has moved in opposite directions. Demand for milk has gone from 35 pounds per person in 1975 to 15 pounds today, the reverse of the trajectory cheese has followed. But championing dairy also means DMI has promoted lots of saturated fat and cholesterol, which has created its share of controversy. "Americans rely on the USDA for dietary guidance," says Parke Wilde, a food economist at Tufts University who studies the checkoffs. "All these fast-food restaurant-chain partnerships must be pretty embarrassing for the people at the agency working to promote healthy eating." Still, DMI's benefit to the dairy industry is clear: a cost-benefit analysis done by Texas A&M University economists in 2012 shows that every dollar a dairy producer invested in DMI returned $2.14 for milk, $4.26 for cheese, and $9.63 for butter industrywide.

Americans may buy less dairy from the grocery store than they used to, but they still like to eat it. After McDonald's switched from using margarine in its restaurants to real butter in September 2015 —a change DMI lobbied for—the company said Egg McMuffin sales for the quarter increased by double digits. "It wasn't easier, it wasn't cheaper, but it was the right thing to do with our food," says McDonald's executive chef, Dan Coudreaut, of the changeover. "As our guests' tastes evolve, McDonald's is obviously going to evolve as well. If we don't, then we become a dinosaur." To help McDonald's execute the shift, DMI's food scientists developed procedures for storing and softening it (one of margarine's primary advantages is its spreadability straight from the fridge), then helped the company locate suppliers for its 14,000 high-volume restaurants.

One of those suppliers was Grassland Dairy Products Inc. in Greenwood, WI, the largest family-owned butter manufacturer in the U.S., which operated its factory seven days a week to churn out 2.4 million pounds of butter to satisfy McDonald's prelaunch butter needs. In April, Grassland announced that its exports to Canada, worth millions, had evaporated because of protectionist pricing guidelines and quotas the Canadian government instituted, causing the conglomerate to suspend milk contracts with fifty-eight dairy farms. Grassland president Trevor Wuethrich said in a statement to Bloomberg that the company has seen an overall increase in demand despite the quotas, which it attributes to "changes made by McDonald's" as well as consumers "seeking simple and natural products," something else DMI takes partial credit for.

Wisconsin governor Scott Walker wrote a letter of complaint to President Trump in April over the Canadian policy. During a visit to Kenosha later that month, Trump publicly blasted Canadian milk subsidies as "a disaster" and "very, very unfair," and predicted they're "not going to be happening for long."

Canada aside, DMI is betting hard that the industry's future will be abroad. In 2009 the group commissioned Bain & Co. to study globalization's impact on the industry. The report was optimistic about exports overall but urged producers to "take action now." It predicted milk demand would grow by 7 billion pounds over the next four years as consumer interest explodes in Asia, Latin America, northern Africa, and the Middle East. Bain concluded that U.S. dairy producers were "well positioned" to fill that gap.

DMI is a pro at getting cheese into foods that never had any, but many dairy farmers are nostalgic for the days when milk was boxed in cartons and served in every kid's lunch rather than ultrafiltered for use in cheese manufacturing. Harry Kaiser, an economist at Cornell University who for years oversaw DMI's annual report, argues that farmers' disillusionment stems from changing consumer habits. When the checkoff got its start twenty-plus years ago, "milk really was just a commodity," he says. The current consumer emphasis on quality and simplicity would seem to create an opportunity for small-time producers with a story to tell. DMI, however, is not a small-time business, which has made certain farmers averse to checkoffs. "They're saying, 'Well, look, I sell organic milk,' or 'I make really great cheese, and it's not a commodity now, it's a brand,'" Kaiser says.

Other farmers complain that DMI was pitched as a self-help program for everybody but it disproportionately benefits Big Dairy. According to DMI, half the industry's 43,000 farmers have 500 cows or fewer, but that's not who gets tapped to fulfill major food-service contracts (e.g., Grassland).

Farmers such as Skip Hardie, a dairy farmer in upstate New York who's on DMI's board, argue that the benefits filter down. "You have to keep in mind that the raw product to make that cheese or butter or yogurt is milk," he says. "So if McDonald's all of a sudden switches to butter, a lot of dairy farmers in the United States are going to sell more milk. Any time you create new demand for a dairy product, it's removing milk from the market that would have had to find a home someplace else."

Others, such as Brenda and Joe Cochran, beg to differ. The Cochrans raise 130 cows on 283 acres in north-central Pennsylvania, and in 2003 sued the USDA and the National Dairy Promotion Board, DMI's parent group, arguing that by paying into the checkoff, they were being forced to subsidize speech — "Got Milk?" — they didn't agree with. "To us, it doesn't matter if it's a small Amish farm with Jersey cows on a pasture system or a big multigenerational family farm, we feel the farmer is still being misrepresented by what the checkoff is communicating," Brenda says. "We produce our milk in a certain way, then it gets commingled with other production paradigms, and then somehow it's generically abracadabra'd into a standard product offered to consumers. That's not truth."

A Pennsylvania district court sided with the USDA, but its decision was reversed on appeal by the Third U.S. Circuit Court of Appeals. The Cochrans' legal victory was short-lived: the following year the Supreme Court took a case brought by the Livestock Marketing Association against USDA and the beef checkoff, alleging that "Beef: It's What's for Dinner" elided the difference between, say, a chuck steak and a grass-fed porterhouse.

Checkoff critics had high hopes. Legal scholar Laurence Tribe was the ranchers' attorney, and Justices Antonin Scalia and Ruth Bader Ginsburg both seemed annoyed by the government's protected-speech defense. ("What is the government speech?" Ginsburg asked. "If you went to the surgeon general, probably that message would be 'Eat meat moderately.'") But the court ruled against the ranchers, rejecting Tribe's argument—identical to the Cochrans'—that the government was forcing them to "engage in speech they don't agree with." Armed with legal precedent, checkoff groups have invoked protected speech as the basis of every defense they've mounted since.

Congress is feeling pressure from agricultural groups to limit checkoffs, largely because of the American Egg Board's two-year effort to kneecap eggless-mayonnaise maker Hampton Creek Inc., which came to light in 2015. (Hampton Creek effectively kneecapped itself later by having contractors buy its Just Mayo spread in bulk from stores, creating artificial demand. A trickle of board resignations culminated in mid-July, when the entire directorship, except for the CEO, resigned.) In March, Republican senator Mike Lee of Utah and Democratic senator Cory Booker of New Jersey, simultaneously with Republican representative David Brat of northeast Virginia, introduced the Opportunities for Fairness in Farming Act, which is designed to "bring much needed reforms to federal checkoff programs" by "cracking down on conflicts of interest and anticompetitive practices, and bringing additional oversight and transparency," Booker said in a press release.

O'Brien of DMI defends her group by pointing out that its acting order was never to address the needs of individual farmers—rather, it's built on the philosophy that "all boats will rise." McDonald's Coudreaut says the stakes are much bigger than individual farmers. "I think about the twenty-seven million people eating in McDonald's every day and how they're being exposed to real butter now," he says. "I don't want to bad-mouth margarine, but when I grew up, Mom brought out butter at Christmas and Easter. Now people are exposed to real butter when they eat the food at our restaurants, and I think that's pretty cool."

At Taco Bell, McClintock's next challenge is automating the manual assembly for the Quesalupa 2.0, which is under development and is rumored to come in two new flavors, Volcano and Bacon Club. If she succeeds, it could open up a whole other level of scale. Of course, the 2.0 version of the Press is also shrouded in mystery, but McClintock does mention "figuring out how to get

robots to pick up cheese and put it on tortillas" and things moving "at very, very high speeds." Maybe it will be enough firepower
to truly mass-produce Quesalupas. Get them in the frozen aisle of
Walmart and Kroger, DMI would argue, and now you're moving
miles of cheese.

The Joy of Reading About Cooking

FROM *The New York Times Book Review*

THE IMPERATIVE MOOD can be so intimate in its rudeness, like a mother or a friend speaking plainly: Skin the chicken. Tell me everything. Crush the garlic. I was drawn to it when I was nine, the year my family moved from London to a tiny village east of Paris.

I didn't speak any French, and no one in town spoke English —not my teachers, not the other students. I sat in the back of class, hoping no one would say my name. They said it both sweetly and incorrectly, an accent added to the *e*, the *j* softened out. Children and adults, including my teacher, spoke to me with an insufferable patience. As if I were a baby, they fed me the words one soft, indecipherable syllable at a time. They taught me politeness by demonstrating their own, keeping me at a distance with formality.

As soon as I got home from school, a daily humiliation, I read my parents' cookbooks. These were the only English books in the house I hadn't already read, a random assortment of gifts and last-minute purchases made at airports. It didn't bother me too much that it wasn't Enid Blyton or Roald Dahl. I was a reader, happy to be reading. Every page was new to me, equally precious, and I hung on to the microstories tucked into the recipe introductions, any turns of phrase or quotations I could memorize.

No one in my family had been to Australia, but we had a paperback of the *Australian Women's Weekly Children's Birthday Cake Book*. I studied its pages before going to sleep, lingering over the steps for a vanilla cake lined with chocolate biscuits, topped with finely chopped green jelly and white plastic figurines, which was meant to look like an aboveground swimming pool. It was a book about aesthetics more than cooking, and whether the recipe was for a typewriter with candy keys or a rubber duck with potato chip lips, it began, like a prayer, in the exact same way: "Make cake according to directions on packet."

There were at least two cookbooks by the actor and author Madhur Jaffrey, whose clear, confident voice I latched on to immediately. A pink-and-blue box was filled with recipe cards in different people's handwriting, crusted over in places, stained. I sifted through this box, pretending to reorganize its contents, reading the old newspaper clipping that had gone fuzzy and soft, my grandfather's notes in the margins in runny blue ink.

Maybe I would have learned this reading anything, but I learned it reading cookbooks: words can be used to make an idea more precise or more vague, to make something clear or to blur its edges. Some writers are good at imagining people who don't live a life exactly like their own, and others seem incapable.

A small, peach-colored copy of *The London Ritz Book of Afternoon Tea*, published in 1986, became my comfort reading. There was no explanation for its being in the house. It was filled with nostalgia for Edwardian London, and its recipes mercilessly enforced all sorts of snotty rules, including that when baking one should use "only the best quality chocolate" and that teabags were "never a good idea." But I liked the sentences, and it fit in my school bag, so for two months I took it everywhere with me, reading a recipe for tea cake or meringues on the bus or between orthography classes. Finger sandwiches at a posh hotel seemed like such a fantasy, reading about it would kick in like a sedative, immediately soothing. Foreign cakes, the tea book told me, held "a frisson of wickedness," but won over the English with their "delectable foreign ways."

I started the recipe for rose petal jam, collecting a liter of rainwater in a dirty bucket and snipping the roses that bloomed along the stone wall between our house and the neighbor's. I covered the washed, shredded petals in sugar overnight, but I never made it to the next step.

Before the end of the year, my handwriting changed, the language in my dreams, everything. I made friends, watched French cartoons, read only French books and comics. I wrote my name with an accent on the *e*, showing people in advance how to mispronounce it. Marielle was my best friend, and she came to school on Wednesdays, which were half-days, with wet hair that smelled like lavender. She'd laugh and correct me if I got something wrong —a gendered article, usually—but it wasn't that often anymore. And after I had slept over a half-dozen times, Marielle's mother stopped fussing, stopped asking me what I would and would not like, stopped talking to me delicately, like a thing that might break. "Come downstairs," she'd shout, when dinner was ready. "Wash your hands. Eat."

Oysters: A Love Story

FROM *The New York Times Magazine*

I MET A man from Long Island—at a bar, by chance, a year after I moved to New York—and right away I liked him. We walked from the bar to a twenty-four-hour diner in the East Village and got grilled cheese sandwiches and french fries and drank bad room-temperature coffee and talked for hours, until a stranger came over and asked if we would like him to officiate our wedding, right there, in the church of Veselka, at this sticky table by the bathroom.

By then it was light outside. I'd known the man for nine hours, and I was powered by an engine of pure enthusiasm. I said sure, why not, yes. Our waitress rolled her eyes but agreed to be the witness as we smeared an unofficial document with ketchup. Not long after, I learned that the man I'd diner-married had worked for many years opening clams and oysters in bars, and it had left him with a calm, clear-eyed appreciation. What I mean is, he didn't get worked up when he talked about oysters, not like some people I knew. And he didn't insist that I try one particular variety, grown off one remote island, with nothing but a squirt of lemon, of course, because anything more would be disrespectful to the oyster.

I liked oysters just fine, but not that much. When I ate them raw, by the dozen, they were occasionally delicious—fat and intact and salty, slipping out of pristine shells. Just as often they were nothing special. Like mouthfuls of bland, brackish jelly, or the sweat off coins from deep pockets, or the fermented milk of a mythical sea creature. Now and then, at a bar with a careless shucker, I got one that had been pried open with a dirty knife. It would be flipped out of shape, hiding grit or sharp, calcified fragments that cut at my tongue. It didn't seem worth the hassle.

But there was something about the way he liked oysters—keenly and quietly, without fetish or hyperbole—that made me reconsider. We carried about a hundred, along with a jar of chopped shallots in vinegar, to my friend's apartment one New Year's Eve, in part because I wanted to get good at opening them; I could manage only one or two in the time he opened six. Later on we ate them smoked, on crackers, and hot, in pan roasts and sandwiches, and, when we visited friends in New Orleans, roasted in garlic butter, freckled with pulverized anchovies and cayenne pepper. Then we walked down the street with grease stains on our clothes, toward music.

When my parents came to visit the apartment we'd shared for three years, I blitzed butter in a food processor with hot sauce, lemon zest, and garlic until the streaks disappeared and the mixture was a pale peachy pink. Outside, the man sat at the table and talked and opened oysters with them while I lit the charcoal for my tiny travel-sized grill. I dropped lumps of cold butter into each shell, crowding them on a piece of crinkled foil so they didn't tip over. I could hear voices behind me, gossiping about family, gasping at rude things, bursting into what I recognized as a mix of both nervous and real laughter.

It took a few minutes for the butter to start bubbling, to make a tangy, fatty sauce with the oyster liquor, and for the meat to heat through. Then we ate in rounds, with grilled bread to clean out the grooves in the shells, and a big, simple salad of romaine and sliced radishes, putting a dozen or so half-shells on the grill every time we ran out.

What my mother wanted to know, after we'd emptied a bottle of wine, was if he and I ever talked about getting married. Not that she minded us living together, no, it wasn't that, and not that it mattered these days, not at all. She wasn't old-fashioned, she insisted, but it would be so nice to know more about my long-term plans. I told her the truth, that I didn't have any long-term plans, but that the oysters on the grill couldn't wait—oysters were like that. I had to go check on them right this second.

Mario Batali and the Appetites of Men

FROM *The New Yorker*

IN THE PANTHEON of American celebrity chefs, Mario Batali is a figure of appetites so legendarily large that his name is scarcely invoked without one of several modifiers: hedonistic, Falstaffian, Dionysian. He is also, according to reports published this week in *Eater*, the *Washington Post*, and the *Times*, a serial sexual harasser whose years of abuse of employees and others have included crude language, unwanted physical contact, and—as allegedly witnessed, in real time, by a server on a security camera, according to the *Times*—kissing and groping an unconscious woman. In response to these revelations, Batali, who owns or co-owns more than two dozen restaurants, hosts the ABC morning show *The Chew*, and has extensive licensing partnerships, has issued a number of apologies. The first, to *Eater*, includes an explanation: "We built these restaurants so that our guests could have fun and indulge, but I took that too far in my own behavior."

Celebrity chefs sell more than food; they sell stories. In October the *New Orleans Times-Picayune* published a report on the culture of harassment and sexual predation in the thousand-employee restaurant empire of the chef John Besh. Part of the shock of those revelations came from the dissonance between the allegations against Besh, which include engaging in a "long-term unwelcome sexual relationship" with a female employee (Besh has called the relationship "consensual"), and the story he had sold of himself. An ex-Marine with a Sunday-school side part and Chiclet teeth, Besh had marketed himself as a family man, a good dad and a loving husband, a churchgoer and a patriot who liked to mention offhand that the aroma of toasting almonds for trout amandine was similar to the scent in the air that his Desert Storm platoon was trained to recognize as a chemical attack. For people plugged into the restaurant-industry whisper network, however, Besh's comeuppance was no surprise.

There is no such clash between public image and private reality in the revelations about Batali, because Batali has always in a sense been selling sex. It's there in his worshipful gazes at ingredients held aloft, his exhortations to his friends, viewers, and dining companions to taste whatever rests on the tongue—to really *taste* it, to pour your body and brain into it, to concentrate yourself into nothing but a single scintillating bud of physical sensation. It's there in his body itself, in an abundant, flushed fatness that seems to physically manifest a flagrant rejection of the superego. And it's there in his language, his voice. As a food writer and editor, I've crossed paths with Mario over the years, and I can report that it is almost an intoxicant. He has whispered in my ear about the rice in a paella, how the grains are both soft and firm. He has growled across a recording booth about the cornmeal dusting a po' boy from Domilise's, in New Orleans. In a 2002 *New Yorker* profile that trembles with carnality, Bill Buford immortalized the chef's grandiloquent libidinousness: "In Batali's language, appetites blur: a pasta made with butter 'swells like the lips of a woman aroused,' roasted lotus roots are like 'sucking the toes of the Shah's mistress,' and just about anything powerfully flavored—the first cherries of the season, the first ramps, a cheese from Piedmont—'gives me wood.'"

It's worth noting that appetites like Batali's are, for the most part, not permitted to women; neither are bodies like his, with their evidence of hungers fulfilled. (Batali has been held up as something of an icon within the wildly misogynist pickup-artist community, where he's considered an archetype of a man who "can be seductive and yet completely visually unattractive.") A woman's hunger, by contrast, "always overreaches, because it is not supposed to exist," Jess Zimmerman wrote in her 2016 essay "Hunger Makes Me." "If she wants food, she is a glutton. If she wants sex, she is a slut." The world does not extend to women the courtesy we have granted Batali, that of reserving our condemnation until his indulgences cross the line into abuse.

For years Batali's behavior has been a subject of gossip: his vul-

gar comments, his roving hands, his propensity for bad behavior in
the public privacy of the Spotted Pig, the West Village gastropub
in which he is an investor. That establishment is co-owned by the
restaurateur Ken Friedman, whose own persistent pattern of sexual harassment was also exposed, on Tuesday, in the *Times*. ("Some
incidents were not as described, but context and content are not
today's discussion," Friedman said in a statement to the *Times*. "I
apologize now publicly for my actions.") We learned in that report
that among employees, the Spotted Pig's VIP-only third floor had
been nicknamed "the rape room" and Batali the Red Menace. "He
tried to touch my breasts and told me that they were beautiful,"
a former server at the Spotted Pig told the *Times*. "He wanted to
wrestle. As I was serving drinks to his table, he told me I should sit
on his friend's face." Behold, in these stories, the insidious duality
of a powerful man's rapaciousness (the word shares a root—the
Latin *rapere*, to take by force—with both *ravenous* and *rape*): Batali's
disregard for boundaries has in the past been a foundation of his
mythology, a thing not to recoil from but to admire; in the context
of the current #MeToo movement, his behavior is just repugnant.

Buford's profile—and the terrific book into which it was later
expanded, *Heat*, a touchstone for food writers of my generation
—is packed with other anecdotes that now seem troubling. Revisit-
ing the book this week, I was appalled that my earlier self, reading
Heat a decade ago, hadn't even registered them as reason for concern. Batali says to Buford's wife, for instance, during dinner at the
Batali-owned restaurant Lupa, "You will eat your pasta or I will rub
the shrimp across your breasts." He says to a waitress, at the same
meal, "It's not fair I have this view all to myself when you bend
over. For dessert, would you take off your blouse for the others?"
Elisa Sarno, a cook at Babbo, complains to Batali about a prep chef
referred to as "the Neanderthal," who jokes about rape and eventually gets fired for his inappropriate behavior. "Mario told her there
was nothing he could do," Buford writes. "'Really, Elisa. This is New
York. Get used to it.'" At a taping of the Food Network series *Molto
Mario*, Batali unleashes an "anarchic spilling out of naughtiness,"
complete with "dancing, butt slapping, kissing." "Why am I not of-
fended?" the set manager asks. "Why is that not a lawsuit?" a guest
responds. Sometimes, Buford writes, "I wondered if Batali was less
a conventional cook than an advocate of a murkier enterprise of

stimulating outrageous appetites (whatever they might be) and satisfying them intensely (by whatever means)."

More recently, in a 2009 profile by the British critic Jay Rayner, virtually every woman who appeared—in person or in reference—was defined relative to Batali's sexual proclivities. There is the female sommelier ("This wine is treating me like a hooker in Florida, baby," Batali tells her); the accomplished British chef Angela Hartnett (Batali likes her "very much," Rayner writes, "though that doesn't really do justice to the completely filthy way he expresses his admiration"); and Gwyneth Paltrow, Batali's cohost, at the time, on a TV series about the cuisine of Spain ("You haven't asked me if I fucked Gwyneth . . . No, I did not fuck Gwyneth"). It is a testament to the power of the post-Weinstein reckoning that each of these comments now seems so starkly out of line.

Hunger and lust are twin evolutionary urges, and Batali is hardly the first to find them intertwined. Both offer intensely intimate, intensely physical rewards. Both are classically disdained—the two pleasures, according to Plato, that a true philosopher should forsake. But even if food and sex partner well, they do not occupy the same plane of experience. Feeding one's hunger is a mortal need; acting on one's sexual impulses is a choice. In his statement to *Eater,* Batali implied that his acts of sexual harassment were "indulgences" gone "too far." The problem is that this casts the recipients of his actions not as people but as objects, with no say in the matter, to be possessed or consumed. I asked Batali, in an email on Tuesday, whether he really thinks that his behavior can be defined as a form of excessive fun. "NO," he emailed back, the word in all caps. "I am ashamed of the way I behaved and am not making any excuses." It is entirely possible to build one's brand on overt sensuality without perpetrating abuse. What it requires is an awareness that frolicking in a thousand-dollar blizzard of white-truffle shavings or opening a fifth bottle of Barolo will never be the same as pawing an employee's breasts or asking her to take off her clothes.

KHUSHBU SHAH

Pawhuska or Bust: A Journey to the Heart of Pioneer Woman Country

FROM *Thrillist*

I RECENTLY PURCHASED my first piece of camouflage. It's a powder-blue tunic with pale flowers cascading down the fabric that I bought on Amazon for $8 after reading in Food Network star Ree Drummond's new magazine that a "floral top" is an essential part of her daily uniform. My new shirt may not provide tactical cover as well as the splotchy green-and-brown print associated with hunters and soldiers, but I was hoping it would help me blend in on this trip to an America very different from my own.

Northeastern Oklahoma is not only hot in the middle of June but humid, and I can attest that sandals would have been a much wiser packing decision than the camo top. But I hadn't endured two flights and a 3.5-hour drive in a compact rental car to get here from New York City to complain about the torrents of sweat drenching my knockoff Vans. I'd come to eat hefty portions of chicken-fried steak and biscuits drowned in gravy, and specifically those served up at Drummond's restaurant in the tiny town of Pawhuska.

Pawhuska has just 3,600 residents and one traffic light (and it only blinks red), but that didn't stop Drummond, better known as the Pioneer Woman, from opening a sprawling two-floor "destination bakery, deli, and general store" in an abandoned building on the corner of Kihekah Avenue and Main Street last October. The Mercantile—or the Merc, as it is fondly referred to by customers and staffers alike—is essentially Drummond's glorified take on a Cracker Barrel, only with better coffee, fewer rocking chairs, and a three-hour wait for a table.

The restaurant is an important addition to her ever-expanding comfort-food empire, which originated in 2006 with the cooking blog that put her signature folksiness on full display. ("Howdy! I'm a desperate housewife. I live in the country. I'm obsessed with butter, Basset Hounds, and Ethel Merman. Welcome to my frontier!" reads the blog's welcome note.) Since then, in addition to landing the Food Network show, Drummond has published cookbooks, teamed up with Walmart on a line of home goods, gotten into the denim game, announced plans to open a hotel, and launched the print magazine that inspired my decision to dress in florals today.

My hopes to interview Drummond in her natural habitat didn't pan out—she was in meetings at Walmart's Arkansas headquarters. But I did get to talk to her briefly on the phone as she drove back from the airport to her sprawling ranch just outside Pawhuska, and she was every bit as genial and modest as she is on TV. When I asked about the restaurant's success, she said, "When we planned the Merc, I never imagined there would be a line out the door! I hoped that the tables would maybe be full. The fact that people are waiting in line really makes me want to continue to make sure everyone's experience is wonderful."

Drummond's devoted fans—whose passion for all things Ree nearly caused the debut issue of *The Pioneer Woman* to sell out in less than a week—are now making pilgrimages to Pawhuska in surprising numbers. I was curious about what types of people were flocking to a place that multiple locals described to me as "a ghost town" and how quickly things change when a celebrity restaurant opens for business.

The lobby of my hotel, located thirty minutes outside Pawhuska in the small city of Bartlesville, was sanitary and sunny—a pleasant-enough space to graze on the free breakfast included with my room as part of a "Pioneer Woman Special" before heading off to the Mercantile. As I picked at the unremarkable omelette on my plate, I couldn't help but listen in as four white women sitting nearby talked in thick Texan accents about their plans to visit Drummond's restaurant later that morning. They'd built their annual mother-daughter trip around an expedition to the "mer-can-teel," as they pronounced it, even though it was a six-hour trek from their hometown of Turkey, Texas.

When I introduced myself, making sure to enunciate my name

clearly, one of the ladies responded with disbelief. "Khushbu? Aren't you mad your momma gave you a name like that?" she asked, bursting out in laughter at the combination of syllables that made up my very Indian name. She then informed me that Turkey is even more rural than Pawhuska. "I have to drive nearly an hour to get to a real grocery store," the woman said. "That's why I like Ree, she is just like me. She has to cook all of her meals."

"And she makes *real* food," drawled another member of the group.

"It's nice to see someone like us on the TV. It's rare," the first woman added. "Plus, she's really clean and wholesome—what is there not to like?"

Similar sentiments were later echoed by every Pioneer Woman fan I spoke to, the vast majority of whom were white and from the Midwest or the South, like the three tall and husky female friends who told me they'd driven thirteen hours from Indiana because Drummond makes "real American food" and "the stuff you actually want to eat." That message is even echoed by Drummond's staff. "Ree promotes a way of life that is so relatable, or it takes you back to that [nostalgic] time and place that is so family-centered and agricultural," Taylor Potter, the Merc's director of operations, told me. "It's authentic. It's America. It's that true small-town, in-the-middle-of-the-country feel." Drummond's fans yearn for the good old days of homesteading and the pastoral farm, a "real America" where recipes are free from "scary, foreign" ingredients and made by hardworking "prairie folk" with "good Christian values."

Drummond has never gotten overtly religious on *The Pioneer Woman*, but the success of her brand very much centers on her appeal as a good Christian. In a strong marriage, with no children born out of wedlock, and given to replacing swear words with terms like "Oh, my gosh!," she's wholesome to the extreme. She might not always quote Bible passages while she's making her recipes on TV, but her pastor will come up in conversation, and the Mercantile does sell bracelets stamped with prayers like "Lord, make me an instrument of your peace."

At forty-eight, Drummond is arguably Food Network's biggest star right now, a feat she's accomplished under the artifice of a traditional stay-at-home wife cooking for a hardworking, manly husband and their four well-behaved children. Her house is always pristine, her signature red hair is always perfectly shaped into loose curls, and her food is always plated in some extremely photogenic form of cast iron. The mistakes she makes are never catastrophic but are instead presented as "teehee oops! silly old me!" moments that only serve to endear her to the audience more.

In many ways she's filled the deep-fried hole left by the ousting of southern butter queen Paula Deen following a slew of racism scandals. Not even a controversy of her own, after a resurfaced clip from an old episode of *The Pioneer Woman* in which Drummond disparages Asian hot wings made the rounds online earlier this year, slowed the rise of the Food Network's new queen of "down-home cooking." That's in part due to building a career on aspirational relatability; her fans don't just want to be friends with her, they want to *be* her, and may even believe that they can be. After all, she's just a cattle rancher's wife running a little Internet blog where she shares recipes and stories of her family that just happened to blow up into a multimillion-dollar empire.

But the perceived Pioneer Woman image is at constant odds with Drummond's backstory. Born Anne Marie Smith, the daughter of a prominent surgeon right here in Bartlesville, she was reared in a home that overlooked a golf course. Drummond went to college at the University of Southern California and had dreams of becoming a lawyer and moving to Chicago after graduating in 1991. But that changed when, as recounted in the memoir *The Pioneer Woman: Black Heels to Tractor Wheels — A Love Story,* she met a "Wrangler-wearing cowboy" with "big and strong" hands. That cowboy, whom she married in 1996 and affectionately refers to on her blog as Marlboro Man, was Ladd Drummond; as of 2013, he and his cattle-ranching family owned more land in the United States than all but sixteen others, with 433,000 acres throughout Oklahoma. But if the giant economic canyon between Drummond and her fans bothers them, you'd never know it.

To understand the passion of Pioneer Woman disciples, it's important to note that getting to Pawhuska is neither easy nor quick. The closest airport, in Tulsa, is more than an hour away. Other options include flying into Oklahoma City and driving two and a half hours north, or flying into Kansas City and tacking on a three-and-a-half-hour drive across three state lines. To get to the area from New York City, a colleague and I had chosen the latter route, which cuts through hundreds of miles of mesmerizing Kansas farmland. (Did we do this so that we could blast "Wide Open Spaces" by the Dixie Chicks while recording an Instagram story? Maybe.)

And just when fans think they've arrived, they're told they still have hours to go. I learned this as we pulled up to the Mercantile after the short drive over from Bartlesville. When I spotted the line snaking around the building, I was thankful to have eaten the mediocre hotel omelette. It was just past 10 a.m. and already the wait to be seated was two and half hours long.

"Oh, honey, people frequently line up at five a.m.," said Linda, the tall, sturdy woman stationed at the large, wood-framed glass door leading into the Merc, when I expressed surprise about the wait. Linda—a gravelly voiced former oil worker with shoulder-length jet-black hair who asked me to keep her real name private and jokingly demanded that I credit her as the Mercantile's "door greeter, concierge, docent, historian, storyteller, and bouncer"—directed foot traffic while fielding endless customer questions, and prodded new and departing diners through the door using two phrases: "You can go on in, folks" and "You can come out, folks." While dutifully taking a photo of a mother-and-daughter duo, she said, "I came out of retirement for this job, but I didn't expect to be this busy. The waits are usually around three hours, but between Christmas and New Year that number got as high as six hours."

While not typical, it's not unheard-of for 15,000 visitors to descend upon the Mercantile in a single day, said Linda. (The city has addressed this onslaught of tourists with upgrades to its infrastructure, including the installation of a new public toilet for line-waiters to use.) The majority of customers are out-of-towners from various corners of the country. In its first week alone, Potter informed me as she walked me into the dining area, the Merc received at least one visitor from each of the fifty states. But Linda told me that she'd also been seeing a steady influx of international vacationers, and recalled meeting people from Germany, Sweden, and Australia.

This swell of customers has made Drummond the second-largest employer in town, after the Osage Indian Nation. While a handful of high-level employees—such as the Merc's pastry chef and culinary director—moved to Oklahoma to work here, most staffers are locals. "Ree doesn't talk about this much," Potter said, "but she has gone out of her way to ensure that everyone is being paid living wage." According to MIT's living-wage calculator for Oklahoma, that works out to at least $10.15 per hour, nearly three dollars above the federal minimum wage.

And it isn't only employees who are feeling the extra money in their pockets these days. Nearly a dozen new businesses have opened up downtown on or just off Main Street in the past year, and the success of the Merc has also been a boon to existing businesses in town, including restaurants. Directly next door sits the Brick Teepee, a cluttered establishment selling, according to a placard displayed in the window, "shabby chic" and antique items. The line to get into the restaurant portion of the Merc frequently extends past the Brick Teepee, and bored diners-in-waiting take turns browsing in the shop to break up the monotony and get out of the glaring Oklahoma sun. The woman at the store's register told me that the owner had initially planned to put a salon in the space but decided on opening a vintage store to take advantage of the foot traffic.

Across the street from the Mercantile at the Prairie Dog, which has been selling hot dogs and self-serve frozen yogurt since 2011, owner Marlene Mosely told me that the change has been notable and swift. "When I first opened my store, there was nothing really around me," she said while finishing up a bowl of fro-yo. Mosley, like Drummond, is married to a cattle rancher and has lived in Pawhuska for decades. "Most of my clientele these days are the annoyed and hungry husbands, fiancés, and boyfriends of the women who dragged them to the Merc," she said with a laugh and a wink. "It's been very good for business."

Since the Mercantile's opening, the city of Pawhuska has seen a 33 percent rise in sales-tax revenue collectively across all businesses, said Joni Nash, the executive director for the Pawhuska Chamber of Commerce, adding that the city finally has enough money to fund its long-gestating "streetscape" program, aimed at beautifying the area around the storefronts. "We're very thankful Ree opened the Mercantile," she said.

For years Pawhuska has been a town that needed saving. "For the longest time we've only had two industries: oil and cattle," says Nash. With the Merc, Ree's brought back a crucial third industry, one chicken-fried steak at a time. "For the state of Oklahoma, tourism is the third-largest industry, so we're finally parallel with the state in that," Nash adds. According to the Oklahoma Historical Society, the town is the most sizable community in Osage County, the state's largest. At 2,304 square miles, Osage is nearly twice the size of the state of Rhode Island. It's also home to the Osage Nation, who opened a settlement in 1872, naming it after a local chief named Paw-Hiu-Skah (meaning "White Hair"). By the time Oklahoma's statehood became official in 1907, Pawhuska had a population of just over 2,400 people.

By 1908 the town was home to twenty retail shops and four separate banks to go with its thriving cattle-ranching industry. Then came the oil boom, and for a brief and flitting juncture in history, Pawhuska was one of America's wealthiest places. The town spent the majority of the 1910s and a large chunk of the Roaring '20s flush with cash. While the streets weren't paved with gold, they were lined with tall buildings and luxury retailers—including an outpost of Tiffany & Co. and Rolls-Royce's first dealership west of the Mississippi River. Money seemed to be flowing in as rapidly as the oil gushing from the wells, and at its height the city was home to 6,400 people. But when the money drained out during the Great Depression, so did the people, kicking off a continuous decline.

The luxury stores and opulent car dealerships are gone. There aren't even any chain restaurants except for a solitary Sonic on the outskirts of town. There used to be a Walmart, but even it struggled to thrive. The corporate succubus, which usually feeds off of small rural communities, gave up on Pawhuska and retreated out of the town in 1995. There are also no hotels to accommodate visitors, only a handful of quaint B&Bs. "It's pretty much been a ghost town for a long time," says Angie Terronez, an Oklahoma native and the director of sales for the Hilton Garden Inn in Bartlesville, where I was staying. "When I was married, we would have to go through Pawhuska to get to my in-laws' house. You never stopped. You never said, 'Oh, let's go through Pawhuska' by choice."

That might still be the case had Drummond and her husband not purchased, in 2012, the downtown building that now houses the Merc. Built in 1903, it has been home to the Osage Mercantile Company, a telephone company, and a popular department store chain, but, like many structures in Pawhuska, it was eventually deserted and left derelict. The renovations on the 22,000-square-foot building had taken four long and trying years to complete, but upon completion, there stood the town's salvation, equipped with a grab-and-go deli, a sit-down restaurant, and a general store on the bottom floor and a coffee shop–cum–bakery on the top.

The abandoned Walmart now serves as Drummond's warehouse, where she stores boxes of the nearly four thousand different items she sells in the retail portion of her store. The Mercantile has no storage space of its own, and because it sells through so much product, trucks haul full loads of goods to the store nearly four times a day. This helps ensure that the shelves are always stocked with home, kitchen, and "fun" items like pastel ruffled cake stands, Mason jar shot glasses, and magnetic finger puppets of famous historical figures. Which is another way of saying that in less than a year, Pawhuska has transformed from a quiet, sparse town into a place where people from thousands of miles away come to buy adorable Benjamin Franklin and Helen Keller puppets for their fingers.

I'd regretted pairing the blue tunic with black leggings when I'd put them on in the morning, but at 4 p.m. I was silently praising the genius who invented stretchy elastic waistbands. I was on my second meal of the day at the Mercantile, and it would also be my final meal there, so in went my order for yet another round of comfort foods that only seemed to be served in punishing portion sizes. I felt like Joey showing up to Thanksgiving dinner in maternity pants in that infamous *Friends* episode.

After a young and jovial server, who looked better suited to being in a boy band than working the floor of a rural restaurant in Oklahoma, took my order, I gazed around the room. Though there were still long lines out the door, many of the seats were empty and waiting to be filled. My coworker and I had somehow won the seat lottery and been seated at a small round table in the corner, where the two walls of cushioned leather benches intersected, allowing us to avoid the awkward dance of figuring who would sacrifice their gluteal comfort and sit in the stiff wooden chairs. The dining room consumed nearly half of the lower level and sported just enough coffee-colored wood and woven Navajo print pillows to be the envy of anyone's "Rustic Home Decor" Pinterest board. At every turn there was a piece of decor to remind you that you were in "cowboy country," lest anyone forgot.

Even though I'd been in this room earlier in the day, my eyes still darted distractedly from one piece of decor to the next: the bright yellow espresso machine on the pine-green counter up front, the semi-open kitchen with arachnidian lamps dropping from the tin-tiled plafond to my right. But the most ineluctable feature was the large wall to my left that acted as a barrier between the dining and retail areas. The bottom half was covered by distressed wood paneling, broken up by a prodigious laser-cut floral pattern, and the top half was an exposed brick mural advertisement for the National Biscuit Company (the earliest iteration of Nabisco), discovered during the renovation of the building. It's all very "antique farmhouse," an aesthetic that feels less disingenuous here than when executed in a high-rise New York City apartment.

The servers fastened a table for ten by cramming together the remaining two-tops that lined the Nabisco wall. An all-female church group—part of the GLOW women's ministry, as a chatty member later explains—piled into their seats, relieved to be inside after a nearly three-hour wait in the blistering Oklahoma sun. I saw more church groups in the dining room of the Mercantile in two days than I had seen in my entire lifetime. Our server later revealed that these groups frequently leave religious pamphlets instead of tips.

The woman sitting at the end, closest to my table, patted down her graying hair, in an attempt to tame the frizz that appears when someone stands in palpable humidity for hours. A member in the middle of the table, who had her long salt-and-pepper strands pulled back into a thick braid, kept tapping her friend's shoulders in an attempt to take a group selfie, not realizing that she would need the wingspan of Kevin Durant to make it happen from her seat. I walked over and offered up my photo-taking services. While the women, all of them from neighboring towns, hadn't traveled as far as many of the other customers I met during my time here, this outing was clearly a big social occasion for them. Not counting wealthy superfans who can afford to jet into Pawhuska aboard a private plane, most visitors to the Merc need to plan ahead to afford the trip. "Many people have saved for months to be able to come and see us," said Potter.

The women thanked me and I sat back down as they offered to pray for us to have a smooth journey home. (They maybe cursed us instead—it took thirty hours, instead of three, to get home.) We agreed, and focused our attention toward the cast-iron skillet of macaroni and cheese, alfredo-drenched lasagna, vaguely Asian-inspired "Ginger" salad, and a chicken-fried steak that was large enough to make four separate chicken-fried steaks the server had just dropped off at my table. Having been there just five hours earlier for breakfast, I could still feel the remnants of my order—an elephantine breakfast pork chop, a biscuit sandwich with a bowl of thick gravy for dunking, a stack of pancakes armed with three flavored syrups, and a spinach-and-mushroom breakfast burrito ordered for the sole purpose of having a vegetable—sticking to the inside of my digestive tract. But I was on a mission.

The majority of the Mercantile's menu is designed to keep the customers planted firmly within their comfort zone—it keeps the clientele happy without challenging them to expand their horizons. That is, except for the store's coffee program. The restaurant is outfitted with not one but two top-of-the-line espresso machines that would make any hipster barista's heart soar, and Drummond worked with Topeka, a popular Tulsa roaster, to make her own signature coffee blend. But the clientele tends to struggle with the espresso-based menu. Jackie Cade, a barista (and now the bakery manager), became visibly giddy when I asked if they could make my standard summertime order of an iced Americano.

"We never get to make those around here," she tells me. "I love getting to use the espresso machine." What does sell, however, is the Spicy Cowgirl, one of the Merc's signature drinks, made with espresso, chocolate, cayenne, and a heavy pour of sweet cream. Drummond is the first to admit that the iced drink is more like a milkshake than a coffee. She also later admitted to me that she'd built the coffee program largely for herself. "I felt that I really did this whole thing just so that I could have a good cup of coffee every day," she said.

I was washing my hands in the Merc's cavernous bathrooms when a gaggle of three women rushed in. They hurriedly painted fresh coats of lipstick onto their lips while attempting to add extra volume to their hair at the same time. "I can't believe he is upstairs!" exclaimed one of the women, referring to Ladd Drummond's unexpected arrival at the bakery on the Merc's second floor. "He is so handsome. We have to go get a picture with him." The trio bolted out the door.

Though it may come as a surprise, Ladd is deeply involved in the Pioneer Woman brand. It was he who convinced Ree to go ahead and start a magazine. He was also behind the design and construction of the Mercantile and is heavily embedded in the store's day-to-day operations. "Ladd is here the most of them all," Linda later revealed to me. And though the menu is technically all Ree's recipes, he is involved with the food to a degree too.

Virginia Fistrovich, the Merc's executive chef of bakery operations, who once worked with famed chef Thomas Keller, recounts the story of Ladd insisting she figure out how to make a "flat" strawberry pie, a dish she had never heard of. (It looks like she figured it out.) Together, Ree and Ladd carefully manage the image of the brand, which is more manufactured than it might seem. Every single item sold at the Merc is picked by Drummond herself, and they are direct representations of her brand. Ceramic colanders sporting a vintage design (Americana vibes) are just as at home next to the decorative wall piece proclaiming "Cowboys are my weakness" (a ranch lifestyle) as they are to the collection of bacon- and pickle-shaped bandages (low-brow humor) Drummond also hawks.

This is especially evident when it comes to operations at the Mercantile. I was not allowed to take any photos of dishes the kitchen hadn't plated for me. The story of Paige Drummond, Ree's youngest daughter, working in the Merc as a barista is slightly exaggerated. ("She's here maybe once a month," said Linda.) And Ree insists on running the social media for the Mercantile herself, even though the staff always offers to help her out, Potter said. Drummond even went so far as to write the directions given to visitors looking to drive out to Drummond Ranch, so that every facet would be in her voice.

But none of that seems to matter much to her fans, who are deeply loyal, almost to the point of being militant. Write one thing that can be perceived as slightly negative about Drummond and brace for an onslaught of defensive comments. Anything she sells, they are willing to buy. When I spoke with Drummond, she admitted with a laugh that many people doubted the finger puppets would sell, but she was obsessed with them. It turns out her fans are too. I personally saw three people add finger puppets to their overflowing piles as they browsed in the store during my two days there. I never witnessed one person walk out with fewer than two bags of purchases from the Merc. One of the most popular items? A $5 roll of plastic wrap, called Chic Wrap, that Drummond uses on her show and her fans were lining up to buy. I picked up a roll and stared at it. There was nothing remarkable about it, except that it is endorsed by Drummond herself.

But Drummond also goes out of her way to repay her fans and

her community for their loyalty. "The Ree you see on television is the Ree you get in real life," Potter told me. And I believe there is definitely some truth to that. She seems genuinely flattered by her own success. And both Ree and Ladd are deeply obsessed with ensuring that visitors to the Mercantile feel taken care of. There are staffers tasked with doling out water bottles and umbrellas to ensure that the people in line remain hydrated and cool.

And this summer the Drummonds opened up tours to the Lodge, the posh house located on the family ranch that serves as a guesthouse and luxury studio space for her Food Network show. The tour is free and only requires the patience to drive 20 miles west of town, through the twists and turns across the bumpy gravel roads that outfit the Drummond Family Ranch. "Opening up the Lodge was actually one hundred percent my husband's idea— most of the good ideas are his," Drummond told me. "His thinking was that so many people have traveled from so far to come to the Merc, we should just add another little layer of memory to the trip. I'm glad he stuck to it."

This past Fourth of July the Drummonds even went so far as to throw a Fourth of July party for the town of Pawhuska out of their own pockets. The family usually hosts a soiree at their ranch, where attendees include the who's who of northeastern Oklahoma, including a number of local politicians. But this year they moved the affair to the center of town, across from the Mercantile, where Ladd and his brother personally set off a fireworks show for the town, according to Nash. "Ree got up and addressed the crowd that evening from the stage before the fireworks . . . and had her pastor pray," she added.

For as far back as Nash could remember, Pawhuska had been a "ghost town" on the Fourth of July, with everyone dispersing after the yearly parade held in the morning. But this year's festivities were packed. "We hadn't seen the town that alive at night," she said. "There was traffic leaving, and it was so exciting. It was a re-kindling of a town that has seen those times before and it's exciting to see those times again."

ANYA VON BREMZEN

The World's Last Great Undiscovered Cuisine

FROM *Saveur*

MEHRIBAN KAZIMOVA, THE sixty-nine-year-old mother of my Baku friend Zulya, is sticking long iron nails of the hardware variety into a pomegranate the size of a baby's head. She then lowers her spiky work into a pot bubbling with a slurry of ground walnuts and pomegranate molasses. Then she heats a horseshoe over a burner. A *horseshoe*. Grabbing oven mitts, she screams an incantation in Azeri and drops the red-hot horseshoe—*splosh! clunk!*—into the pot, leaving the whole fairy-tale brew to simmer just short of forever, until it's time to strain out the metal.

And that, dear comrades, is how you concoct *fisinjan*, the Azeri version of a chicken, pomegranate, and walnut stew of Persian origin that hereabouts comes black as the blackest Oaxacan moles and just as layered and rich. "Screaming scares the stew into blackening," Mehriban explains matter-of-factly. And if it doesn't do the job, why, oxidation from the horseshoe and nails will.

Welcome to Azerbaijan, a onetime Soviet republic, where you'll dine on *fisinjan* and other saucy (though un-nailed) stews called *khurush,* along with ethereal pilafs bejeweled with dried fruits, nuts, and barberries. Where the table is always laden with lavish sprays of whole opal basil and tarragon. Where you'll wrap briny village cheeses in flatbreads, dab tart homemade yogurt on fluffy omelettes called *kükü,* and savor lamb so flavorful it doesn't need salt. Then, over quince compote (or vodka), you'll gossip (surely) about another Mehriban—Mehriban Aliyeva, the current first lady of Azerbaijan, who looks like Gina Lollobrigida and loves launching eye-popping new cultural projects.

The tarragon, the saffron-stained rices, the sexy accents of unripe plums and verjus, the gigantic stuffed meatballs bobbing in broth—they are one reason my boyfriend, Barry, and I have returned for the second time in a year to Baku, the windy capital of this Caspian country of close to 10 million people wedged in between Iran and Russia in the easternmost corner of Europe. This most fascinating of places has a Turkic language, heavy Russian cultural baggage from its years attached to czarist and then Soviet empires—and the world's last great undiscovered cuisine, mostly indebted to sophisticated Persian palace cooking but with enticing inflections of Georgia, Russia, and Ottoman Turkey.

As a former Muscovite born in the USSR, I've brought my own family baggage to Baku. During World War II, my grandfather Naum, then a dashing Soviet intelligence chief, was stationed here to help prepare for the Tehran Conference—the first meeting of Stalin, Roosevelt, and Churchill, held south across the Caspian Sea. His family, including my seven-year-old mother, joined him here. Mom still describes Baku as an Orientalist mirage amid the devastation and hunger of wartime. Fishing in the Caspian was Naum's spy cover. His aides, she recalls, would haul in a sturgeon the size of a sailor, split open its stomach, and scoop out the caviar. To this day she can't look at fish eggs without feeling guilt at her family's luck while the rest of our ravaged country was starving. Equally vividly, my mother remembers Baku's stench of petroleum.

Oil. It was why Hitler veered calamitously toward Baku, but his Luftwaffe held off bombing. The führer wanted the city's vast energy reserves intact. Since ancient days, oil and natural gas have fueled the unexpiring flames of Azerbaijan's Zoroastrian cults, and now they underwrite post-Soviet Baku's futuristic high-rises, malls, and Dubai-worthy starchitect showstoppers—while the city's ornate fin-de-siècle façades testify to the late-nineteenth-century heyday when Azerbaijan pumped half the world's crude and local peasants turned overnight into oil barons. On my previous trip here I'd ogled the fantastical architecture, toured a Zoroastrian fire temple, and filled a plastic bottle, amazed, from black oil pools oozing in the arid moonscape outside Baku. And then I met Zulya, cousin of an Azeri friend in New York and such a fiercely formidable cook that the trip turned into my own Ottolenghi-esque mirage of charred eggplants, yogurt swirls, and dried rose blossoms.

So now I'm back, to pry out Zulya's and her mom's kitchen secrets. In between dolmas and pickles and syrup-drenched sweets, I'll try to untangle Baku's complicated cultural layers.

Mehriban, Zulya's mother, lives between Burberry and Dolce & Gabbana boutiques in a graceful nineteenth-century quarter—not the kind of hood, you'd think, where folks ritually scream at their pots. Entering her building, Barry noted the tomato-red Maserati parked across the street outside Z-style, a chic takeout food shop Zulya owns with her husband, Rufat. Mehriban belongs to a caste of old Soviet-educated elites. A former engineer, she's married to Azerbaijan's retired traffic-police chief. I prod her now about the horseshoe in the simmering *fisinjan* stew. She shrugs. "It's how they do it in Lankaran," she informs me, "my birth city of amazing cooks down on the Iranian border." Soviet times, though, were very different, annotates Zulya. "Then Mom mostly cooked borscht and stroganoff. My parents vacationed in Moscow." But the folkloric foodways held fast in Azeri DNA—and I'm now primed for Mehriban's *plov,* or pilaf.

Anyone familiar with Iranian cooking will recognize the basic pilaf technique: Dump aromatic basmati rice in a huge pot of water. Drain when half done. Steam again long and slow under a towel-swaddled lid until each grain is as eloquent as an Omar Khayyam quatrain. Most crucially, line the pot with lavash or a layer of rice mixed with butter and yogurt to create that addictively crunchy bottom crust called *kazmag* (*tahdig* to Iranians).

"In Azerbaijan we have perhaps two hundred *plovs,*" proclaims Mehriban. "I know at least fifty." For now she's showing off the *borani* pilaf, steamed with pumpkin cubes drizzled with sweet condensed milk and eaten with smoked *kutum,* a Caspian whitefish. The funky contrast of sweet pumpkin, buttery rice, and salty shreds of *kutum* is reason enough to fly to Baku. Ditto the stuffed cabbage Zulya supplies, not the leaden Slavic variety but delicate pouches elegantly filled with meat, dried fruit, chestnuts, and herbs.

As I watch Mehriban reach for enormous jars of preserves—white cherries, rose petals, and *feijoa,* the intoxicatingly fragrant pineapple guava—to accompany our sage tea, I try to unpack the

Azeri obsession with preserves and compotes: Ottoman influence or Soviet-era fixation with putting up *everything* dictated by shortages? Mehriban's household is its own cultural mash-up. Turkish soap operas blare on her Azeri-channeled TV, while beyond a flimsy partition her husband, the ex-traffic-police chief, watches old Soviet films on his own TV.

The next morning Barry and I survey Baku's architectural mix from our eighteenth-floor window at the Marriott Absheron, our glossy high-rise hotel near the Bay of Baku. The Government House, a Soviet-Gothic relic of Stalinist gigantomania, hulks right below. In the distance the Flame Towers, a trio of wavy 2012 glass-and-steel skyscrapers, loom like friendly earthworm monsters from a Miyazaki film. Closer, Beaux Arts oil-boom mansions line Baku Bulvar, the leafy promenade running along the crescent-shaped Caspian waterside. Just inland, the UNESCO-protected walled medieval Persian Old City has been pristinely restored, a stage set of honeyed-sandstone hammams, caravansaries, and carpet shops. Its highlight is the squat Maiden Tower, a marvel of twelfth-century brickwork that looks uncannily art deco.

Then again, not even an architect could tell which layer is which, because recently the whole city center has been sandblasted, refaced, and melodramatically lit to resemble Haussmann's Paris —by way of Vegas—at the whim of First Lady Mehriban, a twenty-four-carat Francophile. And yet Baku isn't an artificial desert folly like Dubai. The history behind its faux-French façades is real and resonant.

Zulya now swings by in her praline-colored Mercedes to whisk us to Yal Bazar, her favorite market. Tanned, coiffed, and sporting torn skinny jeans over Gucci wedges—a vision of Baku by way of Beverly Hills—Zulya had never planned to become the city's premier food diva. She trained as a concert pianist. But as a teenager, she says, she was more seduced by the frilly Soviet tortes baked by Valya, their Russian neighbor, than by sonatas and nocturnes. She begged Valya for recipes, surprised her parents with perfect éclairs, pestered Mehriban to recall old Lankaran dishes. In 2000, on a whim, she opened Z-style in her father's former garage space. "On opening day I stood mortified," she recalls. "Customers swiped every last *piroshki* from my lovingly arranged display!" That night an earthquake shook Baku—but the next day Z-style was even more mobbed. Now with five Z-style shops, a thriving catering business, and a new Caspian-side restaurant about to open, Zulya aspires to be Baku's Ottolenghi (her hero).

Like everything in Baku, the Yaşil market is extremely clean, more boutique than souk. Black and white mulberries are arranged in precise checkerboard patterns; pretty baskets overflow with fava beans and thin wild asparagus. In a spice row Zulya sifts bejeweled fingers through artful pyramids of plump, tart *zirinc* (dried barberries) and sumac in every shade of purple and burgundy. "What decadence!" she gasps in the preserves and pickles shop, where for one jam they stuff each yellow cherry with walnuts. Farther on a lady is selling fig vinegar, *abgora* (verjus), homemade rosewater, and *narsharab* (pomegranate molasses) under a portrait of Lenin. At each stall Zulya schools me in Azerbaijan's fruity-tart-herbaceous seasonings. "These flavor *levenghi,* the walnut paste for stuffing chicken or fish," she says of the sun-dried fruit leathers that shine like sheets of edible fabric in flavors such as Cornelian cherry. These plums? Puckery green *alycha* brings zing to herbed stews; amber dried *albukhara* commingles with chestnuts in a *khurush* called *turshu govurma,* or fills giant soup meatballs that Zulya plans to prepare. We stop at the verdant *sabzi* (greens) counters loaded with some twenty species of herbs.

"Herbs are essential to our Azeri table, as palate teasers by themselves," says Zulya, "and as elements in our dishes." Here's tarragon for chopping into *dovga,* a refreshing cold yogurt soup, and *kever* (garlic chives) and cilantro for a green stew called *sabzi govurma.* "Ours is the world's greenest cuisine!" Zulya declares. A strange thought, given that Baku sits on a diabolically parched, dusty peninsula.

After the market comes a quickstep food crawl: some *gutabi* to start, floppy filled flatbreads singed on convex griddles inside the Old City; then a whole Caspian fish, crisp-fried, then braised in a luscious sour plum sauce at a waterside fish restaurant on the southern edge of town; then a pastry high at Zulya's nearby catering kitchen — where smiling white-coated dames brush syrup over fourteen layers of *pakhlava,* stencil elaborate herringbone patterns on pastries called *shekerbura,* and shape *mutaki* (dainty sweet rolls) around cardamom-scented walnuts.

*

Heading back, we stop at the Bibi-Heybat Mosque, perched above a hauntingly ugly-beautiful graveyard of rusting old oil derricks and tankers. The mosque is a venerated thirteenth-century shrine that was destroyed by Soviet atheists in 1936, then resurrected with showy sleekness in the '90s with the blessing of Heydar Aliyev, Azerbaijan's monumental ruler, now dead and succeeded by Ilham, his (less monumental) son. Azerbaijan is a paradox: a predominantly Shiite country whose citizens love Russian vodka. Another paradox: Heydar Aliyev, who was an atheist, communist KGB chief before he started blessing mosques.

In Baku, Aliyev *père* is immortalized not by a somber stone mausoleum but by a swooping, quasi-extraterrestrial fantasia of white curves that from some angles resembles whipped cream piped in from the cosmos. I mean the Heydar Aliyev Center, one of Zaha Hadid's most breathtaking buildings. Here in this white apparition conjured by power and petro-fortune, we behold Heydar Aliyev's vintage cars, Heydar Aliyev's many medals, Heydar Aliyev's manifold gifts from other world leaders. (Putin gave a macho rifle, Romania's president an old-ladyish tea set.) There's some space for international art exhibitions too, and a pretty swell ethnographic museum.

"At least someone's willing to spend a country's billions for global cachet," Barry quips the next day, as Zulya's husband, Rufat, threads sweet nuggets of sheep's tail fat onto skewers. We're gathered at Mehriban's dacha, a short drive east of Baku, for a multigenerational family feast to celebrate Azerbaijan's Independence Day. By late afternoon Mehriban's airy bourgeois kitchen is a green, aromatic blur of parsley and chives sautéed for the *sabzi govurma,* of dill bouquets snipped for the herbaceous *pahla plov,* a delicate pilaf studded with fava beans. Eggplant whirs in the food processor for the baked *kükü* omelette textured seductively with walnuts and barberries. Mehriban is stuffing softball-sized meat orbs with dried fruit. These will be floated in saffron broth with chickpeas and chestnuts in *küfta bozbash,* a soup garnished with a zesty flourish of sumac-dusted onions.

Because one pilaf is never enough, Zulya now brings her celebratory rice tour de force out of the oven. It's called *khan* (also *shah* or something else royal) *plov,* and it's rice baked inside a golden lavash pastry case bathed with a truly indecent amount of butter. *Whoosh!* Zulya inverts the royal pilaf onto a platter. *Crunch!* She slices open its casing. And a fragrant cargo of saffron rice, barberries, candied lemon peel, dried fruit, chicken, and nuts — Zulya's modernized take on the classic — cascades out of the pastry. Toasts ascend to the sky. I marvel at the bright bowls of trompe l'oeil cherries and grapes decorating the table; they look fresh but are actually pickled. As a Muscovite with homes in New York and Istanbul, I feel as if all my life I've belonged at this generous Turco-Russian-Persian table. Rufat refills our glasses with vodka. I think of the complicated Soviet past we all share, of my small mom finding a brief wartime paradise in Baku, of the natural resources and geopolitical forces that have separated our former "fraternity" of Soviet republics into the haves and have-nots . . . of all the Azeri dishes I still haven't savored.

Zulya taps my shoulder, as if reading my mind. "Anya . . . Anyechka," she cajoles. "Next time you come to Baku, we'll make you a whole huge Caspian fish stuffed with walnuts!"

After Oranges

FROM *Oxford American*

ANY PIECE OF fruit has a story inside. You could say the seed is the beginning, the plant that grows is the middle, and the fruit that falls is the happy ending. Plant another seed and you can tell it all over again. These are lies, of course. Stories never turn out that way. Lives don't neatly fit into three parts. The structure won't ever follow a straight line. You have to ignore a world of context to pretend a story is that simple. Take an orange.

We know that the orange is in fact green. The fruit changes to its namesake color when exposed to cool air. Yet when the temperature drops below 28 degrees for longer than four hours, ice will form within an orange. The peel will show no injury, but the frozen flesh will turn mushy and the orange will fall from the tree, inedible. When the force that makes us can also ruin us, when a lethal irony is at play, we call the story a comedy or a tragedy, depending on the ending. Even if it is just an orange.

A tree damaged by a freeze may need to be pruned. Afterward, the tree's wounds can become infected, much the same way the body might react after an amputation. The scab pustules caused by *Elsinoë fawcettii* are unsightly and wartlike, though edibility is not altered. A scion infected with *Phytophthora* will develop rotting lesions which can extend down below the ground, turning the roots into wet, useless tendrils. The canker blisters of *Xanthomonas citri* are black but surrounded by vivid yellow haloes. They will eventually kill the fruit, a mottled and rotten waste on the ground.

Orange trees, like hurricanes, thrive near the wet, tropical zones. When a storm approaches with winds of less than 74 miles per hour, minor fruit loss can be expected, with some broken twigs, branches, and oranges tossed to the ground. Faced with hurricane-force winds, an entire crop can be ripped from the branches, along with most of the leaves. If the hurricane reaches category five, the groves themselves will be uprooted, trees carried and flung to the whims of the wind.

By the time the brown fungus of *Alternaria alternata* is spotted on the leaves of a Minneola tangelo tree growing in a low, wet grove, it is probably too late. The tree will be helpless to do anything but drop the fruit. The eggs of the Mediterranean fruit fly are laid below the skin of a host orange. After seven days the larvae will hatch and feed on the sweet flesh. The symptoms of citrus tristeza virus include small leaves and twig dieback. Beneath the bark, the tree's trunk will resemble a honeycomb. A tree like that can't support itself. That's one way the story can end. *Tristeza* is the Spanish word for sadness.

In the winter of 1965 an ambitious writer met with William Shawn, the famously autocratic editor of *The New Yorker,* to discuss his next story. After some considerable effort, the young man had published an expansive profile of a basketball star in the January 23 issue of the magazine. While going over final proofs of that story with Shawn, he had even talked his way into a job as staff writer. But now they couldn't agree on the writer's next assignment. The writer would suggest subject after subject, only to be told that the idea had already been reserved for another writer or that Shawn wasn't interested in it. This is the moment, as the story goes, when John McPhee finally just said, "Oranges."

According to the version he told in an interview with the *Paris Review* decades later, "That's all I said—oranges. I didn't mention juice, I didn't mention trees, I didn't mention the tropics. Just—oranges. Oh yes! Oh yes! [Shawn] says. That's very good. The next thing I knew I was in Florida talking to orange growers."

It is a fitting origin story for an idiosyncratic writer whose work has followed the furthest limits of his interests wherever they lead. Descriptions of McPhee's career inevitably fumble with the broadness of it—he has written books about sports and nature and canoes and doctors and fish and nuclear physics. McPhee is a patient writer, aware of time and yet existing a little outside of it. Around the same cultural moment that, say, Joan Didion was collecting her essays for *The White Album,* a book that spans the upheaval of a decade, McPhee was beginning to map out a comprehensive survey of North American geology, a book that spans the upheaval of billions of years. Twenty years later, when he finally published *Annals of the Former World,* a seven-hundred-page monument to rocks, he was awarded the Pulitzer Prize in nonfiction.

McPhee has published steadily since the late sixties, until recently never going more than a few years between books—his oeuvre currently runs to thirty-one titles—and he remains a regular presence in *The New Yorker,* which features excerpts from his developing projects and, in recent years, essays about his craft. Since 1975 he's taught nonfiction writing at Princeton in a course called "The Literature of Fact." He is sometimes accused of being a boring writer or one who writes about boring subjects—*forty-five hundred words about picking up golf balls?*—but the accusations miss the point. Maybe *you* get bored, but John McPhee does not. The unifying subject of McPhee's work is his sometimes overwhelmed, occasionally zigzagging, but always endless desire for knowledge of the world.

Take a random survey of nonfiction writers today—published or unpublished, successful or emerging—and you will invariably hear some opinion, if not three, about McPhee's career and influence. Lately my in-box is full of them.

"Nothing has given me more license to try to be interesting about boring things than reading John McPhee."

"McPhee makes me want to slow down."

"I've read every single book McPhee published and yes, it's all goddamn good, inhumanly gentle and smart, precise, painful."

"The one book I read was mostly a snore; it was about shad. I really like the articles."

"It's funny that he's become an authority on narrative structure, because you rarely encounter a prominent nonfiction writer who seems to care so little about the mechanics of reading."

"McPhee has been something of a password to me, a secret coin."

"*Pine Barrens* was the one for me. And the one about the Swiss Army. Sheesh, that one."

"Everyone talks about writing Great Sentences, but really wouldn't it be obnoxious, in fact, to read six-hundred-plus pages of perfectly Great Sentences? Only just in the sense that it's devastating, that *Annals of the Former World* is devastating to any serious writer."

But before all of that, half a century ago, McPhee was a young writer who'd landed an assignment: he had to go down to Florida to look into oranges.

"Why oranges?" McPhee later wrote. "There was a machine in Pennsylvania Station that cut and squeezed them. I stopped there as routinely as an animal at a salt lick." He noticed the juice change color, "light to deep," over the course of a winter and puzzled over an ad "that showed what appeared to be four identical oranges, although each had a different name. My intention in Florida was to find out why, and write a piece that would probably be short for *New Yorker* nonfiction of that day—something under ten thousand words." He returned with 40,000.

Shawn ran most of what McPhee brought back in the *New Yorker* across two issues in May 1966. Farrar, Straus and Giroux published the full version in a slim volume the following year. The book has aged well. Fifty years later, it reads as an agile survey of world history, a vivid period piece of changing American foodways, and an early classic by a master just beginning to find his form.

In the decades after World War II, the methods of industrial manufacture and production were transforming American food. New processed foods were introduced by the dozen. A product from the C. A. Swanson & Sons company called "TV Brand Frozen Dinners," made with cryogenic flash-freezing technology, sold by the millions. Cheese spread was spraying out of Nabisco's Snack Mate cans. ("It makes a cheeseburger an easeburger.") A company called Sweet'N Low promised to sweeten up your drink without a grain of sugar. And when McPhee arrived in Florida, a glass of fresh orange juice was rapidly becoming a thing of the past. The groves there, which grew a quarter of the oranges in the world, were putting almost all of their fresh fruit into "small, trim cans, about two inches in diameter and four inches high," McPhee wrote, "containing orange juice that has been boiled to high viscosity in a vacuum, separated into several component parts, reassembled, flavored, and then frozen solid."

We gather this in the early pages of the book, where no one in Florida will hand McPhee a taste of fresh-squeezed orange juice.

He gets cup after cup of concentrate from Floridians who tell him it is really so much better, the industrially balanced flavors and sweetness. In a small act of defiance, he grabs a couple of oranges off a tree near his motel and juices them on a reamer bought from a hardware store's dusty shelf.

McPhee's book about oranges in the age of concentrate production is not a screed against industrial food or agribusiness priorities. There's no scolding chapter explaining which oranges to buy at the grocery store. For that matter, there's no hand-holding "what will happen in this book" chapter or really even much in the way of plot or main character, aside from the regular presence of our reporter guide. In that way, it doesn't much resemble the books published about food today. If you read it a couple of times, trying to ascertain some kind of narrative structure, you may get the impression that McPhee is simply peeling an orange, circling his subject and handing out segments of the beauty and contradiction contained within.

In January I drove to Florida to look for the oranges McPhee wrote about. For research he had traveled to a place called the Ridge in central Florida. The area is a geological phenomenon, not unlike the sort that would consume a large part of McPhee's later career, of unusual dimensions:

> The Ridge is the Florida Divide, the peninsular watershed, and, to hear Floridians describe it, the world's most stupendous mountain range after the Himalayas and the Andes. Soaring two hundred and forty feet into the sub-tropical sky, the Ridge is difficult to distinguish from the surrounding lowlands, but it differs more in soil condition than in altitude, and citrus trees cover it like a long streamer, sometimes as little as a mile and never more than twenty-five miles wide, running south, from Leesburg to Sebring, for roughly a hundred miles. It is the most intense concentration of citrus in the world.

I crossed the Florida-Georgia line on 301, a highway that bridges St. Marys River, looking for the Florida Welcome Center that served McPhee a glass of concentrate to begin his trip. It's gone now, of course. Shortly after you cross the bridge, a large blue sign reads WELCOME TO FLORIDA with an orange instead of an *o* in the state's name. To the right of the sign is the empty, abandoned parking lot, the asphalt cracked through with weeds and scrubby pines. To the left is a drive-through discount liquor store that also sells lottery tickets.

A couple hours down the road, I pulled off I-75 to visit a place that very unofficial-looking billboards promised was an OFFICIAL FLORIDA WELCOME CENTER. This seemed odd, that the center would be welcoming drivers into the state long after they'd arrived, but maybe it made sense for the people who believe they aren't in Florida until they've arrived at Disney World or the beach. This Lake City welcome center is attached to an outlet store for boots and a restaurant called Country Skillit. Inside, there is a 14-foot-long stuffed alligator in a glass case, several long racks of brochures, and a few women behind the counter who would be more than happy to sell you a timeshare at a Westgate brand resort. There aren't any oranges.

"I thought you'd have oranges," I said to the woman behind the counter.

"Next exit," she replied.

"I mean, it's just kind of funny, a Florida welcome without orange juice, you know?"

She smiled silently, saying nothing until she realized I was waiting for her to reply.

"Next exit."

The next exit was a rest area with vending machines, but the exit after that had oranges. It was a gas station with towering, faded signs, cheap coffee, and a rather diverse selection of Florida citrus. A woman handed out slices from hand-labeled Tupperware. I bought a sack of red navels, a winter delicacy, thick-skinned and juicy and sweet, with flesh as red and bright as a grapefruit. Inside the station a few baby alligators floated in an aquarium next to a dead, stuffed adult, 13 feet long. Outside, in between the gas pumps, a box had gone moldy and the bright orange peels were growing with blue-gray fuzz.

The orange is, of course, synonymous with color. If you say you're having a yellow for breakfast, no one will have any clue what you're talking about. An orange? Well, of course. It seems so simple, that an orange is orange, but it is much more complicated than that. McPhee leads us down a rabbit hole:

> The color of an orange has no absolute correlation with the maturity of the flesh and juice inside. An orange can be as sweet and ripe as it

will ever be and still glisten like an emerald in the tree. Cold—coolness, rather—is what makes an orange orange. In some parts of the world, the weather never gets cold enough to change the color; in Thailand, for example, an orange is a green fruit, and traveling Thais often blink with wonder at the sight of oranges the color of flame. The ideal nighttime temperature in an orange grove is forty degrees. Some of the most beautiful oranges in the world are grown in Bermuda, where the temperature, night after night, falls consistently to that level. Andrew Marvell's poem wherein "the Bermudas ride in the ocean's bosom unespied" was written in the sixteen-fifties, and contains a description, from hearsay, of Bermuda's remarkable oranges, set against their dark foliage like "golden lamps in a green night." Cool air comes down every night into the San Joaquin Valley in California, which is formed by the Coast Range to the west and the Sierra Nevadas to the east. The tops of the Sierras are usually covered with snow, and before dawn the temperature in the valley edges down to the frost point. In such cosmetic surroundings it is no wonder that growers here have heavily implanted the San Joaquin Valley with the Washington Navel Orange, which is the most beautiful orange grown in any quantity in the United States, and is certainly as attractive to the eye as any orange grown in the world. Its color will go to a deep, flaring cadmium orange, and its surface has a suggestion of coarseness, which complements its perfect ellipsoid shape.

In one paragraph, ostensibly about the relative orangeness of an orange, McPhee moves from biological fact to globe-trotting observation to seventeenth-century poetry of the imagined tropics to the top of a snow-covered mountain to a present-day agricultural epicenter, before returning to his original line of inquiry with the lavish description of a single beautiful orange. There is a touch of Thoreau—who likewise could take us from the proper price for a shirt to the complications of the pronoun *they* to our relationship with authority to mummies in Egypt in the span of a paragraph —and like Thoreau's, this virtuosic essaying is not noise but the signal itself. The prose, the actual structure of the paragraph, is telegraphing a message: even the most basic of things, the color of an orange, contains within it the whole world's complications. And he still brings home the surface point, which is "Wow, yeah, oranges, they're beautiful, aren't they?"

Yes, they are beautiful. When McPhee pulled off Interstate 75 around Leesburg, Florida, to drive the state highway that runs along the Ridge, he was moved by the sight of it to quote the eighth-century Chinese poet Tu Fu: "Two big gardens planted with thousands of orange trees. / Their thick leaves are putting the clouds to shame."

As I traveled south on Highway 27 past the Florida Citrus Tower, the only words that came to mind were the ones on the signs, the terse poetry of corporate dining: Golden Corral, Buffalo Wild Wings, Texas Roadhouse, Red Lobster, Olive Garden. The shift he saw coming, the world of industrial food indicated by orange juice concentrate, has fully arrived here. The view has changed.

When McPhee came to Florida, Disney World had yet to begin construction. The suburbs of Orlando have since sprawled far west, and for several miles around here there are now more parking lots and cul-de-sacs than orange groves. Eventually, though, Highway 27 does give way to the groves, to the endless rows of dark-green trees, but even this is different from what McPhee observed.

About a decade ago the color of the orange trees in Florida began to change. The dark-green leaves began to mottle, their solid tones turning to yellow-green splotches. The men in the groves knew this was a bad sign. The fruit grew smaller or sometimes odd, misshapen, lopsided. The trees produced less fruit and then even less and then died. It started in the south of the state, spreading from tree to tree, row to row, grove to grove. No quarantine could contain it. By the time a tree showed symptoms, it was too late. The disease had already been in the roots for years, slowly crippling the tendrils until they pulled back, useless, unable to feed the leaves and changing their color.

The disease has a scientific name, huanglongbing, given by the researchers who first identified the bacteria in China's Chaoshan and Pearl River Delta plains. The damage it caused had been familiar in orange groves since at least the late nineteenth century. The disease was sometimes called jitouhuang (yellow chicken head) or genfu (root rotting). It ruined the industry there, more or less. A century later, the bacteria arrived in Florida. No one knows how.

The Asian citrus psyllid, a brown insect only a few millimeters long, carries the bacteria. Psyllids leap more than they fly, flittering among the branches of the trees and feasting on the tender young leaves. As they eat the plant, they also infect it, passing the disease to every tree in their path. The folks on the Ridge in Florida mostly just call it by the color, greening. You can see it in the leaves, the way they've turned from dark green to light. Greening. Today no one is quite sure if Florida's oranges will survive.

In 1965 the Florida Agricultural Statistics Service commissioned the first aerial survey of commercial citrus acreage in the state. Chartered planes flew in a series of 3-mile-wide flight paths while cameras, loaded with black-and-white panchromatic film and calibrated to make exposures at a precise scale of 1 inch for every 2,500 feet, photographed 14,000 square miles of the state. Each geometric grid of orange trees was then identified, measured, and indexed by variety, age, and identifying features. The resulting report, Florida's Commercial Citrus Inventory, has been repeated and improved upon ever since. The level of detail is meticulous; if a photograph presents some kind of discrepancy—say, a large number of missing or newly planted trees—a ground crew is sent to inspect and verify the acreage.

It is hard to imagine a more comprehensive form of survey than this: a photographic archive of every working orange tree in Florida. We've become accustomed to the story of our agriculture being told by numbers: every single head of cattle slaughtered, every pound of corn grown, every pound of honey produced, every egg laid. The results of the first Commercial Citrus Inventory, published the year before *Oranges*, determined that there were 858,082 acres of commercial citrus groves in Florida.

McPhee's work is similarly comprehensive, but different, of course. He is more interested in qualities than quantities, more a poet than accountant, too present to be a historian, a writer capable of recording the stories that numbers and archives cannot. By focusing his work this way, the book accomplishes a number of subtle illusions. It is a small thing—not even a hundred fifty pages—but the volume seems to contain much more than its length. My many returns to *Oranges* have never quite explained it. I always come up short, not sure why this book works at all and yet reaffirmed that it does. It is like one of those houses that looks like it should fall over but never does, as if unconcerned with gravity.

The opening pages are a prose poem, a single unbroken paragraph that vividly arranges images of orange consumption around the globe: "A Frenchman sits at the dinner table, and, as the finishing flourish of the meal, slowly and gently disrobes an orange . . .

English children make orange-peel teeth and wedge them over their gums on Halloween. Irish children take oranges to the movies, where they eat them while they watch the show, tossing the peels at each other and the people on the screen. In Reykjavik, Iceland, in greenhouses that are heated by volcanic springs, orange trees yearly bear fruit."

At one point McPhee describes sitting down under a tree to read a stack of books recommended by the pomologists at the University of Florida's Citrus Experiment Station. It is not unlike the story we know about the Buddha and the Bodhi Tree, the place where he is said to have attained enlightenment. There is a pleasant sense in the book that McPhee has filtered all human knowledge of oranges to this moment, that all the stories of kings and orangeries and poets and groves that he weaves through his version of the history have arrived with him at this age of oranges in Florida. There is a kind of mastery, of control, demonstrated in this kind of knowledge. It is the same kind of control that lets us take the fruit of an ancient tree and remake it into a 2-by-4-inch can.

The Florida Agricultural Statistics Service report was repeated biennially, so that the past fifty years of oranges can be glimpsed within them. One can read between the numbers that in, say, 1971 or 1977, a hard freeze occurred in January. Some towns near the Ridge have hopeful, talismanic names, Frostproof and Winter Haven and Winter Garden and Winter Park, but names offer no protection from cold winds.

The numbers have other stories in them. You can guess that production peaked in the late nineties. You can sense a little of what happened in the 2004 and 2005 hurricane seasons, when storm after storm hit the state, destroying more than a third of the acres of oranges. As the numbers continue to decline after that, you can see how those storms spread canker, a disease that can be carried on water and wind, into every grove in the state.

Not long after, the leaves started to change color.

That afternoon in Florida, I met with Ben Hill Griffin III. The final pages of *Oranges* are a portrait of his father, Ben Hill Griffin Jr., one of the most successful orange barons in history. Ben Hill III's wood-paneled office in Frostproof is filled with evidence of his family's success. There is the scale model of the University of Florida football stadium named for his father, the framed magazine and newspaper pages, the honorary degrees and plaques. He has an air of generosity. He asked his secretary to bring us cups of coffee.

I'd come in part because I noticed a passing mention on the second-to-last page of *Oranges:* "an empty lot where Ben Hill III was about to start building a house." I thought that it would be nice to see the finished house where McPhee had once noted an empty lot. Ben Hill III agreed that this was a nice idea, but he explained that he had built the house, lived in it, and sold it long ago. He didn't know who lived there today.

I asked about the processing and packing facilities, the ones that McPhee had toured with Ben Hill III's father. Those had been sold too, to Procter & Gamble in 1981. It was meant to be one of the biggest deals in orange juice. With those properties, P&G had assembled the components to compete with Minute Maid and Tropicana, but it never could get out of third place. In 1991 the FDA decided its use of the word *fresh* on concentrate products constituted false advertising. P&G tried to fight the ruling, but the FDA charged it in court for making false and misleading claims and seized all of the Citrus Hill products in a nearby warehouse. The brand ran into the ground not long after that. Ben Hill III estimated that P&G lost hundreds of millions of dollars on the deal.

But these were old stories. To talk about the industry today is to talk about greening. Ben Hill III wanted to impress upon me the numbers. He had typed out a few pages of notes that contained the boiled-down facts:

"Industry produced 250 million boxes per year in 2010. 70 million boxes in 2016."

"Millions of dollars of research have been spent to date in search of cure but to no avail."

"Cost of production has grown from $850/acre to $2,400/acre with reduced production."

"Through time, production declines to zero."

"No cure in sight."

When McPhee had come, the work was nearly around the clock. Now, Ben Hill III runs his packing house only a couple of days a week. There just aren't enough oranges to pack. I asked him what greening could mean for Florida oranges. In my notes from the day, his response is in all capital letters: "THE END OF THE INDUSTRY."

That evening I had a blackened redfish sandwich at the local bar in Frostproof. When the bartender asked, I told her I was in town on a story about oranges, that I'd come to see the orange capital of the world.

"Yeah, more like meth capital of the world," a waitress said under her breath. She and the bartender laughed uneasily.

The bartender turned to me, her face serious. "No, really, it is like *Breaking Bad* around here."

I looked at her, took another bite of my sandwich.

"But, yeah, oranges, I hear they're having a hard time too," she said.

I moved to Florida in the nineties, when I was in grade school. My mother had remarried and we moved to a property west of the Ridge, where the curling shapes of suburban cul-de-sacs were slowly carving into strawberry fields and cattle pastures and orange groves.

During those years I had a friend named Jeff. I don't remember ever talking with him about oranges, though we drove past them every day—acre after acre, miles and miles of oranges—on our way to school. We talked about music and girls and skateboarding and which gas stations were the best for buying beer without an ID. I don't remember anyone we knew ever talking about oranges either. These farms, their long expanses along the country roads, were just an inconvenience to us, a thing in the way of the rest of our lives. We were always driving to some party an hour away. It was always either a suburban house, abandoned by parents for the weekend, or a pasture somewhere bordered by groves, a place where adults couldn't see us. One night we pulled his car to the side of the road and ran into a grove with a garbage bag and filled it with oranges we picked from the trees. We ran with the bag as if someone might be watching. We ran because that's what we'd seen criminals do on television. At the party later, we sliced them in half and found the absent parents' electric juicer. It was the sort of machine that turned on when pressed with an orange, that gave its golden juice down a little metal spout. Everyone drank it with vodka, of course. We'd told Jeff's parents that he was staying at my house and my mother that I was staying at his house. We drove another hour and slept on some quiet beach we'd never seen before.

I don't remember the first time I saw someone bring a different bag of oranges to one of those parties. I remember hearing about them more than I saw them, small bags filled with perfectly round little pills. This was fifteen years ago, when no one really knew Oxy-Contin would be such a problem, when you could crush half of one of those pills on the coffee table and snort it and not worry about a thing. I didn't think about them much at the time, though they're everywhere in my memory now.

Florida became the place to get OxyContin. People drove across the country to get their prescriptions filled, to get their little bottles and bags of oranges. By 2010 manufacturers would sell 650 million oxycodone pills in Florida in a single year, five times the number of boxes of oranges.

I haven't seen those pills in so long that I had to look up a picture to remind myself. They look a little more yellow than I remember, more like a sour lemon than a sweet orange. I moved away and fell out of touch with Jeff. He's dead now, and I'm the one looking up pictures of pills on my computer in a motel room and remembering the way the drip would taste coming down the back of my throat.

The morning after seeing Ben Hill III, I met with Ellis Hunt Jr., an heir to and president of the Hunt Brothers, Inc., in Lake Wales. Hunt Bros. is almost as old as any business in the Florida citrus industry today. For much of that history, many orange groves were owned in relatively small blocks, ten acres here, twenty acres there. It didn't make much sense for those small owners to build their own packing houses, so they would pay a cooperative like Hunt Bros. to tend their groves and pick and process the oranges.

Fifty years ago McPhee explained the business like this: "If an owner has bearing trees on his property, the cooperative gives him a drawing account, advancing the costs of production against eventual profits, and sending him a check for the difference at the end of the season. Owners with new groves are sent monthly bills until their trees come into bearing." That's more or less how a cooperative would work today too, except that there are no eventual profits for most small owners. To keep a grove going in the midst of greening requires intense, expensive rotations of fertilizer and pesticides. After a few years of losing money, many have walked away from their groves and stopped paying into the co-ops. By his own estimate, Hunt believes as many as 230,000 acres have been abandoned across the state. The groves that Hunt Bros. tends today are largely its own.

Hunt was born into the industry. He picked in the groves as a teenager, studied citrus in school. Aside from a brief prodigal period—long hair, VW van, the seventies—he has been here in Florida, working with oranges, his whole life. The Hunt Bros. packing house is a technological marvel, a Rube Goldberg machine of whirring, spinning, weighing, cleaning, sorting contraptions capable of marvels that McPhee would have delighted in. As we walked through, though, it was hard not to notice the way the machine was sorting out so much fruit, the small, useless harvest of greening. All the sorting technology in the world makes no difference if you don't have the right fruit to put in it. We went for a drive in the groves after.

Only a person with Hunt's experience can navigate a grove. To an outsider, it is like entering a hedge maze, an endless geometric trap of rows and rows of citrus trees. As we cruised the acres in his truck, there was never a spot where you couldn't see some effect of the disease. When an owner abandons a grove, it creates problems for the neighbors. Without maintenance, a deserted grove is a breeding ground for psyllids, the bugs that carry the disease. The only way to stop them from spreading is to push and burn the infected trees. That's what they call ripping the trees from the ground, pushing them into a pile, and lighting them on fire. Hunt pointed out evidence of this, swaths of land scarred with rows but no trees. He saw that as a good thing, evidence of owners who had taken care of their property. All around he pointed to abandoned groves, crippled-looking gnarled trees with useless fruit. These were the bad neighbors, he said, ones who cut their losses and walked away and left the problem for everybody else. One day their trees will have to burn too.

The next day I visited a very different grove. The man who showed it to me, Michael E. Rogers, compared it to a library. We were riding in a golf cart, moving very slowly between the trees so that I could understand the description. Most groves are planted with trees of the same variety, hundreds and thousands of Valencias or Hamlins or Midsweets. Here in the Library, every single tree was different, like books on a shelf. Some were tall, others were short, some fat, some skinny. Some contained sweet fruit, others bitter and full of seeds. Some peels were difficult, others came off easy. Some trees in here were sick and dying from greening. Others were alive and well.

Rogers is the director of University of Florida's Citrus Research and Education Center. If the Ridge was once the greatest concentration of citrus in the world, the CREC is still the greatest concentration of citrus knowledge in the world. This is the place where McPhee came and, as he has said, his "short article turned into a book."

Rogers showed me just about everything on the CREC campus that day—laboratories, processing facilities, experimental groves, taste tests, heavy-duty machinery, proof-of-concept videos—and everything, all of it, was in some way fighting the disease of greening. There are still other concerns in citrus, other aspects to be studied, other problems to be solved, but nothing will take priority until they solve greening.

McPhee arrived here at a time of relative peace and prosperity. He wrote, "Lightning kills as many orange trees as any disease," which is a comical ratio today. The CREC is now a central command, a military base in an urgent war. There are many fronts and battles, many treatments and stopgap measures to slow the spread of the disease. But in the end the result will be decided by a single plant, a tree that is resistant to greening. If the CREC can develop such a tree, Florida oranges will survive. If it can't, well, no one really likes to talk about not winning.

Rogers explained that they're now testing genetically modified trees, ones in which the genes that are affected by greening have been simply deleted from the DNA. They're testing all sorts of varieties, like an easy-to-peel, greening-resistant variety to compete with the California-grown Cuties. They call that one Bingo! The researchers have hope, but the trees in the Library are like books in so many ways. They're complicated and slow. They take time, years in fact, to reveal how the story ends.

McPhee returned to the subject of oranges years later, when he wrote about what he calls California's second gold rush. After the arrival of train tracks in Los Angeles, the "people rushing in were farmers, and the gold was oranges," he wrote. He described the evolution of a giant grove assembled from a collection of small, sin-

gle-farmer-owned orchards on the north side of the city. Though
nowhere near as big as the Ridge, the grove grew large enough
to serve as a kind of moat between Los Angeles and the San Gabriel Mountains, which irrigated the groves with their mountain
watersheds. For a time the grove became an accidental buffer, a
protective distance put between the citizens of Los Angeles and the
mountain's violent cycles of wildfire and landslides. But it didn't
last. Floods of debris eventually came raging down through the
groves and killed dozens of people. During the Second World War,
a new rush of people moved to Los Angeles to work for the war industry, and orchards were clear-cut to make room for new housing.
A virus broke out. The new neighbors didn't care for the oranges.
They stole them or dumped junk and trash behind the trees; they
passed laws against farmers' smudge pots but drove their cars until
the toxic smog choked the fruit. In a matter of just a few pages, the
grove comes and goes.

The story is a passing anecdote, a digression contained within
"Los Angeles Against the Mountain," the closing section of *The Control of Nature.* Published about twenty years after *Oranges,* the book
tells three stories, unconnected aside from the spirit of McPhee's
interest, the echoing allure of "any struggle against natural forces
—heroic or venal, rash or well advised—when human beings
conscript themselves to fight against the earth, to take what is not
given, to rout the destroying enemy, to surround the base of Mt.
Olympus demanding and expecting the surrender of the gods."

Humans don't win in the end. We take a battle on occasion
—dam an undamable river, halt a volcanic eruption in its tracks.
We're even sometimes foolish enough to believe we've wrested
control, that we can learn and adapt to defy any force and that
we're too powerful to be stopped. But there's no winning. However much we know, there is always more. Whenever we think we've
seen the big picture, we are only glancing at the smallest of scenes.

In the broad strokes of McPhee's career you can see a little of
that. When looked at with fifty years' hindsight, his books appear
less about mastering his subjects and more about the patient, hard
work of continuing to try to understand. It is perhaps the highest
compliment I can think of to say that his work resembles an old,
slow-growing, wide-branched tree.

Before I went to Florida to look for McPhee's fruit, I had been
returning to *Oranges* for years. I read to figure out how to do it,

looking again, looking closer, as if it were only a matter of learning each move, imitating each flourish, then the whole mysterious thing could be known and repeated and controlled. I've heard this story again and again from friends, writers who have done the same but with Didion or Wallace or McCarthy or Baldwin or whoever. Young writers—those of us still looking for a subject to open the world the way oranges did for McPhee—need books to aspire to, guides off in the distance, green fruit glowing on the high branches of a tree. Ask anyone who's been in that affair, though, and they'll tell you the relationship is dangerous. Eventually admiration and imitation lead you down a wrong path. You'll go looking for things that aren't there anymore. Most writers I know hate the books they love. I didn't understand it until later, but I went to Florida in January so I could stop reading *Oranges,* so that I could see the trees for myself and move on. We all have to learn to grab for the fruit we can reach.

At the CREC that afternoon, I casually mentioned to several people the scene where McPhee sits down under a tree and reads everything about oranges. I had the foolish idea that the tree might still be around, that it would be standing right outside the research library like a hallowed spot. Nobody else quite remembered that part.

I headed to my car in the visitors' lot, but I wasn't ready to leave. The story that Ellis Hunt Jr. had told me, about the people who had abandoned their groves without burning them down, was turning over in my head. Those trees contained two stories, two endings—not one. The owners who had abandoned them believed the story of their trees was over, that it was done because they had walked away. For everyone else, the story kept on going, unfinished as of yet.

I decided to walk for a few minutes in the afternoon sun, and think about which tree might be nice to sit under, to try not to think about anything else. There are trees all over the campus, not just orange trees. This is Florida, so there were palm trees, tall and skinny, and there was a little clump of regular pines with a blanket of brown needles below it. There were live oaks tall and thick with Spanish moss that spread their shade all around. They were all books—just ones that hadn't been written yet.

In other words, there were plenty of fine places to sit.

Contributors' Notes

Other Notable Food Writing
of 2017

Contributors' Notes

Jane Black is a Washington, DC–based food writer who covers food politics, culture, and sustainable agriculture. Her work appears regularly in the *Wall Street Journal*, the *New York Times*, and the *Washington Post*, where she was previously a staff writer.

Karen Brooks holds one of the food world's most prestigious honors: James Beard Craig Claiborne Distinguished Restaurant Review Award 2017. After this, it's all gravy. Brooks eats, drinks, and thinks about food for *Portland Monthly*, as the magazine's food critic and editor. Though she prefers takeout to home cooking, she has written nine food books to date, most recently *The Mighty Gastropolis: Portland: A Journey Through the Center of America's New Food Revolution*. Best life experiences: TEDxPortland speaker (and now advisory board member), *Today* show appearance, guest judge on *Top Chef Masters* (Bravo), harrowing trek through the Machu Picchu jungle. In her spare time Karen is an NBA baller, action-movie junkie, and board member for Urban Gleaners, a grassroots nonprofit serving reclaimed food to needy kids.

Mary H. K. Choi is a YA novelist living in New York. Her debut, *Emergency Contact*, has been dubbed by the *New York Times* as "blushingly tender and piquant." She has written for *GQ, Wired, New York*, and Marvel and DC Comics and is the host of *Hey, Cool Job!* a business podcast. She can also be seen on *Vice News Tonight* on HBO as a culture correspondent. Visit her at choitotheworld.com.

Amanda Cohen is the chef and owner of Dirt Candy, the award-winning vegetable restaurant on New York City's Lower East Side. Dirt Candy was the first vegetable-focused restaurant in the city and the leader of the vegetable-forward movement. The restaurant's original location had only eighteen seats and was open for seven years, during which time it became the first vegetarian restaurant in seventeen years to receive two stars from the *New York Times,* was recognized by the Michelin Guide five years in a row, and won awards from *Gourmet* magazine, the *Village Voice,* and many others. Its new location opened in January 2015 and was the first restaurant in the city to eliminate tipping and share profits with its employees. Amanda was the first vegetarian chef to compete on *Iron Chef America,* and her comic-book cookbook, *Dirt Candy: A Cookbook,* is the first graphic novel cookbook to be published in North America. It's currently in its seventh printing. In 2018, *New York* magazine named Dirt Candy "The Absolute Best Restaurant on the Lower East Side."

Lauren Collins is a staff writer at *The New Yorker* and the author of *When in French: Love in a Second Language.* She lives in Paris.

John T. Edge has served as director since the 1999 founding of the Southern Foodways Alliance, an institute of the Center for the Study of Southern Culture at the University of Mississippi. Winner of the M.F.K. Fisher Distinguished Writing Award from the James Beard Foundation, he is the author of *The Potlikker Papers: A Food History of the Modern South.* He holds an MA in southern studies from the University of Mississippi and an MFA in creative nonfiction from Goucher College. A columnist for the *Oxford American* and *Garden & Gun,* Edge wrote the "United Tastes" column for the *New York Times* for three years.

Ted Genoways, a three-time James Beard Foundation Award finalist, is the author of *The Chain: Farm, Factory, and the Fate of Our Food* (2014) and *This Blessed Earth: A Year in the Life of an American Family Farm* (2017). He is currently completing a history of the early years of the tequila industry, to be published in 2020.

Jonathan Gold is the restaurant critic for the *Los Angeles Times.* He won the Pulitzer Prize in criticism in 2007 and was a finalist again in 2011. A Los Angeles native, he began writing the "Counter Intelligence" column for *L.A. Weekly* in 1986, wrote about death metal and gangsta rap for *Rolling*

Stone and *Spin*, among other places, and is delighted that he has managed to forge a career out of the professional eating of tacos.

Dana Goodyear is a staff writer at *The New Yorker* and the author of three books, including *Anything That Moves: Renegade Chefs, Fearless Eaters, and the Making of a New American Food Culture*. Her work has been nominated for a National Magazine Award, and she has twice won the James Beard Foundation Award for journalism. She lives in Venice, California.

Alex Halberstadt is the author of *Lonely Avenue: The Unlikely Life and Times of Doc Pomus* and the forthcoming *Young Heroes of the Soviet Union*, a family memoir. His writing has appeared in *The New Yorker*, the *New York Times Magazine*, the *New York Times Book Review*, *GQ*, *Saveur*, *Food & Wine*, the *Paris Review*, and elsewhere. He was nominated for a James Beard Award in 2013 and 2014 and teaches at Eugene Lang College and NYU's Gallatin School for Individualized Study.

Marissa Higgins is a queer writer and editor based in Washington, DC. Her nonfiction appears or is forthcoming in the *Sun*, *The Atlantic*, the *Washington Post*, *Guernica*, *Salon*, *NPR*, *Slate*, *Rumpus*, and elsewhere. Her work centers on poverty, LGBTQ issues, and how food intersects class and culture. She is working on a book of essays.

Based in Los Angeles, **Baxter Holmes** is a national NBA writer focusing on features, projects, and other enterprise stories for ESPN.com and *ESPN The Magazine*. He previously covered the Lakers for ESPN, the Celtics for the *Boston Globe*, and a variety of subjects as a staff writer for the *Los Angeles Times*. He attended the University of Oklahoma and hails from Tuskahoma, Oklahoma, a town smaller than the period at the end of this sentence.

Lauren Michele Jackson is a doctoral candidate in English at the University of Chicago and a writer based in Chicago. Her work has appeared in *The Atlantic*, *The Awl*, *The Journal*, *New Republic*, *New York*, and *The Point*, among other places. She is currently working on her first book, a collection of essays about race and appropriation, forthcoming.

Beth Kowitt is a senior writer for *Fortune*, where she primarily covers the business of food and consumer behavior. She is a winner of the Front Page Award for business journalism from the Newswomen's Club of New York, the New York Press Club's food-writing magazine award, and the NYSSCPA Excellence in Financial Journalism Award for beat news reporting. She has a BA degree in sociology and English from Bowdoin College and an MS degree from Columbia University Graduate School of Journalism. She and her husband, photographer Karsten Moran, live in New York City.

Francis Lam is the host of public radio's *The Splendid Table*, is the editor-at-large at Clarkson Potter, and serves on the board of the Southern Foodways Alliance. His writing has won numerous awards from the James Beard Foundation and the International Association of Culinary Professionals. As an editor, he was responsible for the *New York Times* best-selling cookbooks *Cravings*, by Chrissy Teigen, and *Koreatown*, by Deuki Hong and Matt Rodbard, as well as the two-time James Beard Award–winning *Victuals*, by Ronni Lundy. In past lives he was a columnist for the *New York Times Magazine*, a regular judge on *Top Chef Masters*, the features editor at *Gilt Taste*, a senior writer at *Salon*, and a contributing editor at *Gourmet*. His work has appeared in ten editions of the *Best Food Writing* anthology. He believes that in professional football, that would count as a dynasty; in ancient China, not so much.

Harold McGee writes about the science of food and cooking. He started out studying physics and astronomy at the California Institute of Technology and then English literature at Yale University. In 1984 he published *On Food and Cooking: The Science and Lore of the Kitchen*. Twenty years later, the revised and enlarged edition of *On Food and Cooking* was named best food reference of 2004 by the IACP and the James Beard Foundation. In 2005 *Bon Appétit* magazine named McGee food writer of the year, and in 2008 *Time* magazine named him to its annual list of the world's most influential people. From 2006 to 2011 he wrote a monthly column, "The Curious Cook," for the *New York Times*. Since 2011 he has been a visiting lecturer at the Harvard University course "From Haute Cuisine to Soft-Matter Science."

Ligaya Mishan grew up in Honolulu, Hawaii, the daughter of a Filipino mother and a British father. She is the "Hungry City" columnist for the *New York Times* and a contributing editor at *T Magazine*, and has written for the *New York Review of Books* and *The New Yorker*.

Shane Mitchell is a *Saveur* contributing editor. Formerly she was *Travel + Leisure*'s special correspondent. Her writing has also appeared in *Australian*

Gourmet Traveller, Afar, Bon Appétit, The Bitter Southerner, Departures, Serious Eats, and other publications. She is a James Beard Foundation Award finalist and has received the IACP culinary writing prize. She kayaks on the St. Lawrence River and collects handmade knives wherever she travels. When not on the road, she lives in New York's North Country.

John O'Connor is from Kalamazoo, Michigan. His writing has appeared in the journals *Open City, Post Road, The Believer,* and *Quarterly West* and the anthologies *The Best Creative Nonfiction Vol. 1* and *They're at It Again: An Open City Reader.* He has also written for the *New York Times, GQ, Saveur, Men's Journal,* and the *Oxford American* and for two years was a foreign correspondent for Japan's largest daily newspaper, the *Yomiuri Shimbun.* He teaches journalism at Boston College.

Chris Offutt writes a food column for *Oxford American* magazine. He is the author of *Country Dark, Kentucky Straight, Out of the Woods, The Same River Twice, No Heroes, The Good Brother,* and *My Father, the Pornographer.* He also wrote screenplays for *True Blood, Treme,* and *Weeds.* His work is in many anthologies, including *The Best American Short Stories, The Best American Essays,* and *The Pushcart Prize.* He grew up in the hills of eastern Kentucky and currently lives in rural Lafayette County near Oxford, Mississippi. Reach him at offuttchris1@gmail.com.

Julia O'Malley, a third-generation Alaskan, is an editor at the *Anchorage Daily News* and a freelance writer who lives in Anchorage. She has written for the *New York Times,* the *Washington Post,* the *Guardian, High Country News, Eater, Saveur,* and *National Geographic,* among other publications. She was Atwood Chair of Journalism at the University of Alaska Anchorage from 2015 to 2017 and has taught food writing around Alaska. The essay included in this book was nominated for a James Beard Award in 2018. Find her work at juliaomalley.media.

Clint Rainey covers the food industry for *New York* magazine's *Grub Street.* He is a *Businessweek* contributor and a James Beard Award winner who has appeared on *Marketplace,* WNYC, the BBC, and others. The last time his writing got anthologized, it was for an infographic about men's bracelets.

Tejal Rao is a Brooklyn-based writer. She works as a reporter for the *New York Times* and a columnist for the *New York Times Magazine.*

Helen Rosner is *The New Yorker*'s food correspondent. Her 2016 essay "On Chicken Tenders," published in *Guernica*, received a James Beard Award. She lives in Brooklyn.

Khushbu Shah is a senior food editor at *Thrillist* and currently resides in Brooklyn.

Moscow-born **Anya von Bremzen** is a writer based in New York and Istanbul. She is the recipient of three James Beard Awards and the author of six acclaimed cookbooks as well as a memoir, *Mastering the Art of Soviet Cooking*, which has been translated into fourteen languages.

Wyatt Williams is writing a book about meat.

Other Notable Food Writing of 2017

ALAN RICHMAN

Drew Nieporent May Be the Last Old-School Restaurateur Standing. *New York Times*, September 12.

HELEN ROSNER

Christ in the Garden of Endless Breadsticks. *Eater*, October 3.

JAYA SAXENA

Women Aren't Ruining Food. *Taste Cooking*, October 30.

JOHN SEABROOK

Behind the Cellar Door. *The New Yorker*, January 23.

PARUL SEGHAL

Thanksgiving Wins a Convert. *New York Times*, November 14.

MAYUKH SEN

The Sad, Sexist Past of Bengali Cuisine. *Food52*, July 5.

KHUSHBU SHAH

What Happens When a Brown Chef Cooks White Food. *GQ*, April 25.

MIMI SHERATON

The Big Apfel. *Saveur*, February/March.

JESSICA SIDMAN

Spies, Dossiers, and the Insane Lengths Restaurants Go to Track and Influence Food Critics. *Washingtonian*, December 6.

CRAIG S. SMITH

Burrowing Under Luminous Ice to Retrieve Mussels. *New York Times*, March 17.

GARRETT SNYDER

The Zen of Ken. *Taste Cooking*, May 18.

ZACH STAFFORD

Burned Out. *Eater*, September 21.

JOSHUA DAVID STEIN

Noma Mexico Goes Beyond Delicious. *Food & Wine*, May 8.

SADIE STEIN

Ode to the Buttered Roll, That New York Lifeline. *New York Times*, August 1.

RYAN SUTTON

Ranking America's Fast-Food Chicken Nuggets. *Eater*, January 27.

MARK SYNNOTT

The Last Death-Defying Honey Hunter of Nepal. *National Geographic*, July.

CHERYL LU-LIEN TAN

For the Love of Welsh Rarebit. *Foreign Policy*, July 24.

JAKE TUCK

What Comes After the Beer Snob. *Eater*, January 18.

MARI UYEHARA

The Fake Rolex of Canned Foods. *Taste*, June 20.

The 10th Anniversary of the Kale Salad as We Know It. *Taste Cooking*,
     October 24.

PETER VIGNERON

The Curious Case of the Disappearing Nuts. *Outside*, May 24.

JEFF VRABEL

The Never-Ending Quest to Breed (and Somehow Consume) the World's
     Hottest Chili Peppers. *GQ*, January 19.

THE BEST AMERICAN SERIES®

FIRST, BEST, AND BEST-SELLING

The Best American Comics

The Best American Essays

The Best American Food Writing

The Best American Mystery Stories

The Best American Nonrequired Reading

The Best American Science and Nature Writing

The Best American Science Fiction and Fantasy

The Best American Short Stories

The Best American Sports Writing

The Best American Travel Writing

Available in print and e-book wherever books are sold

hmhco.com/bestamerican